"This book brilliantly captures the essence of school leadership and real collaboration, offering leaders a roadmap amid the complexity of our educational world. It is a must-read for anyone committed to growing their leadership practice—especially in today's complex educational world—because it offers what we need most: a research-based, heart-centered framework to guide our way forward."

Ellie Drago-Severson, *Professor of Education Leadership and Adult Learning and Leadership Director, Leadership Institute for School Change, Teachers College Columbia University, USA*

"Gould's Six-Point Conceptual Framework offers clarity and adaptability, presenting practical yet inspiring strategies that have profoundly shaped my understanding of leadership, and his framework has truly been a cornerstone of my practice. *School Change is a Collaborative Process* is essential reading for anyone dedicated to authentic leadership, meaningful teaching, and creating lasting change in education."

Christopher M. Strickland, *Assistant Professor of Art Education, University of Nebraska Kearney, USA*

School Change is a Collaborative Process

School Change is a Collaborative Process is an essential resource for PK–12 leaders committed to increasing student learning. Presenting a Six-Point Conceptual Framework that demystifies the change process, this book guides readers through practical steps to establish values-driven inclusive leadership, build relational trust, assess contextual needs, set a collective focus, plan strategically, monitor progress, and celebrate gains. Written in an engaging workbook style, each chapter includes prompts to foster reflection and translate chapter content into leadership practice. This guide empowers educational leaders, whether they are teachers, instructional coaches, principals, or district administrators, and provides a clear roadmap to take initiative and lead sustainable, impactful change that will make a lasting difference in schools.

Stephen Gould was the Founder and Director of the Educational Leadership PhD program at Lesley University and is a nationally and internationally recognized educational leader and practitioner-scholar with extensive experience as a PK–12 teacher, principal, assistant superintendent, executive coach, consultant, and university professor.

Also Available from Routledge Eye on Education
(www.routledge.com/eyeoneducation)

A Blueprint for Teacher Retention: Leading Schools that Teachers Don't Want to Leave
James A. Bailey

Your School Leadership Edit: A Minimalist Approach to Rethinking Your School Ecosystem
Tamera Musiowsky-Borneman, C.Y. Arnold

Game-Changing Leadership in Action: An Educator's Companion
Kim Wallace

How to Have Difficult Conversations as an Educational Leader: Self-Reflections and Strategies for Success
Patty Corum

The Respected School Leader: Developing your Character Traits and Transformational Leadership Skills
Howard J. Bultinck, Lynn H. Bush, Noreen A. Powers

The International Education Leadership Companion: Lessons and Best Practices from Expert Leaders
Lindsay Prendergast, Catarina Song Chen, Colin Brown

Leadership Teams in America's Best Schools: Improving the Lives of All Students
Joseph F. Johnson, Jr., Cynthia L. Uline, Stanley J. Munro, Jr., Francisco Escobedo

Making Community Schools a Reality: Harnessing Your Power as a School Leader through Collaboration
Emily L. Woods

Wholehearted School Leadership: Rewiring our Schools for Courage, Justice, Learning, and Connection
Kathryn Fishman-Weaver

Data Analysis for Continuous School Improvement, 5th Edition
Victoria L. Bernhardt

Culturally Conscious Decision-Making for School Leaders: A Toolkit for Creating a More Equitable School Culture
Shauna McGee

Teacher Leadership Practice in High-Performing Schools: A Blueprint for Excellence
Jeremy D. Visone

School Change is a Collaborative Process: A Step-by-Step Guide to Improve K–12 Student Learning
Stephen Gould

School Change is a Collaborative Process

A Step-by-Step Guide to Improve K–12 Student Learning

Stephen Gould

Routledge
Taylor & Francis Group

NEW YORK AND LONDON

Designed cover image: © Getty Images

First published 2026
by Routledge
605 Third Avenue, New York, NY 10158

and by Routledge
4 Park Square, Milton Park, Abingdon, Oxon, OX14 4RN

Routledge is an imprint of the Taylor & Francis Group, an informa business

© 2026 Stephen Gould

The right of Stephen Gould to be identified as author of this work has been asserted in accordance with sections 77 and 78 of the Copyright, Designs and Patents Act 1988.

All rights reserved. The purchase of this copyright material confers the right on the purchasing institution to photocopy or download pages which bear a copyright line at the bottom of the page. No other parts of this book may be reprinted or reproduced or utilised in any form or by any electronic, mechanical, or other means, now known or hereafter invented, including photocopying and recording, or in any information storage or retrieval system, without permission in writing from the publishers.

Trademark notice: Product or corporate names may be trademarks or registered trademarks, and are used only for identification and explanation without intent to infringe.

ISBN: 978-1-041-14295-9 (hbk)
ISBN: 978-1-041-14294-2 (pbk)
ISBN: 978-1-003-67379-8 (ebk)

DOI: 10.4324/9781003673798

Typeset in Warnock Pro
by Apex CoVantage, LLC

Access the Support Material:
https://www.routledge.com/9781041142942

THE 6-POINT CONCEPTUAL FRAMEWORK

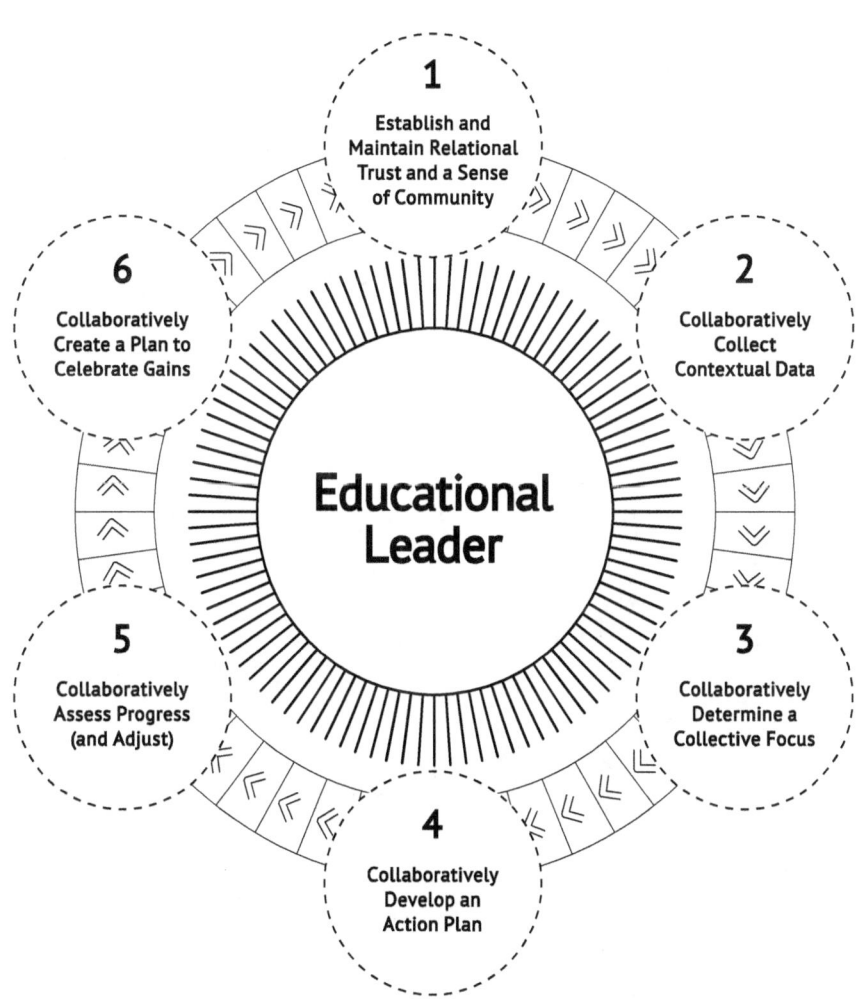

Conceptual Framework design and chapter openers designed by Christian Arichabala.

Contents

Support Materials   *xi*
Meet the Author   *xiii*
Acknowledgments   *xv*
Preface   *xvii*

▶ Chapter 1   The Six-Point Conceptual Framework and New Expectations for Educational Leaders   2

▶ Chapter 2   Establish and Maintain Relational Trust and a Sense of Community   44

▶ Chapter 3   Collaboratively Collect Contextual Data   77

▶ Chapter 4   Collaboratively Determine a *Collective* Focus   116

▶ Chapter 5   Collaboratively Develop an Action Plan   137

▶ Chapter 6   Collaboratively Assess Progress   153

▶ Chapter 7   Collaboratively Develop a Plan to Celebrate Gains   174

▶ Chapter 8   Collaboratively Create a Context-Specific Innovation Plan   188

Conclusion   199

Appendices   *205*

Support Materials

Some of the resources in this book are also available on the book product page online, so you can easily print them for use. To access these downloads, go to https://www.routledge.com/9781041142942 and click on the "Support Material" link.

Table 3.2	Professional Learning Communities Survey	96
Table 3.3	Aligned Factors and Conditions in a Standards-Based Instructional System Protocol	99
Table 3.6	Equity, Diversity, Inclusion, and Justice (EDIJ) Assessment	106
Table 4.1	Factors and Conditions to Determine a Collective Focus	127
Table 8.1	Rubric to Assess a Collaboratively Developed Innovation Plan	193

Meet the Author

▶ **Dr. Stephen Gould** is an educator, builder, and bridge-maker whose leadership journey spans classrooms, principalships, doctoral programs, international reform, and artistic expression. Known for his deep commitment to collaboration, equity, and human-centered change, Dr. Gould brings both vision and practicality to every setting he serves.

He began his career in PK–12 education, later serving as a principal and assistant superintendent, where he championed inclusive leadership, teacher agency, and student-centered innovation. At Lesley University, he founded and directed the Educational Leadership PhD program, where he taught and mentored aspiring school and district leaders. His work helps educators lead with authenticity, navigate complexity, and design meaningful change rooted in context and community.

Dr. Gould's leadership has extended far beyond US borders. As a consultant with the National Institute for School Leadership (NISL) and in collaboration with the World Bank, he traveled to Kuwait to support the Ministry of Education in training school leaders to lead democratic, collaborative, and transformative reform. Across three visits, he helped shift leadership mindsets toward inquiry, relational trust, and sustained innovation.

A prolific writer and thinker, Dr. Gould has contributed to national and regional organizations including the National Association of Elementary School Principals (NAESP) and the Massachusetts Elementary School Principals' Association (MESPA). At the Ikeda Center for Peace, Learning, and Dialogue, he explores the intersection of leadership, human potential, and creativity, most notably in his reflective interview, "The Music of Leadership," posted on their website.

Outside the world of education, Dr. Gould is also a songwriter, arranger, and djembe drum player. He brings rhythm, resonance, and creative energy to his work, seeing leadership as both an art and an act of service. Through every role he inhabits, he helps others listen more deeply, lead more courageously, and collaborate more meaningfully for the sake of student learning, social justice, and innovation in schools.

Acknowledgments

To my Father, who was a role model without ever saying a word and whose life was cut short before actualizing his dreams; to my Mother, who was on her own too soon and whose opinions mellowed and expressed love increased with age; to my wife Sharon, and sons Adam and Travis, who bring so much joy and happiness to my life; to Satchmo, Duke, Monk, Mingus, Orff, Kodaly and Tibor Serly who influenced my music and imagination; to my 4th grade teacher, Miss Norma K. Pease for her encouragement and kindness; to my many teachers whose lack of pedagogical skills challenged me to figure out how to become a better teacher; to Noreen Sullivan who was an exemplar and first showed me how to differentiate instruction followed by Dr. Margaret Wang; to Mohamed Kalifa Kamara, my djembe teacher, for his patience and always seeing the glass half full; to Dr. Robert Sinclair and Dr. Ralph W. Tyler who I had the good fortune to have as teachers and advisors and whose perspective on the purpose of schools in a democratic society and leadership greatly influenced me and is woven into the fabric of this book; to my PK–12 faculties, students and parents; educational leadership, PhD. colleagues, doctoral students, and all communities working hard to transform schools and make the world a better place.

Preface

I remember the first time I stood in front of a classroom with nervous anticipation. It was not my teaching goals and objectives that set the tone that day. It was the students. One girl with dancing eyes showed her hopes and expectations for a humane and compassionate teacher. A boy doodled in his notebook, barely looking up. It wasn't until I noticed the detail of his sketches that I realized he wasn't disengaged. He was dreaming on paper. That was the moment I knew teaching was about observing, listening to their stories of challenges and hopes, and creating a classroom learning environment where every voice matters.

Educational leadership, for me, is about those moments where trusting relationships meet vulnerability and courage overcomes difficult circumstances. Over the years, I've worn many hats as a musician, teacher, principal, assistant superintendent, consultant, and professor. Each role has deepened my understanding of what it means to lead with purpose and authenticity. Leadership is not about 'command and control' authority. It's about dismantling the barriers that keep too many students from having success in PK–12 schools and inspiring teachers to take collaborative action.

As principal, one experience was in a school where resources were scarce and inequities loomed large. I recall a veteran teacher saying, "Why should I try something new when this school is about compliance over creativity." In response, I shared a story about a struggling student who turned his failing grades around when I shifted my thinking as a teacher and leader from mandates to relevance, rules to relationships, and started asking him what he needed to succeed.

The COVID-19 pandemic magnified inequities that had long been brewing beneath the surface. I think of Maya, a high school sophomore who logged in from her kitchen table at home every morning, juggling schoolwork and caring for her younger siblings while her parents worked multiple jobs. I think of Mr. Stewart, a veteran teacher whose passion for his craft waned under the relentless pressure of mandates and initiatives that were disconnected from the realities of his students. These deeply human stories reinforce my conviction that we cannot return to "business as usual." Our schools need to move away from technical fixes, face the adaptive challenge of changing instruction and leadership behavior, and embrace transformation and innovation.

Change is a collaborative process that begins with trust. I've seen trust when a student lights up in response to a teacher who believes in her potential. I've witnessed it when despite difficult teaching and learning factors and conditions, resilient teachers come together to collaborate and reimagine what's possible for their students. Trust is the currency of meaningful change and cannot be built by enforcing top-down mandates. Trust and change grow in the fertile seedbed of shared purpose, mutual respect, and authentic connection.

As a musician, I find that educational leadership is like encouraging every member of a band to contribute their own distinctive voice. The educational leader's role is to nurture individuality, create harmony, and blend diverse voices into a sound that resonates and communicates shared meaning. This metaphor illustrates my approach to leadership as an art that balances vision with collaboration, structure with improvisation, and strategic thinking with heart and soul.

Public education stands at a crossroads. The complexity of today's social, economic, and political challenges has converged with limitations of the traditional school model and persistent inequities. Educators, families, and communities are being called to reimagine how schools can better serve all students, not only as learners, but as developing citizens of a democratic society. This book was born from that call.

Change is a Collaborative Process: A Step-by-Step Guide to Improve PK–12 Student Learning is a practical and value-laden response to one of the most pressing questions in education today: how do we design school improvement efforts that are not only effective and sustainable, but also inclusive, democratic, transformative, and innovative? Too often, change efforts in schools are driven by external mandates and one-size-fits-all solutions. They ignore context, disregard important new content, and lack a moral compass. This book argues that real and lasting school improvement begins with collaboration, not as a buzzword or an occasional practice but as a foundational commitment to working *with* others.

For the purposes of this book, teachers, teacher teams, instructional coaches, department heads, special education directors, principals, superintendents, university professors teaching educational leadership courses, and policymakers are all considered to be educational leaders. At the center of this book is the belief that change must emerge from shared values, collective inquiry, collaboration, and coordinated action. This book is for those who recognize that school improvement is not just a technical fix, but also an adaptive challenge rooted in relationships, guided by contextual factors and conditions, and propelled by a shared vision of what schools *can* be.

Grounded in research and informed by years of teaching and leadership practice as a principal, assistant superintendent, workshop presenter, national and international consultant, university professor, and PhD program director in educational leadership, this book introduces a research-backed Six-Point Conceptual Framework. The Framework is designed to help educational leaders, with or without a position of authority, collaboratively lead with purpose, build trust, collect and interpret contextual data, set a collective focus, develop plans for action, monitor progress, celebrate and acknowledge those who contributed to school improvement gains, and create a context-specific innovation plan. Many of the communication examples in the book have been shared with educational leaders and students. As new understandings regarding teaching, learning, and leading surfaces in new research, the Six-Point Conceptual Framework will continue to be tweaked.

Each step in this framework is explored in depth, with reflective prompts, assessment protocols, examples, and leadership tasks to support collaborative change, improvement, and transformation and to make innovation a lived reality. More than a framework to guide improvement efforts, this book is a call to reclaim the democratic purpose of education. At a time when public trust in institutions is eroding and social divisions have deepened, schools must not only teach democratic principles, but they must also model them. When schools operate collaboratively, and reflect the values of dialogue, equity, and shared responsibility, they become places where students learn not just to achieve at high levels, but also to belong and contribute.

As Dewey (1938) said so long ago, "If we teach today's students as we taught yesterday's, we rob them of tomorrow." There are many who have been waiting a long time for things in PK–12 education to change. I offer this book with humility and hope, to all who are working to make schools more responsive, more just, more humane, and more democratic. In a way, much of this book functions as my leadership platform. My deepest belief is that change, improvement, transformation, and innovation when deep-rooted in collaboration truly becomes possible.

School Change is a Collaborative Process is a step-by-step guide that provides the structure, tools, practice and inspiration to help you lead change and innovation. If you're ready to transform schools so that they truly meet the needs of today's students, it's time to trust and embrace the collaborative change process and begin by completing the following Leadership Task before reading Chapter One. Let's get to work!

With appreciation, optimism and hope for what we can reimagine and accomplish together!

—Stephen Gould

Leadership Task: *Develop a One-Page Written Statement*

- In your statement address the question, "What do you value as a person and educator?"

Describe how values influence your leadership practice as an educational leader with or without formal authority. Keep this written statement as a Word document so that you can refer to it in a future chapter. After you have completed your one-page written statement, turn the page and step into Chapter One.

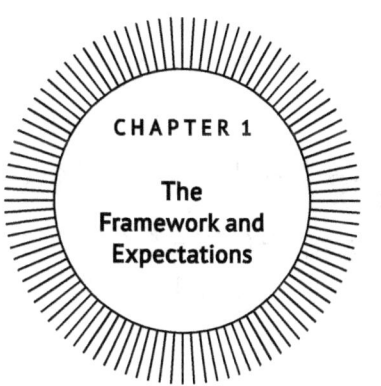

CHAPTER 1

The Framework and Expectations

CHAPTER 2 — Establish and Maintain Relational Trust and a Sense of Community

CHAPTER 3 — Collaboratively Collect Contextual Data

CHAPTER 4 — Collaboratively Determine a Collective Focus

CHAPTER 5 — Collaboratively Develop an Action Plan

CHAPTER 6 — Collaboratively Assess Progress (and Adjust)

CHAPTER 7 — Collaboratively Create a Plan to Celebrate Gains

CHAPTER 8 — The Innovation Plan

The Six-Point Conceptual Framework and New Expectations for Educational Leaders

▶ INTRODUCTION

In today's rapidly changing educational landscape, leadership is no longer defined by titles or hierarchy. Whether teachers, teacher teams, department heads, instructional coaches, special education directors, principals, or superintendents, educational leaders are called to adopt a visionary, collaborative approach to drive meaningful change, improvement, transformation, and innovation. This chapter introduces the *Six-Point Conceptual Framework*, a systems-thinking, strategic-planning model designed to help leaders navigate the complexities of organizational development and the turbulent waters of school improvement. In addition, it delves deeply into *expectations for educational leaders, reflection, communication, and leadership identity*.

At its core, the chapter explores the intersection of democratic purposes of schooling, evolving leadership theories, new leadership expectations, and the role of leadership identity. It emphasizes how reflective, value-driven, inclusive, and collaborative leadership, grounded in clear, consistent communication, can catalyze systemic change. Educational leaders and students aspiring to be leaders are invited to reflect deeply on who they are, what they value, and how they lead. Growth begins with self-awareness, a commitment to lifelong learning, and a mindset that values reflection and inquiry as much as action and results. This requires challenging unconscious, deeply ingrained assumptions and mindsets that shape decisions and behaviors, like leadership identity, positionality, power, and privilege.

A key challenge for today's leaders is to recognize how outdated solutions often perpetuate the very problems they aim to solve. As Einstein noted, "The significant problems we face cannot be solved with the same level of thinking we were at when we created them." Effective leadership demands awareness of one's role in the system, ethical decision-making, empathy, compassion, curiosity, and the ability to lead amid uncertainty and ambiguity. Leaders must understand how systems should interconnect to meet the needs of all students of all families. Good intentions alone are not enough.

Educational leadership is not just about managing tasks or achieving outcomes. Educational leadership involves developing a clear vision and the capacity to see the gap between a preferred future and current reality. A shared vision is connected to individual visions. Educational leaders should be designers, teachers, and facilitators who listen to the personal visions of faculty and families and work collaboratively to create an inspired shared vision rather than impose their personal vision on school community members.

A shared vision is more than an idea. A shared vision fosters a sense of common purpose, fuels commitment, aligns and motivates efforts, and reduces resistance. It becomes a living part of daily school life. True school change comes from people working together with purpose, trust, and persistence to create high-performing learning environments where all voices are valued and teachers and students learn at high levels. The process of collaborative school change cannot be mandated. It is something to build together!

In this chapter educational leaders with or without authority will learn

- How to use the Six-Point Conceptual Framework to guide, facilitate, sustain, and maintain a step-by-step, structured, iterative process for change innovation and transformation.
- How to utilize a structured, iterative process for change innovation and transformation.
- How to align the Framework's six interconnected subsystems to unite faculty to address factors and conditions inhibiting and promoting school improvement.
- How leadership theories and models have shaped practice.

- How new expectations have influenced current leadership roles.
- How self-reflection on values, identity, mindset, vision, and communication underpins effective, collaborative leadership to increase student learning.

Ultimately, this chapter serves as an invitation to embark on a path of self-discovery and to learn how to apply the Six-Point Conceptual Framework to guide the collaborative improvement of PK–12 student learning. It is assumed that educational leaders have completed the Leadership Task assigned in the Preface. If not, please step back and complete the Leadership Task before going forward in this chapter.

▶ THE SIX-POINT CONCEPTUAL FRAMEWORK

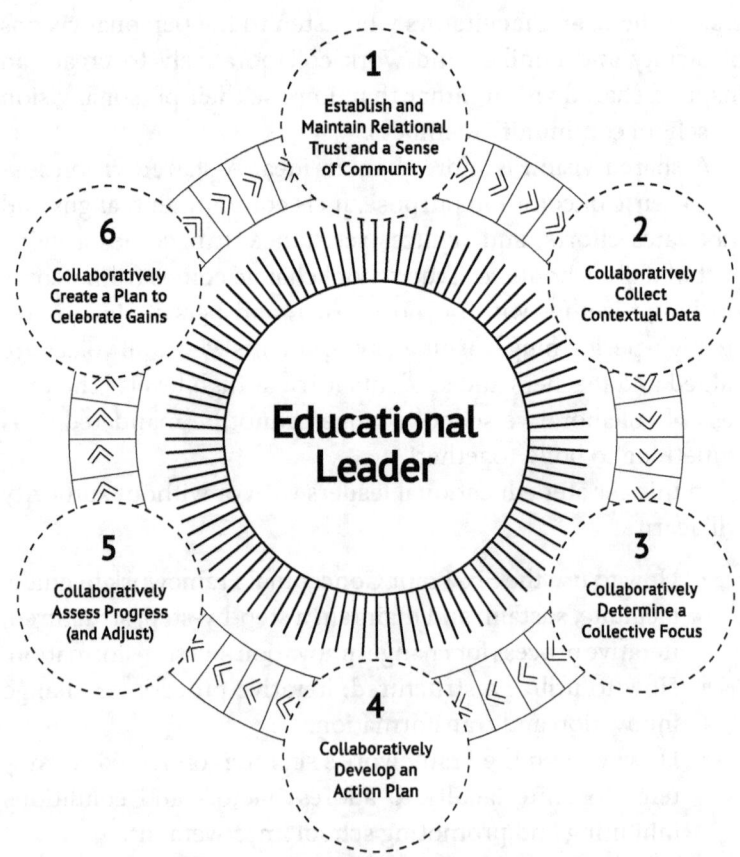

At a time of urgent need for system-wide change, improvement, and transformation, the Six-Point Conceptual Framework supports innovation at the classroom, grade level, department, school, or district level. To guide this process, the Six-Point Conceptual Framework presented in this book offers a practical and visionary roadmap for leaders. Tackling challenges through reflective practice; establishing and maintaining relational trust and a sense of community; and collaboratively collecting contextual data, determining a collective focus, developing an action plan, assessing progress, and creating a plan to celebrate gains function as vital stages in the journey of continuous improvement.

The Six-Point Conceptual Framework offers a coherent, research-informed approach to collaboratively lead the PK–12 school change process. It empowers leaders at all levels, with or without formal titles, to work with faculty colleagues to co-create context-specific solutions that address teaching, learning, and dysfunctional organizational factors and conditions.

The Six-Point Conceptual Framework is a system. A classroom, grade level, teacher team, department, school, or district are all systems. Curriculum content and performance power standards; assessment utilization; instruction; linked, multi-leveled materials; connected safety nets; job-embedded professional development; collaboration; and aligned parent outreach are all systems.

The Framework integrates systems thinking and strategic planning and emphasizes the need to understand the relationships among subsystems that are part of a larger system, rather than viewing factors and conditions in isolation. Each of the six points of the Framework functions as a subsystem within the Framework. By considering how subsystems interact and influence one another, educational leaders and faculty gain a holistic perspective that reveals systemic factors and conditions that are persistent barriers and hinder student learning.

The Framework is iterative and flexible, allowing leaders to move between subsystems based on school context and developmental stages of improvement. For example, a new leader may begin by building trust and assessing context, while an experienced leader might focus on data collection and targeted improvement. Regardless, relational trust often requires ongoing attention. Grounded in shared purpose, values, reflection, vision, relational trust, a sense of community, and collaborative effort, the Framework helps leaders commit to and guide approaches to school improvement. The Framework is not a checklist, but a dynamic change process that cultivates collective agency and builds the conditions for sustainable change. Focusing on subsystems of the Framework ensures that innovation is not random or reactive, but intentional, grounded in shared inquiry, and responsive to the specific needs of a school community.

At the heart of this step-by-step guide to improve PK–12 student learning is the belief that the most enduring and meaningful transformations in education emerge from within, through the collective will and wisdom of educators, students, families, and communities. But this belief is not just educationally sound. It is fundamentally democratic. The very practice of collaboration in schools echoes the values and principles of a democratic society, which include shared responsibility, inclusive participation, mutual respect, reflective dialogue, and collaborative decision-making. When we commit to working together, across roles, identities, and perspectives, we enact democracy in one of its most vital public institutions, the school. The Six-Point Conceptual Framework is, quite simply, an indispensable system and change process for leading the improvement of teaching, learning, leading, and innovative school improvement.

▶ THE PURPOSE OF SCHOOLS

The purpose of schools in the United States has been defined in multiple ways over time, depending on the historical, political, and philosophical context. Thomas Jefferson, in his 1779 Bill, "A Bill for the More General Diffusion of Knowledge," stated that an informed citizenry is essential for a functioning democracy to prevent tyranny, enable reasoned decision-making, and ensure government accountability. He believed that public schools would give all citizens the knowledge to understand their rights and duties, discern facts from falsehoods, and that an education was the great equalizer. John Dewey (1916) argued that the fundamental purpose of education is to prepare individuals to participate fully in democratic life. He believed that schools should cultivate critical thinking, communication, and social responsibility. According to the U.S. Department of Education (2010), the purpose of education is preparing students with skills for the labor market and economic development.

Darling-Hammond (2010) maintains that "The mission of public education must be to guarantee all students, regardless of race or income, access to a high-quality education that prepares them for college, careers, and citizenship." The Association for Supervision and Curriculum Development (ASCD) and Center for Disease Control (CDC) (2014) affirm that the purpose of education is to develop the whole child academically, socially, and emotionally and nurture mental health and physical well-being. Tyler (1973), reinforces the sentiments of Jefferson and Dewey and contends that, "Carrying on citizenship is the most important reason for public education. A democratic society cannot long exist unless its citizens participate actively in its affairs and assume responsibility for its continued welfare."

▶ THE EVOLUTION OF EDUCATIONAL LEADERSHIP THEORIES AND MODELS

Educational leadership theories and models have evolved significantly over time, reflecting changes in societal priorities, organizational needs, and educational contexts. In all likelihood, early leadership models were derived from historic, heroic, positional leaders who led their followers to great conquests and other monumental accomplishments. The theories and models presented next indicate when they were first introduced and provide ways to understand and guide educational leadership behaviors.

Democracy in Education (1779-Present)

Thomas Jefferson presented a rationale for the need to have public schools: "If a nation expects to be ignorant and free, in a state of civilization, it expects what never was and never will be." The Democracy in Education model is a call to action for educational leaders to not only lead democratically but to foster democratic values within their schools. John Dewey (1916) said, "Every generation needs to rediscover democracy." Schools should serve as democracy's workshop and provide students, teachers, and families with opportunities to experience and be part of a democratic process. Tyler (1973), mentions the critical role schools should play in reinforcing the importance of democracy and modeling its practice. *Professional Standards for Educational Leaders* (2015) emphasizes the need for leaders to initiate, facilitate, and sustain improvement through collaborative efforts. Collaboration is an example of democratic practice. School leaders promote democratic values in teaching, learning, leading, and decision-making and emphasize and celebrate democratic values at national holiday times.

Trait Theory (1840-1940)

This early leadership Trait Theory model suggests that great leaders are not made but born with inherent traits such as intelligence, charisma, and decisiveness. Early studies of principal effectiveness and leadership qualities were rooted in the "Great Man Theory" (Carlyle, 1841), and educational leaders were often chosen based on this perspective. Trait Theory overemphasizes innate qualities and overlooks situational or environmental factors.

Behavioral Theory (1940s-1950s)

Kurt Lewin (1890–1947), a pioneer in social and behavioral psychology, emphasized that effective leadership and school improvement depend on understanding behavior as shaped by both people and their environment. He argued that leaders foster positive change by building trust, clarifying purpose, and creating supportive conditions rather than relying on pressure or compliance. Viewing the school as an interconnected system, Lewin highlighted the importance of collaboration and collective responsibility through group dynamics, which later inspired Professional Learning Communities and shared leadership models. His three-stage change model, "Unfreezing, Changing, and Refreezing" continues to guide educational leaders in challenging existing practices, implementing innovation, and embedding new approaches into school culture and policy.

Situational Leadership (1950s-1970s)

Hersey and Blanchard (1969) contend that principal and superintendent leadership effectiveness depends on the situation and the leaders' ability to adapt approaches to improvement based on school culture and community needs.

Instructional Leadership (1970s-Present)

Researchers like Webber and Edmonds began to explore the connection between school leadership practices and student outcomes. The Instructional Leadership model (Hallinger and Murphy, 1985a) emphasizes the principal's role in improving teaching and learning by setting academic goals, monitoring instruction, supporting teachers, and fostering teacher development. Instructional leadership emerged as a response to the demand for accountability in schools. The major criticism is that the model focused heavily on academics, at the expense of a social curriculum. Regarding the role of the principal in utilizing this model, Fullan (2003a) said,

> The principal as instructional leader is too narrow a concept to carry the weight of the kinds of reforms that we need for the future. We need, instead, leaders who can create a fundamental transformation in the learning cultures of schools and the teaching profession itself.

Currently, Instructional Leadership 2.0 broadens its approach to include broader student needs.

Ethical and Moral Leadership (1980s-Present)

Ethical and moral leadership is grounded in principles, emphasizing fairness, and is focused on the moral dimensions of leadership, justice, and integrity (Gilligan, 1982). It is useful when involving diverse stakeholders in decision-making and resolving dilemmas. Ethical and moral leadership is receiving a resurgence in this post COVID-19 period.

Leadership for Renewal (1980-2000)

John Goodlad's idea of leadership for renewal focuses on preparing, supporting and changing the daily practice of PK-12 and higher education leaders so that they become critical adapters of curriculum and work effectively to promote inquiry, equity and continuous learning.

Transformational Leadership (1985-Present)

Leaders inspire and motivate followers to align with a shared vision and achieve at higher levels. This model emphasizes charisma, intellectual stimulation, and individualized consideration (Burns, 1978; Bass, 1985; Leithwood & Jantzi, 2000) and is adopted in schools to promote school-wide reforms and foster shared purpose, collaboration, teacher empowerment, and innovation. Transformational Leadership continues to focus on inspiring and motivating followers to achieve more than they thought possible.

Servant Leadership (1990s-Present)

Servant Leadership emphasizes the leader's role as a servant to their followers, prioritizing their needs and growth and focusing on the well-being of students, teachers, and the community. According to Sergiovanni (1992), servant leadership focuses on principals fostering inclusive, nurturing school cultures; community-building; and teacher empowerment. This model, too, has a following given the newfound understanding of the importance of building relational trust and the stress of high-stakes testing.

Adaptive Leadership (1990s-Present)

Adaptive Leadership (Heifetz, 1994) emphasizes the ability to respond to complex, changing environments by mobilizing others to tackle tough challenges and learn from them. The model promotes collaboration and organizational learning and differentiates between technical problems solvable with existing knowledge as opposed to adaptive challenges requiring new learning and innovation. Heifetz is a pioneer of adaptive leadership and expanded on approaches for adaptive change, which helps leaders navigate rapid changes and crises in education like COVID-19.

Leadership for Social-Emotional Learning (1994-Present)

As awareness of the importance of social-emotional learning (SEL) continues to grow, school leaders are increasingly called upon to prioritize the well-being of the whole child as well as that of faculty and staff. This responsibility includes fostering a safe, caring, and supportive school culture where students feel emotionally secure and valued. In the aftermath of COVID-19, leaders are also expected to cultivate a positive school culture that promotes teachers' emotional health, helps prevent burnout, and actively encourages practices of self-care.

Culturally Responsive Leadership (1995-Present)

This model emphasizes equity and cultural competence in addressing the diverse needs of all students, particularly in response to gaps in achievement often highlighted by standardized test results (Ladson-Billings, 1995). It supports multilingual learners, promotes culturally relevant pedagogy, and fosters inclusive school environments. Leaders center cultural competence and responsiveness to diverse student and community needs (Gay, 1982; Khalifa et al., 2016).

Distributed Leadership (2000-Present)

Originally introduced in the 1950s by Gibb, it wasn't adopted until later. Elmore (2000), in "Building a New Structure for School Leadership," challenges the traditional notion of leadership, suggesting that it should be distributed among teachers. He advances the idea that a single individual (e.g., the principal) is no longer the sole decision-maker. Instead, educational leaders are expected to empower teachers to take on leadership roles within their schools. Elmore's ideas have been influential in shaping contemporary approaches to school leadership and improvement, emphasizing the importance of shared responsibility, collaboration, and a focus on whole-systems student learning. Spillane (2006) contends that distributive leadership fosters a sense of ownership and collective responsibility for student success. In addition, distributive leaders involve the broader school community by collaborating with parents, community organizations, and local businesses. In this way, leaders can create partnerships beyond the classroom that support teaching, learning, and leading.

Leadership for Accountability and High-Stakes Testing (2001-Present)

The No Child Left Behind Act has placed additional pressure on school leaders to ensure that students meet specific benchmarks. This model, with its mandated, summative assessment, high stakes standardized testing, expects teachers to utilize data to assess student progress and determine necessary improvement efforts. While standardized testing remains a key measure of success, school leaders are expected to ensure that the emphasis on testing does not undermine the integrity of the curriculum and instructional quality. Seashore teachers often feel the pressure and stress of high stakes testing.

Leadership for Learning (2010-Present)

Leithwood et al. (2010) contends that educational leadership makes a difference in improving student learning. There are five guiding principles of leadership for learning: maintaining a focus on learning as an activity; creating conditions favorable to learning as an activity; leading a dialogue about leadership for learning; sharing leadership; and sharing a sense of accountability. The four dimensions of leadership for learning identified by Hallinger (2010) are values and beliefs; leadership focus; contexts for leadership; and sharing leadership.

Leadership for Equity, Access, and Social Justice (2010-Present)

The Equity and Access model (Darling-Hammond, 2010) includes making curricular and instructional adjustments that respond to the needs of diverse learners so that all students feel supported, have access to high-quality instruction and technology, and are given the opportunity to succeed. In this model, leaders continue to focus on addressing systemic inequities and fostering equity, inclusion, and empowerment (Shields, 2010); challenge discriminatory practices; promote equity; and ensure all students have access to quality education (Theoharis, 2007).

Leadership for Innovation and Personalized Learning (2012-Present)

Zhao (2012) consistently challenges traditional approaches to education by urging leaders to innovate, foster personalized learning, help teachers learn how to empower students to take ownership of their learning, and provide learning activities so that students are engaged in solving meaningful problems. He argues that students should be seen as active participants in their learning, with agency to explore their passions, identify their needs, and chart their educational pathways. Zhao advocates for leaders to distribute leadership that empowers all faculty to contribute to innovation. He suggests leaders and teachers nurture innovation by moving away from solely addressing student weaknesses and instead focusing on cultivating and developing each student as a unique individual with their own interests, strengths, and potential. He encourages leaders to practice open communication, empathy, compassion, and active listening; build trusting relationships; and create a school culture where teachers feel comfortable trying new approaches, knowing that they have support for risk-taking.

In this model, teachers act as guides, coaches, community organizers, and project managers, supporting students as they pursue their personalized learning goals and helping them develop crucial skills like creativity and entrepreneurship. Zhao criticizes the current education system's overreliance on standardized tests and advocates for alternative ways of measuring student progress that capture a broader spectrum of learning and development. Zhao encourages educators to drive progress and break away from outdated practices. While technology can be a useful tool, Zhao warns against equating personalized learning solely with technology.

In essence, Zhao's vision for personalized learning and innovation centers on creating an education system that values and nurtures each student's unique potential; fosters a student-centered approach that embraces individual strengths; cultivates a culture of continuous improvement and creative exploration; and empowers students to become lifelong learners.

In summary, there has been a shift from individuals working and making decisions in isolation to teacher teams working collaboratively on a collective problem that they share. Leadership has transitioned from trait and behavioral theories to distributed and innovation leadership. In recent years there has been an increasing emphasis on equity, access, and justice with leadership efforts addressing systemic inequities and social justice. Theories and models like Adaptive Leadership and Leadership for Innovation and Personalized Learning respond to modern, complex educational challenges. Educational leaders should take into consideration the effects of COVID-19 on students, teachers, and families and implement a social curriculum and social emotional learning (SEL).

▶ NEW EXPECTATIONS FOR EDUCATIONAL LEADERS

Educational leadership has significantly evolved in response to shifting societal needs, educational reforms, and increased accountability. A review of current research and leadership models highlights a set of new expectations that redefine what it means to lead in schools today. In this book, *educational leadership* refers broadly to anyone working in schools who influences teaching, learning, and school culture regardless of formal title. This includes teachers, instructional coaches, department heads, guidance counselors, special educators, principals, and superintendents. These individuals are key agents of change. Today's leaders are expected not just to manage operations, but also to model learning, lead innovation, and act with moral purpose even when doing so means swimming against the current and challenging the status quo. Elmore (2000) defines leadership as "the guidance and direction of large-scale, sustained, and continuous improvement of instructional practice and performance." This involves guiding faculty, collaboratively, to improve curriculum and instruction and the conditions in which they occur. This shift moves leadership away from traditional command-and-control models toward approaches that build relational trust, shared decision-making, teacher empowerment, continuous learning, and system-wide alignment. According to Fullan (2003a) "Leaders must be lead learners modeling inquiry, openness to change, and deep engagement with the moral purpose of schooling." Leithwood et al. (2010) emphasizes that even if principals do not work directly with every student, their influence on school culture and instructional quality is profound.

Modern school leaders face a diverse array of challenges including managing operations and resources, improving instructional quality and student achievement, using data to inform decisions, supporting the holistic development of students, facilitating professional growth, and engaging families and communities (Power, 2004). Challenges like technological advancement, the lasting impacts of COVID-19, and growing cultural and linguistic diversity add layers of complexity and public scrutiny. In this context, culturally responsive leadership is essential. Leaders must foster inclusive environments where all students can thrive, develop civic awareness, and feel emotionally supported. This includes promoting equity, closing opportunity gaps, supporting SEL, and embracing cultural diversity across the school community. In addition, school leaders often face dilemmas with no clear solution, a solution that is controversial, or an imperfect solution at best. Courageous leadership is going forward in the face of ambiguity. Leaders are also expected to co-develop with faculty a shared vision set school-wide goals, engage families in decision-making, and build leadership capacity across the school.

Contemporary leadership models emphasize shared responsibility. Leaders are no longer expected to make all the decisions alone. Instead, they must empower teachers to take on leadership roles, especially in areas such as curriculum, instruction, professional development, and community engagement. Distributing leadership sustains improvement efforts. As Hargreaves and Fink (2006) write, "Sustainable leadership spreads and sustains deep learning for all." Distributing leadership also strengthens partnerships with families, community organizations, and businesses, extending learning beyond the classroom (Sergiovanni, 1992).

Leadership is not limited to those with formal positions of authority. Teachers, team leaders, instructional coaches, department heads, guidance counselors, and others without formal authority can and do lead meaningful change. Leadership is about taking ownership, acting with intention and inspiring improvement. Reflect on your role. What influence do you have over curriculum, assessment, and instruction in your classroom, grade level, department, school, or district? Heifetz (1994) argues that anyone who wants to make a difference can be a leader. How can you foster collaboration, support colleagues, guide professional learning, or engage families?

Gleaned from the research literature on educational leadership policy documents, a number of leadership behaviors regarding what is expected of educational leaders leading in a constantly changing world are identified and described next.

Reflect on Self and the Purpose of Reflective Leadership Practice

Among the most vital behaviors for educational leaders is self-reflection, described as the deliberate and thoughtful examination of one's beliefs, actions, and their impact. Reflection is a catalyst for professional growth and continuous improvement. Foundational thinkers such as Dewey (1933), Schön (1983), and Darling-Hammond (2017) have highlighted reflection as essential to effective teaching and leading. Dewey saw reflection as bridging theory and practice, central to inquiry-based learning, and believed that "we do not learn from experience; we learn from reflecting on experience." Building on Dewey, Rodgers (2002) emphasized that reflection must be communal, methodical, evidence-based, and aimed at growth and change. Schön introduced the concepts of "reflection-in-action" (real-time decision-making) and "reflection-on-action" (post-practice analysis), both critical for continuous improvement.

As Schön noted, "The practitioner allows himself to experience surprise, puzzlement, or confusion. He reflects on the phenomenon before him, and on the prior understandings which have been implicit in his behavior." For leaders, such reflection deepens self-awareness, sharpens decision-making, and lays the groundwork for transformative leadership.

Self-reflection enables educators to refine their practice, improve student learning, and understand their work within larger systems, such as those described in the Six-Point Conceptual Framework. It requires honest examination of values, beliefs, mindsets, identity, positionality, biases, commitments, and vision. As Bennis (1989) wrote in *On Becoming a Leader*, "Know thyself . . . is still the most difficult task any of us faces . . . until you truly know yourself . . . you cannot succeed in any but the most superficial sense."

Reflection also supports ethical leadership. It fosters critical thinking, enhances problem-solving, informs positionality, and promotes inclusive, equitable practice (Greenleaf, 1977; Brookfield, 1995). It enables educators to surface and address implicit biases and align their actions with their values around equity, diversity, inclusion, and justice (EDIJ).

Moreover, reflective educators are more adaptive, resilient, and committed to lifelong learning. Regular reflection not only enhances instructional effectiveness and student engagement but also contributes to emotional well-being and professional sustainability. Kolb (1984) and Darling-Hammond have shown that reflection is a cornerstone of adult learning and collaborative professional communities, where educators work together to improve outcomes for all students.

Identify Values, Beliefs, Mindsets, and Commitments

In every thriving school, behind the visible routines of teaching, learning, and leading, lies something deeper that shapes every interaction, every decision, and every aspiration. That "something" is the set of values, beliefs, mindsets, and commitments held by educational leaders and faculty. These four elements quietly, yet powerfully, determine how schools evolve, educators grow, and students succeed. Educational leaders and faculty often engage in reflective practices through journaling, professional development workshops, and utilizing 360-degree feedback systems.

A clear understanding of values, beliefs, mindsets, and commitments, and the role they play in problem-solving and decision-making, is one of the most critical aspects of leadership. Values, beliefs, mindsets, and commitments are enduring and desirable prevailing sentiments that we have experienced and possess. Beliefs are a firmly held opinion or conviction. For example, effective leadership is the belief that all students from all families can achieve at high levels given differentiated teaching and an adaptive and supportive learning environment. This belief requires a shift in mindset from asking "Can they?" to "Have we created the conditions where they can?" It recognizes, as Howard (1991) and Resnick (1995) argue, that intelligence is shaped more by effort, opportunity, and strategic support than by innate talent. Mindsets refer to a person's natural or prevailing tendency or inclination, disposition, attitude, or mood. Commitments are a dedication to see something through regardless of the challenges. A leader's values, beliefs, mindsets, and commitments shape how they view their role, prioritize, make decisions, and engage with others. When behavior or decisions conflict with shared values and beliefs, leaders need to change their behavior or alter their decisions. Values, beliefs, mindsets, and commitments are related to each other and help shape the culture of a school. They should become the standard for guiding actions and judging what leaders, teachers, and others do morally. Examples of values, beliefs, mindsets, and commitments include the following:

relational trust; a sense of community; integrity; treating others with respect; freedom; respect for differences; openness; transparency; empathy, compassion, equity, diversity, inclusion, and justice; logical thinking; ethical, collaborative and capacity building leadership; all children can learn if provided the right learning experiences and environment; parent, family, and community engagement; service and giving back; and helping students become productive members of a democratic society.

Understand Your Leadership Identity

Leadership identity is rooted in values, beliefs, mindsets, commitments, culture, race, ethnicity, experiences, education, knowledge, and skills. Understanding your leadership identity is a deeply personal journey that begins with self-reflection and leads to transformation. Leadership identity is an awareness of who you are, what you stand for, your positionality, how you see yourself, and how you want to be perceived by others. It reflects what matters most to you as a leader.

Leadership identity is foundational to effective leadership because it shapes behaviors such as being self-aware, authentic, transparent, compassionate, ethical, inclusive, collaborative, equity-minded, culturally competent, and committed to social justice and systemic change. Before leading improvement efforts leaders must first reflect on their own identity. As Bennis (1989) noted, "Becoming a leader is synonymous with becoming yourself. It is precisely that simple, and it is also that difficult." Leadership practice in PK–12 schools is shaped by how leaders view themselves and their role in supporting students, teachers, and families.

True change cannot be imposed by top-down mandates. It must grow from the beliefs, values, and actions of those closest to the learner (Sinclair & Ghory, 1987). At the same time, beliefs carry moral weight. A strong ethical stance is essential, especially when confronting systemic inequities and racism, which remain major barriers to student achievement. Educational leaders must actively commit to antiracist, culturally relevant, and equity-focused practices. This is not a one-time task. It is an ongoing responsibility central to authentic leadership. Educational leaders must regularly examine their leadership identity. The conditions in which teaching, learning, and leading take place greatly impact student outcomes. Educators must become architects of learning, improve current conditions and design inclusive learning conditions where all students feel safe, valued, and capable of learning at high levels.

Communicate Your Vision and Collaboratively Develop a Shared Vision

Vision is the outward expression of leadership identity and values. One of a leader's first priorities should be to communicate clearly and authentically their purpose, leadership identity, and vision. For leaders with formal authority, it's essential to reflect on their own leadership identity when crafting and communicating their personal vision. A compelling vision provides a vivid image of a preferred future and what classrooms, departments, schools, or districts could and should become. Rooted in a leader's understanding of their community and its unique demographics, an effective vision offers direction, coherence, and meaning to the work of school improvement. It sets aspirational goals serving as a guiding set of ideals motivating the school community. Vision is particularly powerful when shared through face-to-face communication followed by opportunities for dialogue, allowing faculty, families, and community members to provide feedback and input. Senge (1990) reinforces these sentiments and affirms that

> Real vision cannot be imposed from above. It is forged through the interaction of people who care deeply about something they want to create together. A vision is not an idea, it is a force in people's hearts, a force of impressive power.

Face-to-face communication of vision, followed by open dialogue with faculty, families, and community members, is crucial to building trust and commitment. But that is not where it ends. After discussion, educational leaders should pivot and engage faculty in collaboratively developing a shared vision. When a vision is collaboratively developed, it captures the minds and hearts of those who actualize it. A shared vision inspires shared purpose, collaborative action, and improvement.

Communicate Frequently

Effective and consistent communication is at the heart of educational leadership. A synthesis of the work of several respected theorists and authors in educational leadership (e.g., Darling-Hammond, Fullan, Hargreaves & Shirley, and Senge) highlights the critical nature of communication in leadership practice. Strong communication skills allow leaders to build trust and credibility, foster collaboration, promote change and innovation, mobilize collective action, encourage stakeholder buy-in, and skillfully navigate and resolve conflicts. Openness, transparency, authenticity, empathy, compassion, humility, and courage are all critical leadership behaviors central to creating shared purpose, mobilizing stakeholders, and building leadership capacity across a school or district, and these should be communicated. Great leadership is about serving others (Sergiovanni, 1992) and what is communicated. Communication is not just about transmitting information. It's about building trust, fostering collaboration, co-constructing meaning, facilitating ongoing improvement, and guiding the improvement of school culture. According to Wheatley (1999), "In organizations, real power and energy is generated through relationships. The patterns of relationships and the capacities to form them are more important than tasks, functions, roles, and positions. And communication is how relationships happen."

Poor communication, by contrast, creates confusion, erodes trust, and leaves stakeholders feeling uncertain. Leaders must communicate clearly and consistently, offering feedback, sharing rationales behind decisions, reporting results, highlighting areas for growth, and inviting input from faculty and the broader community. Locke and Latham (1990) stress the value of clear communication in setting shared goals, while Goleman (1995) emphasizes the role of emotional intelligence in fostering empathetic, trust-building dialogue.

Establish and Maintain Relational Trust

Relational trust occurs when people come to understand each other and that leaders can be counted on to act in ways consistent with personal and community values. Trust is given to those with similar values, whose actions are consistent with what they say and who have a proven track record of getting results by providing services with predictability (Heifetz, 1994). This process will be elaborated later in the chapter.

Practice Collaborative Leadership

Research based leadership approaches emphasize collaboration and shared responsibility for school improvement. Leaders are now expected to collaboratively develop with teachers, students, parents, and community members a shared vision; set school-wide goals; engage stakeholders in the decision-making process; and build the leadership capacity of teachers and teacher teams (DeWitt, 2016).

Prioritize Teaching and Learning

Ralph Tyler (1949), considered the father of curriculum and evaluation, was clear regarding what the schools were expected to teach. Ralph Tyler's foundational "Tyler Rationale," still relevant today, emphasizes a) the goals and objectives schools should seek to attain; b) the educational experiences that are likely to attain the goals; c) the organization of these experiences into a curriculum; and d) assessing whether the objectives have been achieved.

Effective school leaders are now expected to prioritize teaching and learning and take an active role in improving their quality (Leithwood et al., 2004). Regarding building the capacity of teachers, leaders are expected to foster a culture of continuous learning by providing teachers with opportunities for professional development, collaboration, and supportive and corrective feedback. Differentiated instruction, Mastery Learning, instructional coaching, peer learning, and data-driven instruction are some methods used to improve teaching practices. *Professional Standards for Educational Leaders* (2015), formerly known as the *ISLLC Standards*, encourages educational leaders to secure and allocate resources to support ongoing professional development.

Support Equity and Access

New expectations and standards for leaders suggest that leaders need to possess a moral compass. In the current educational landscape, there is a heightened emphasis on equity and access and addressing the diverse needs of all students, particularly in response to gaps in achievement and opportunity that are often highlighted by standardized test results (Darling-Hammond, 2010). Some of these areas where equity and achievement gaps exist include access to high-quality curriculum, instruction, and technology in face-to-face classrooms and online.

Recognizing and mitigating implicit bias, understanding systemic inequities, and developing inclusive classroom practices are essential. This equips teachers to create environments where all students can thrive (Kendi, 2019). Equity in practice includes integrating culturally responsive teaching methods, which validate and incorporate students' cultural backgrounds into the learning process. Research highlights how this approach can increase engagement and achievement for marginalized students (Gay, 2018). Through the use of data from formative and standardized testing, school leaders can help teachers create inclusive learning environments and develop strategies and interventions that support diverse learners, historically marginalized students of color, English language learners, and those from low-income backgrounds. Expanding access to Advanced Placement (AP) courses and advanced programs through targeted outreach, preparatory programs, and eliminating prerequisite barriers ensures all students can pursue rigorous academic opportunities. Providing wraparound services, such as mental health counseling, academic tutoring, and family engagement programs, ensures that students' holistic needs are met. Community schools, which integrate such services, are effective models of equitable practice (Colburn & Beggs, 2020).

Implement Inclusive, Bias-Free Curriculum and Restorative Justice Practices

Revising curriculum to include diverse voices and histories promotes a more inclusive learning environment. Schools adopting frameworks like the "Windows and Mirrors" approach help students see their identities reflected and understand the experiences of others (Sims-Bishop, 1990). Restorative justice practices focus on relationship-building, conflict resolution, and addressing the root causes of behavior. These practices can replace punitive discipline measures and have been shown to reduce suspension rates and improve school climate (González, 2012).

Promote Social-Emotional Learning (SEL)

According to Bruce and McKee, in *Transformative Leadership in Action: Allyship, Advocacy and Activism*, it is critical that

> Learners have an awareness of self and of others, a willingness to uncover internal "records" related to oppression and to engage in critical reflection, possess an understanding of control and cultural domination, and possess a budding ability to expose their own thinking.

With a growing recognition of the importance of social-emotional learning and support, school leaders are now expected to prioritize social and emotional well-being by supporting the whole child, faculty, and staff. In this regard school leaders must ensure that their schools provide a safe, nurturing, and supportive school culture and learning environment where students feel emotionally secure and supported. This involves implementing programs that promote SEL; addressing issues such as bullying, racism, and mental health; and fostering positive relationships between staff and students. In addition, in the post COVID-19 period, just as students require social-emotional support, so too do teachers and families. School leaders are expected to create a positive school culture that supports emotional health and well-being, encourages self-care, and reduces teacher burnout.

Integrate Technology and Online Learning

The rise of digital tools requires leaders to integrate new learning modalities and prepare both teachers and students for a technologically driven future (Zhao, 2008). Leaders are expected to guide their schools in managing and integrating technology in the classroom in ways that enhance learning. In addition, this includes ensuring that teachers are trained in using educational technology effectively and that students have equitable access to digital tools and resources.

Reach Out and Engage Families

New expectations are that educational leaders will reach out and help parents and community members better understand the goals of their school and how they can help support and participate in the efforts of the school to change, improve, and transform teaching, learning, and the conditions in which they occur. Additional forms of engagement include helping their children at home with homework and other educational activities (Epstein, 2011).

Focus on Standardized Testing and Accountability

With the increased emphasis on standardized testing, leaders must find ways to help teachers align instruction with state standards, testing, and teaching requirements while maintaining a focus on holistic student development, creativity, and critical thinking. The new expectations include balancing accountability with instructional quality. While standardized testing remains a key measure of success, school leaders are expected to ensure that the emphasis on testing does not undermine instructional quality. School leaders must be adept at interpreting data and data-informed decision-making (Seashore-Louis, 2017). Leaders are expected to provide guidance to teachers on how to integrate formative assessments and standardized test preparation into the curriculum without sacrificing engaging and meaningful learning experiences. Teachers are expected to utilize formative and summative assessments to identify student needs, inform curriculum adjustments, guide instruction, and assess student progress. Teachers often feel the brunt of high-stakes testing pressure. Adding to the responsibilities of already over-burdened teachers and school leaders, leaders are expected to support teachers' emotional well-being as they both navigate the stress of testing pressures that come with accountability measures.

▶ EXAMPLES OF WRITTEN COMMUNICATIONS

Whether you are new to your role or a seasoned professional, whether or not you hold formal authority, communicating is essential. Who you are and what you stand for should not remain internal. It must be clearly expressed to your colleagues, students, and community. For example, at the start of each school year, consider communicating your values, beliefs, mindset, commitments, leadership identity, or shared vision through a brief face-to-face speech or written message. This communication can set the tone for how you hope to work with others and what you aim to accomplish collaboratively. It serves as a source of clarity during times of challenge or distraction, a compass for decision-making, and touchstone for accountability. When these values are articulated in writing and communicated, preferably face-to-face, they provide scaffolding to approach challenges with integrity, ensuring that decisions are aligned with the leader's ethical compass and the vision and shared values of the school community. When a brief face-to-face speech or written message is communicated authentically, your values, beliefs, mindset, commitments, leadership identity, or shared vision become more than a personal statement; it becomes a catalyst for change, improvement, transformation, and innovation.

Example 1: Shared Values and Beliefs

Dear Faculty,

It's the beginning of a new school year, and I want to share the values and beliefs that influence my practice. Central to my practice is reflection and working with others in a culture of relational trust and a feeling of belonging. I began by reflecting on my values, beliefs, dispositions, and commitments. I continued by asking myself, "Who am I? What do I value? What do I want to make happen? What is required to make it happen? Am I willing and committed to doing what is required?"

Integrity is something I deeply value. In every decision I make and every action I take, integrity is a guiding principle. It means being honest, transparent, and consistent. Trust is earned through actions, and it is the cornerstone of effective leadership and collaboration. By fostering a culture of integrity, we create a foundation of trust where everyone feels safe, respected, and valued.

Empathy is another fundamental value I hold dear. Understanding and appreciating the diverse backgrounds, experiences, and perspectives of our students, teacher colleagues, and community members is crucial. Empathy enables me to connect on a human level, see the world through others' eyes, and genuinely support others. When I lead with empathy, I hope to build bridges, break down barriers, and create an inclusive environment where everyone can contribute to improving student learning and attend to their well-being.

Authentic relationships require that I not only work effectively with others but that I genuinely care about them. This means investing time in building relationships, being present, listening actively, and showing appreciation. When I know and care about others, support their efforts, and celebrate gains together I know that we will be able to withstand the many challenges that confront us every day in schools.

Collaboration is the heartbeat of our community. We achieve more when we work together, leveraging our collective strengths and expertise. This means fostering open communication, encouraging diverse viewpoints, and creating opportunities for meaningful collaboration. By working together, we can tackle challenges, innovate, and accomplish our shared goals.

Lifelong learning is a value that propels our school community forward. In a rapidly changing world, my commitment to continuous improvement and growth is essential. I must cultivate a culture where curiosity is encouraged, mistakes are seen as opportunities for learning, and professional development is provided. By embracing lifelong learning, I not only enhance my own skills, but I also model this mindset for our students.

Equity, access, inclusion, and *justice* are things I deeply and profoundly value. Every individual in our school deserves the opportunity to succeed, regardless of their background or circumstances. I, we, must strive to create an equitable environment where resources, support, and opportunities are accessible to all. Inclusion means recognizing and valuing diversity, ensuring that everyone's voice is heard, and creating a sense of belonging for every member of our community.

In closing, I want to emphasize that these values are not just words. They are commitments. As we move forward together, let us establish and maintain authentic relationships and embody integrity, empathy, collaboration, lifelong learning, equity, access, inclusion, and justice in all that we do. Let us build a community where trust, equity, and access are not just an expectation but a lived reality. By working together, we can create an environment where every member of our school community feels valued, empowered, and connected.

Thank you for your dedication, your passion, and your unwavering commitment to our school. Together, I know we will be able to build a brighter future for our students, each other, the community at large, and our democratic society.

Example 2: Follow-Up Post for Shared Values and Beliefs

As a leader with authority, after sharing a speech, like the preceding one, follow-up with a shortened written version posted in the teachers' or parents' lounge. An alternative is to send faculty an email and include your leadership identity in the school newsletter. Next is a follow-up summary of the aforementioned communication.

Dear Colleagues,

I am deeply committed to the transformative power of education. My leadership journey has been shaped by my values and beliefs that every student deserves a voice and that collaboration is foundational to innovation. As an educator and leader, I am guided by a vision of schools as inclusive, dynamic spaces where every learner, teacher, and parent feel valued and empowered. My leadership identity is rooted in self-agency, empathy, and integrity; values I strive to model and inspire in others.

I believe in the power of listening to students' stories, to educators whose insights enrich our practices, and to families whose hopes illuminate our path forward. Together, we can build a school and district that honor diverse experiences and ensure success for all. My commitment to you as your leader is to cultivate a community defined by shared vision, mutual respect, and a relentless pursuit of excellence. Together we can create a future where every decision reflects our collective values and every action propels us closer to our shared goals.

Thank you for trusting me to lead with purpose, passion, and an unwavering belief in the promise of education.

Example 3: Follow-Up Email or Face-to-Face Communication for Shared Values and Beliefs

The following communication might be shared by a team leader, instructional coach, special educator, or department head without a formal position of authority as a follow-up to a teacher team meeting. It reflects a summary of previously discussed shared values and commitment to fostering a compassionate, creative, innovative, and justice-filled school for all students from all families.

Working Together as a Team

- We believe that serving one another is our primary responsibility.
- We value healthy human relationships; treating one another with respect, forgiveness, compassion, patience, kindness, and tolerance.
- We promote equity and access.
- We act ethically with integrity and honesty.
- We believe in constructive and honest communication, seeking first to understand and then to be understood.
- We believe in an environment that is physically, emotionally, and spiritually safe.
- We believe that all students can learn at high levels if given instruction and a learning environment that meets their needs.
- We believe that small, self-directed, and empowered teams can make responsible and effective decisions for the good of the organization.
- We believe the contribution of each individual is essential to success.

- We keep our commitments.
- We continually improve the quality of everything we do as we serve our co-workers, students, their parents, and the public.
- We promote personal and professional growth and life-long learning.
- We recognize and reward one another's progress and success.

See the Appendices for more examples of communications and additional follow-ups.

▶ DEVELOPING A LEADERSHIP IDENTITY COMMUNICATION

Reflect on the educational leadership models and new expectations for leaders presented earlier. Ask yourself how effective you are as a leader and how you want to be perceived by others. Review your one-page statement developed for the Leadership Task in the Preface. Self-reflect on values, beliefs, mindsets, commitments, leadership identity, new educational leadership expectations, and insights gained. Compare what you wrote for the Leadership Task in the Preface and determine if it was comprehensive enough to inform your colleagues and community who you are as an educational leader, what you hope to accomplish, and the depth of your commitment.

Write down some of the values and beliefs, shared in that initial Leadership Task, that resonated with you. These values, beliefs, mindset, commitments, and content shared earlier in this chapter should help form the foundation of your leadership identity communication. Before you begin writing your leadership identity speech decide on who your audience(s) will be (e.g., students, faculty, families) and choose language appropriate for the particular audience. Perhaps share how your understanding of your leadership identity will help you as an educational leader (e.g., to promote inclusivity in your organization). End your leadership identity speech with an enduring message and/or a call to action. Feel free to use or adapt any of the examples provided earlier.

Example: Post for Leadership Identity

The following is another example of a post that can be used to communicate leadership identity.

Colleagues,

My leadership identity will serve as my guide to all interactions, navigating ethical dilemmas and decision-making, ensuring that my actions remain aligned with my values and my dedication to making a meaningful, positive impact on students, faculty, and parents.

- I will reflect on and remain rooted in my values, beliefs, disposition, and commitments even when faced with challenges or unpopular decisions.
- I will be trustworthy, honest, truthful, and transparent.
- I will treat others as I wish to be treated and interact with others with understanding and compassion.
- I will honor my commitments and keep my promises, guided by my values, moral compass, and ethical standards.
- I will accept full responsibility for my actions, acknowledge shortcomings, and embrace accountability for the consequences of my decisions.
- I will recognize the privileges I hold and will work to support those who are less fortunate.
- I will strive to inspire confidence in others.

The importance of school leaders sharing and discussing their leadership identity with faculty and community cannot be overestimated. It communicates transparency and openness and reinforces relational trust.

▶ DEVELOPING A BULLETED PRELIMINARY PLAN FOR THE SIX-POINT CONCEPTUAL FRAMEWORK

A preliminary plan for each point of the Framework should focus on key actions you, as an educational leader, will take to advance school improvement. Use bullets to describe the leadership steps you will take. The preliminary plan should avoid generic or third-person descriptions and instead detail specific, actionable steps you will take to guide others. Do not describe what you think an educational leader other than yourself would do. Preliminary plans that you develop should make it clear that the step-by-step actions will be taken by you as the educational leader. Highlight how you will lead discussions, facilitate collaboration, and align with the purpose of schools. Include relevant citations to reinforce content, process, the rationale behind your approach and to communicate that the preliminary plan is grounded in evidence-based practices. Your preliminary plan will differ from the preliminary plans of others due to your unique school context and the degree to which you have a position with or without authority.

Looking ahead, each preliminary plan for each subsystem of Six-Point Conceptual Framework is foundational to the one that follows. After creating bullets for each of the six preliminary plans for each point of the Six-Point Conceptual Framework all the bullets are transferred to a Word document and organized using the titles of the six subsystems. Bulleted preliminary plans will be expanded and evolve into a narrative for a context-specific, tailor-made innovation plan in Chapter Eight. The knowledge, skills, and mindset gleaned from developing bulleted preliminary plans form the basis of an innovation plan that will contribute to creating a PK–12 coherent approach for guiding, facilitating, and sustaining school improvement. It will help faculty colleagues collaboratively address persistent factors and conditions needing improvement in classrooms, departments, schools, or districts. Developing preliminary plans and an innovation plan prepares educational leaders for when they will be working collaboratively with faculty colleagues.

Example: Communicating the Purpose and Process of Developing a Preliminary Plan

Here's a suggested script or set of talking points that leaders can use to guide a teacher team or faculty conversation that leads to the development of a preliminary plan aligned with the Six-Point Conceptual Framework. The goal is to make the purpose clear, build ownership, and support staff in generating their own preliminary plan outlining leadership actions.

I want to re-introduce the Six-Point Conceptual Framework, as a tool we'll be using to help guide our school improvement efforts in a more intentional and collaborative way. The Six-Point Conceptual Framework, provides a structure for analyzing school conditions and strategically planning how we can strengthen teaching, learning, and leadership.

This process isn't a top-down model or a new program to implement. It's a way of organizing and aligning the good work we're already doing while identifying areas we want to improve. Each of the six points in the framework represents a different subsystem that contributes to student learning. What I'd like us to begin working on today, and over the coming weeks, is something called a preliminary plan. Each teacher team will think through and begin writing a bulleted list of specific actions we can take, based on our role, to contribute to improvement in each of the six areas of the Framework.

Let me be clear. This isn't about what you think *someone else* should do, and it's not a generic list of best practices. This is about your own leadership, whether it's formal or informal, and how *you* can take purposeful steps to move our work forward. "I will". Be specific and realistic. For example, instead of saying "teachers should collaborate more," you might say, "I will initiate a biweekly planning session with my grade-level team focused on analyzing student work." That kind of clarity helps us build momentum. As we do this, think about how you will lead or contribute to important conversations, facilitate or participate in collaboration, and identify and align your work with our shared purpose and vision as a school.

As we move forward, your bulleted preliminary plan will become the foundation for a fuller narrative innovation plan we'll build together. It will help us create a more coherent and sustainable approach to change that grows from our collective expertise and shared commitment to our students. I'll support you through this process, and we'll make space to share ideas, offer feedback, and refine our thinking together. The diversity of our experiences and perspectives will make our school-wide plan stronger and more responsive to the real needs of our students and community.

▶ CHAPTER SUMMARY

This chapter lays the foundation for understanding educational leadership in PK–12 schools. Today's leaders are expected to do far more than manage administrative tasks. They must reflect on evolving responsibilities; communicate shared values and vision and leadership identity; and lead dialogue-rich meetings to identify and resolve factors and conditions that are affecting student learning. Educational leaders need to collaboratively transform schools so that they prepare students to be productive members of a democratic society and contribute to the greater, common and collective good. This involves prioritizing improvements in curriculum that are equity-focused and responsive to the needs of all students and families. In a post-COVID world, the social-emotional well-being of students, staff, and families is of paramount importance. Perhaps one of the most important leadership tasks is to inspire a sense of stability and hope.

The Six-Point Conceptual Framework offers a strategic, values-based model to guide leadership practice. It supports trust, transparency, inclusivity, collaboration, and ethical decision-making. By reflecting on values, leadership identity, and a shared vision, leaders can stay grounded in purpose while navigating change. Importantly, leadership is not about imposing change. It is about inviting and empowering the school community to engage in a shared journey of continuous improvement, transformation, and innovation.

The future of education belongs to those willing to shape it. Leaders at all levels, with or without a formal leadership position, can foster learning environments where every learner is empowered to learn at high levels. In the next chapter, we will explore the foundational role of relational trust and community building, examine key leadership approaches, and look at communication strategies that improve PK–12 student learning.

Leadership Task: *Reflective Journal*

- Respond in writing to the following prompts. This will be your first journal entry. Use these questions for self-reflection or to guide a faculty or college classroom

discussion. Keep your reflective journal by your side so you can write a reflection or make notes as you read.
- Which subsystem of the Six-Point Conceptual Framework resonated most with you, and why?
- Reflect on a past or current challenge. How could the Framework help address it?
- Which subsystem do you anticipate will be most challenging in your leadership practice?
- How do your values and leadership identity enhance your ability to build trusting relationships?
- How do your values and leadership identity shape daily decisions?
- How do your values and ethics differ from others in your organization, and how do you navigate those differences?
- How can your values and leadership identity help address conflict or resistance to change?
- Recall an ethical dilemma. How might your values influence your response?
- How does embracing diverse identities and equity contribute to school improvement?
- To what degree are you committed to advancing equity for all students?
- Share an example from observing leaders of how their values and ethical stance shaped school or district culture.

Leadership Task: *Develop a Leadership Identity Communication*

- If you are a teacher team leader, department head, principal, special education director, or superintendent at a grade-level, teacher team, department, school, or district meeting, develop a face-to-face leadership identity message to acquaint or reacquaint chosen a larger audience (ex. students, faculty, parents, community members) with what you value and who you are as an educational leader.

Leadership Task: *Create a Bulleted Preliminary Plan to Describe the Six-Point Conceptual Framework*

- As an educational leader with authority (e.g., principal, special education director, superintendent) or without, create a preliminary plan using only bullets to capture the step-by-step process you will take to inform colleagues regarding the purpose and components of the Six-Point Conceptual Framework.

References

The following resources provide additional content to share with faculty or other colleagues. They informed the development of this chapter and offer valuable perspectives on the evolving expectations, knowledge, skills, mindsets, and commitments needed for educational leaders in today's dynamic schools.

ASCD, & CDC. (2014). Whole school, whole community, whole child: A collaborative approach to learning and health. *Journal of School Health*, 85(11), 729–739.

Bass, B. M. (1985). *Leadership and performance beyond expectations.* Free Press.

Bennis, W. G. (1989). *On becoming a leader.* Addison Wesley.

Boyd, J. P. (Ed.). (1950). *The papers of Thomas Jefferson* (Vol. 2: 1777–1779). Princeton University Press.

Brookfield, S. D. (1995). *Becoming a critically reflective teacher.* Jossey-Bass.

Burns, J. M. (1978). *Leadership.* Harper & Row.

Carlyle, T. (1841). *On heroes. Hero-worship, and the heroic in history.* James Fraser of London.

Colburn, L., & Beggs, L. (2022). *The Wrap Around Guide: How to Gather Student Voice, Build Community Partnerships and Cultivate Hope.*

Darling-Hammond, L. (2010). *The flat world and education: How America's commitment to equity will determine our future.* Teachers College Press.

Darling-Hammond, L. (2017). *Empowered educators: How high-performing systems shape teaching quality around the world.* Jossey-Bass.

Dewey, J. (1916). *Democracy in education: An introduction to the philosophy of education.* New York, NY: Macmillan Company.

Dewey, J. (1933). *How we think: A restatement of the relation of reflective thinking to the educative process.* D.C. Heath.

DeWitt, P. (2016). *Collaborative leadership: Six influences that matter most.* Corwin.

Elmore, R. F. (2000). *Building a new structure for school leadership.* The Albert Shanker Institute.

Epstein, J. L. (2011). *School, family, and community partnerships: Preparing educators and improving schools.* Routledge.

Fullan, M. (2003). *Change forces with a vengeance.* Routledge Falmer.

Gay, G. (2018). *Culturally responsive teaching: Theory, research, and practice.* Teachers College Press.

Gilligan, C. (1982). *In a different voice: Psychological theory and women's development.* Cambridge, MA: Harvard University Press

Goleman, D. (1995). *Emotional intelligence: Why it can matter more than IQ.* Bantam Books.

González, T. (2012). Restorative justice from the margins to the mainstream: Equity for all students. *Leadership and Policy in Schools, 11*(3), 283–298. Howard Law Journal.

Greenleaf, R. K. (1977). *Servant leadership: A journey into the nature of legitimate power and greatness.* Paulist Press.

Hallinger, P. (2010). Developing instructional leadership. In B. Davies & M. Brundrett (Eds.), *Developing successful leadership* (pp. 61–76). Dordrecht: Springer.

Hargreaves, A., & Fink, D. (2006). *Sustainable leadership* (Volume 6). Jossey-Bass/John Wiley & Sons. (Leadership Library in Education Series).

Heifetz, R. A. (1994). *Leadership without easy answers.* Belknap Press.

Hersey, P., & Blanchard, K. H. (1969). *Management of organizational behavior: Utilizing human resources* (1st ed.). Prentice Hall.

Howard, J. (1991). *Getting smart: The social construction of intelligence.* Efficacy Press.

Kendi, I. X. (2019). *How to be an antiracist.* One World.

Khalifa, M., Gooden, M. A., & Davis, J. E. (2016). Culturally responsive school leadership: A synthesis of the literature. *Review of Educational Research.* https://doi.org/10.3102/0034654316630383

Kolb, D. A. (1984). *Experiential learning: Experience as the source of learning and development.* Prentice Hall.

Ladson-Billings, G. (1995). Toward a theory of culturally relevant pedagogy. *American Educational Research Journal, 32*(3), 465–491. American Educational Research Association.

Leithwood, K., Harris, A., & Strauss, T. (2010). *Leading school turnaround: How successful leaders transform low-performing schools.* Jossey-Bass.

Leithwood, K., & Jantzi, D. (2000). The effects of transformational leadership on organizational conditions and student engagement with school. *Journal of Educational Administration, 38*(2), 112–129. https://doi.org/10.1108/09578230010320064

Leithwood, K., Louis, K. S., Anderson, S., & Wahlstrom, K. (2004). The Wallace Foundation, in collaboration with the University of Minnesota's Center for Applied Research and Educational Improvement and the Ontario Institute for Studies in Education.

Lewin, K., Lippitt, R., & White, R. K. (1939). Patterns of aggressive behavior in experimentally created "social climates." *The Journal of Social Psychology, 10*, 271–299. https://doi.org/10.1080/00224545.1939.9713366

Locke, E. A., & Latham, G. P. (1990). *A theory of goal setting and task performance.* Prentice-Hall.

Power, P. (2004, August 2). *Breaking the leadership rules: What is the educational 'bottom line'?* Curriculum Corporation.

Resnick, I. (1995). *From aptitude to effort: A new foundation for our schools.* Daedalus.

Rodgers, C. R. (2002). Defining reflection: Another look at John Dewey and reflective thinking. *Teachers College Record, 104*(4), 842–866. https://doi.org/10.1111/1467-9620.00181

Schön, D. A. (1983). *The reflective practitioner: How professionals think in action.* Basic Books.

Seashore-Louis, K. (2017). High-stakes testing and the evolving responsibilities of educational leaders. *Journal of Educational Administration.* https://www.emerald.com/insight/content/doi/10.1108/JEA-01-2017-0001/full/html

Senge, P. (1990). *The fifth discipline.* Double Day.

Sergiovanni, T. J. (1992). *Moral leadership: Getting to the heart of school improvement.* Jossey Bass.

Shields, C. M. (2010). Transformative Leadership Working for Equity in Diverse Contexts. *Educational Administration Quarterly, 46*(4), 558–589. SAGE Publications.

Sims-Bishop, R. (1990). Mirrors, windows, and sliding glass doors. *Perspectives: Choosing and Using Books for the Classroom, 6*(3), ix–xi.

Sinclair, R. L., & Ghory, W. J. (1987). *Reaching and teaching all children: Grassroots efforts that work.* McCutchan Publishing Corporation.

Spillane, J. P. (2006). *Distributed leadership.* Jossey-Bass.

Theoharis, G. (2007). Social justice educational leaders and resistance: Toward a theory of social justice leadership. *Educational Administration Quarterly, 43*(2), 221–258.

Tyler, R. W. (1949). Basic principles of curriculum and instruction. Chicago: University of Chicago Press.

Tyler, R. W. (1973). The Purpose of Education in a Democratic Society. In J. J. Chambliss (Ed.), *Educational Foundations: An Anthology* (pp. 108–113). Boston: Allyn and Bacon.

U.S. Department of Education. (2010). *A blueprint for reform: The reauthorization of the Elementary and Secondary Education Act.* Washington, DC: U.S. Department of Education.

Wheatley, M. (1999). *Leadership and the new science: Discovering order in a chaotic world.* Berrett-Koehler.

Zhao, Y. (2008). *Reach for greatness: Personalizable education for all children.* Corwin.

Zhao, Y. (2012). *Catching up or leading the way: American education in the age of globalization.* ASCD.

Additional Resources

The following books, articles, and websites, although not cited in the text, influenced and contributed to my overall educational leadership knowledge, skills, and practice.

Argyris, C. (2008). *Teaching smart people how to learn* (HBR Classics ed.). Harvard Business Review Press.
Avolio, B. J., & Bass, B. M. (2004). *Multifactor leadership questionnaire: Manual and sampler set* (3rd ed.). Mind Garden.
Blankstein, A. (2017). The principal's role in supporting culturally responsive practices. *Educational Leadership, 75*(2). http://www.ascd.org/publications/educational-leadership/oct17/vol75/num02/The-Principal's-Role-in-Supporting-Culturally-Responsive-Practices.aspx
Bolman, L. G., & Deal, T. E. (1997). *Reframing organizations: Artistry, choice, and leadership.* Jossey-Bass.
Brookfield, S. D. (1990). *The skillful teacher: On technique, trust, and responsiveness in the classroom.* Jossey Bass.
Bruce, J. A., & McKee, K. E. (2020). *Transformative leadership in action: Allyship, advocacy & activism.* Emerald Publishing.
Burns, J. M. (1978). *Leadership.* Harper & Row.
Carlyle, T. (1841). *On heroes. Hero-worship, and the heroic in history.* James Fraser of London.
Covey, S. R. (1989). *The 7 habits of highly effective people: Powerful lessons in personal change.* Free Press.
Darling-Hammond, L. (2010). *The flat world and education: How America's commitment to equity will determine our future.* Teachers College Press.
Darling-Hammond, L. (2017). *Empowered educators: How high-performing systems shape teaching quality around the world.* Jossey-Bass.
Dewey, J. (1938). *Experience and education.* Macmillan.
Elmore, R. F. (2009). *Instructional rounds in education: A network approach to improving teaching and learning.* Harvard Education Press.
Epstein, J. L. (1995). School/family/community partnerships: Caring for the children we share. *Phi Delta Kappan, 76,* 701–712.
Fullan, M. (2001). *Leading in a culture of change.* Jossey-Bass.
Fullan, M. (2003). *The moral imperative of school leadership.* Corwin Press.

Fullan, M. (2013). *The new meaning of educational change*. Teachers College Press.

Fullan, M. (n.d.). *Drivers of whole systems reform* [Video]. https://youtu.be/FLX0NwaFaQQ

Fullan, M., & Langworthy, M. (2013). *Towards a new end: New pedagogies for deep learning*. Hallinger and Murphy – Assessing – The Chicago University Press.

Goodlad, J. (1998). *Educational Renewal: Better Teachers, Better Schools*. Jossey-Bass.

Hallinger, P., & Murphy, J. (1985a). Assessing the instructional management behavior of principals. *Elementary School Journal, 86*(2), 217–247.

Heifetz, R. A., Linsky, M., & Grashow, A. (2009). *The practice of adaptive leadership*. Harvard Business Review Press.

Kouzes, J. M., & Posner, B. Z. (2017). *The leadership challenge: How to make extraordinary things happen in organizations* (6th ed.). Jossey-Bass.

Leithwood, K., Harris, A., & Hopkins, D. (2008). Seven strong claims about successful school leadership. *School Leadership & Management, 28*(1), 27–42.

Sinclair, R. L., & Ghory, W. J. (1997). *Reaching and teaching the disconnected student: Affective education for all children*. Corwin Press.

Sinclair, R. L., & Ghory, W. J. (1987). *Reaching marginal students: A primary concern for school renewal*. McCutchan Publishing Corporation.

Tyler, R. W. (1949). *Basic principles of curriculum and instruction*. University of Chicago Press.

THE 6-POINT CONCEPTUAL FRAMEWORK

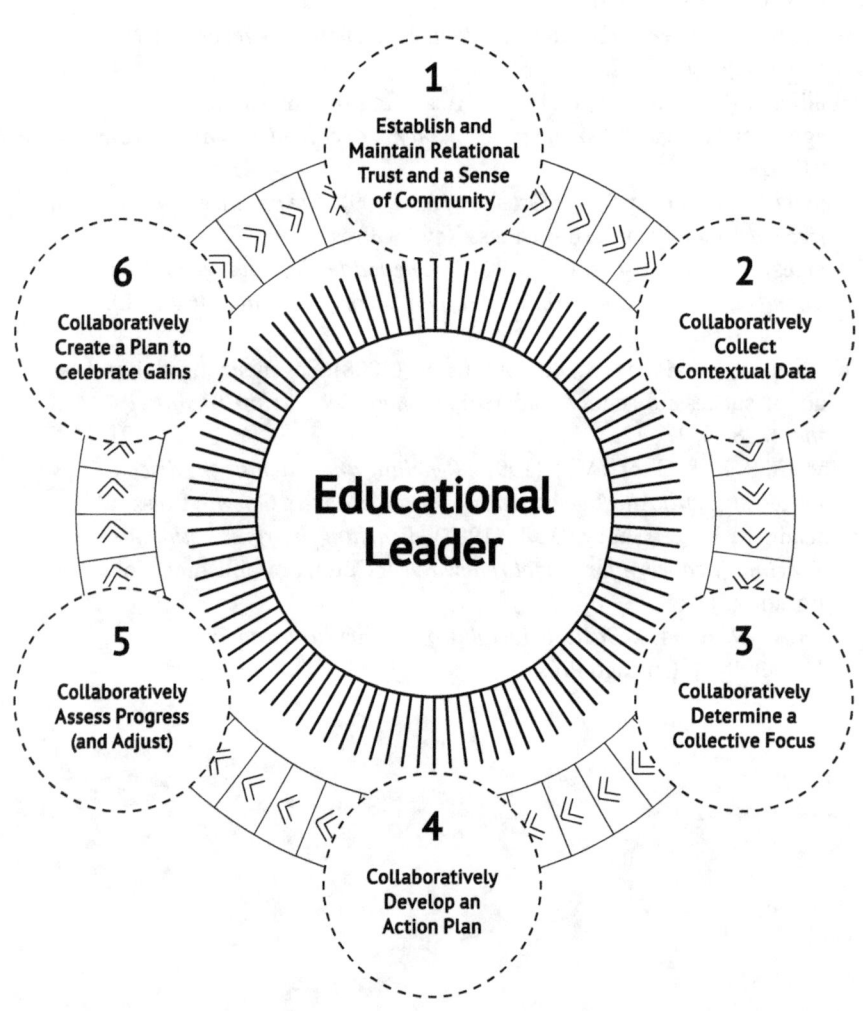

Conceptual Framework design and chapter openers designed by Christian Arichabala.

Chapter 2

Establish and Maintain Relational Trust and a Sense of Community

▶ INTRODUCTION

Establish and Maintain Relational Trust and a Sense of Community is the first subsystem of the Six-Point Conceptual Framework. This subsystem advances a systems-thinking, strategic-planning approach designed to collaboratively lead the change process to transform PK-12 student learning, teaching and leading. This chapter explores the everyday values and actions that build and sustain relational trust and a sense of community, critical elements in today's post-COVID-19 educational landscape.

The pandemic exacerbated long-standing inequities, including learning loss in reading and math (especially for low-income students and students of color), limited access to technology, and growing mental health challenges for both students and teachers (Kuhfeld et al., 2020; Di Pietro et al., 2020; Loades & Chatburn, 2020). In this context, cultivating trust, a sense of belonging and community is more urgent than ever. According to Bryk and Schneider (2002), "Relational trust is the connective tissue that binds individuals together to advance the education and welfare of students."

The chapter positions relational trust not just as a leadership competency, but also as essential for meaningful collaboration, school improvement, and innovation. Trust allows leaders to foster strong, authentic relationships between teachers and students, among faculty colleagues, and families and across all school communities, enabling collaborative progress and shared accountability. Establishing and maintaining relational trust and a sense of community is a foundational component of the Six-Point Conceptual Framework, guiding educational leaders toward transparency, authenticity, and open communication. Insights and practical strategies are offered to help leaders establish a shared sense of purpose, build trust, and lead with values, vision, and integrity.

This chapter examines the critical role of shared values and leadership identity in cultivating a sense of community. It also addresses how systems of oppression can undermine trust-building efforts, underscoring the need for equity-focused, inclusive leadership that ensures every voice is valued and heard. By engaging with the end of chapter leadership tasks and internalizing the chapter's concepts, leaders will gain practical tools to implement the first component of the Six-Point Conceptual Framework, Establishing and Maintaining Relational Trust and a Sense of Community.

In this chapter educational leaders with authority or acting as agents of change will learn to

- Apply the first component of the Six-Point Conceptual Framework to build relational trust and a sense of community.
- Promote trust and belonging among all stakeholders.
- Use integrity, transparency, authenticity, and communication to strengthen trust at all levels.
- Align shared values, beliefs, mindsets, and vision to build trust and community.
- Recognize how systems of oppression impact trust-building and student learning.
- Create a leadership platform speech.
- Develop a preliminary plan to establish and maintain relational trust and a sense of community.

By reflecting on these learning outcomes, internalizing the content and processes presented, and through the leadership tasks presented in this chapter, leaders will deepen their understanding of relational trust and its transformative power. By the chapter's conclusion, educational leaders, will be equipped with practical approaches to apply the first component of the Six-Point Conceptual Framework, which focuses on establishing and maintaining relational trust and a sense of community.

▶ BEGINNING THE JOURNEY OF COLLABORATIVE SCHOOL CHANGE

In a world defined by constant disruption and complexity, leadership is no longer about having all the answers. Instead, it's about asking better questions. As Heifetz (1994) reminds us, "One may lead perhaps with no more than a question in hand." Today's most effective leaders embody this spirit of inquiry. They listen more than they speak, lead with empathy and emotional discipline, and reflect deeply before they act. They build trust not through control, but through curiosity, collaboration, and consistent care for their people. Soft skills, like communication, collaboration, and motivation, are no longer secondary. They're foundational. The leaders who are most effective are those who stay grounded in humility and a continuous learning mindset. Learning keeps us human, and embracing the unknown helps reduce fear and builds resilience. Courage in leadership is the quiet, repeated act of showing up with purpose, even when the path forward is unclear.

Innovation is often stifled not by lack of ideas but by leadership that clings to control. Visionary leaders recognize that they don't succeed in isolation. They resist the urge to be the smartest person in the room and instead strive to build a room full of smart people who feel safe to contribute. They model vulnerability by acknowledging their own missteps and asking questions like, "What would you do if you were me?" and "What do you think is the most important thing for us to explore together?" Leadership today needs to be human, humble, and guided by purpose. Leadership demands urgency, but not panic; clarity, but not rigidity. Leadership is not a title or position; it's a way of thinking, speaking, and serving. It's about aligning empowerment with accountability. When people are trusted with real responsibility, clarity of purpose, and the tools to succeed, they begin to take ownership. Initiative becomes the norm. Energy rises. And cultures shift from compliance to commitment.

Purpose becomes a stabilizing force and a source of trust, direction, and energy when leaders communicate their purpose, share what they stand for, what makes them tick. When leaders invite faculty colleagues to do the same, they cultivate a culture where alignment, authenticity, and shared meaning inspire collaborative action. Great leaders don't just manage tasks, they notice people. They observe not only instructional practice but the social interactions that affect it. They see when someone's contribution should be celebrated, when a team needs support, or when tension signals a deeper issue. Being seen, heard, and valued is often the true source of engagement and innovation. People do their best work when they feel safe, appreciated, and connected to something greater than themselves.

This chapter supports educational leaders in deepening their understanding of relational trust, its underlying role in school improvement, and its power to transform school culture. According to Fullan (2001), "Improvement in schools is not possible unless relationships are at the core of what needs to change. The key is to build collaborative cultures where trust and respect foster learning for all." Establishing and maintaining relational trust begins with leaders sharing and discussing their leadership identity and vision for a preferred future in a leadership platform with faculty. This showing of authenticity, transparency, urgency, and inviting participation regarding the development of the faculty's shared vision rather than adopting the leader's vision begins the process of building relational trust.

Innovation begins with trust. Innovative leadership isn't about repackaging old reforms. It's about reimagining schools. Leading with curiosity rather than solutions invites creativity and collaboration. Heifetz (1996) argues that effective leaders don't start with answers, but with questions. Leaders might begin by reflecting and asking questions like, "Are concerns met with respect?" "Is it safe to speak up?" "Do teachers feel free to disagree without fear of punishment?" "Do actions align with shared values and vision?" "Am I collaboratively creating a culture where innovation is possible?"

Relational trust is a value, belief, and mindset critical to school improvement. In order to create a culture of relational trust, educational leaders need to reflect on their own values, beliefs, mindsets, commitments, leadership identity, and vision and clearly communicate them to students, teachers, parents, and the broader community. They must lead by example, foster inclusive dialogue, and invite feedback. Trust grows when leaders engage four key communities, students, teachers, families, and the broader public, in co-creating shared directions and solutions. Trust is built through transparency, consistency, and genuine care. It cannot be declared. It must be lived. It is reinforced when teachers feel heard, supported, and part of a collaborative decision-making process. Inviting participation in shaping the school's shared values and vision strengthens trust, a sense of belonging, and commitment.

Leaders should first assess the level of trust in their schools, not necessarily through formal tools, although they are provided in the next chapter, but by observing behavior and listening. Trust is not achieved in a single moment. It is a continuous, intentional process that thrives in environments where people collaborate and feel safe to speak out and challenge ideas and proposed actions to increase teaching, learning, and leading. Trust must be experienced, not just stated. When teachers are invited to shape direction, trust deepens and the will to innovate grows. Trust is not "a one and done." It should be communicated and experienced daily. It can't be mandated or relegated to culture statements or policies. Relational trust is not a leadership technique. It's a value, a mindset, a daily practice, and the cornerstone of culture. It is the glue that binds teams and the spark that guides engagement. Trust is increased or diminished depending on how leaders respond when someone disagrees with them, the manner in which they communicate under pressure, and the degree to which they understand the people they are trying to lead. According to Heifetz (1996), trust is built through authenticity, consistency, reliability, and alignment between words and actions. Frei (2023) in a TED Talk further emphasizes that trust is based on authenticity, logic, and empathy as do Bryk and Schneider. Trust collapses without respect, empathy, and compassion. The leaders who are most trusted are the ones who are clear in their communications, consistently empathetic, and authentically human.

For years educational leadership has focused on hard skills like managing operations, but today there's growing recognition that soft skills are just as vital, if not more so. Emotional intelligence (EQ) has become essential to educational leadership. Leaders with high EQ understand their own emotions, communicate effectively, build resilient teams, manage stress, and respond thoughtfully in high-pressure moments. Today's teachers seek more than direction; they want empathy, transparency, flexibility, and humanity. As Maya Angelou reminds us, "People will forget what you said, forget what you did, but never forget how you made them feel."

Collaboration doesn't happen by accident. It is dependent on the degree to which trust is part of school culture, and it must be facilitated. There is a well-known aphorism, often attributed to Drucker, the well-known management consultant and author, but not confirmed, that "Culture eats strategy for breakfast." Leaders can create opportunities for shared leadership, working together, sharing ideas, and co-creating solutions. While principals and superintendents don't need to attend grade level, department, or special education meetings, their presence as facilitators, listeners, or participants can strengthen trust, team alignment, and morale.

Relational trust is shaped by leaders and teachers who believe deeply in their students and each other. Such belief is not abstract. It manifests in everyday behaviors, how teachers collaborate, how leaders lead, and how decisions are made. An endearing and trust building practice is when leaders want input on their decision-making process, they don't ask for feedback they ask for advice. When schools cultivate trust, respect, empathy, and a commitment to collaboration, they build a relational foundation that strengthens every other effort. These relationships among students, educators, families, and communities create the web of connection essential for meaningful improvement. Leaders who model these values of relational trust, collaboration, and democratic processes earn trust and foster the conditions for transformation.

A strong sense of community and belonging is essential to meaningful change and improvement (Deal, 1996; DuFour, 2010). Leaders foster community by encouraging participation and creating inclusive environments. For example, leaders often work with teachers to build culturally responsive classrooms, involve students in rule-making, and celebrate student achievements. Another example is leaders co-creating norms for teacher team meetings and using teacher teams for shared leadership. Providing breakfast on Fridays and supporting dress-down Fridays reinforces a sense of community. When trust and belonging are present, collaboration flourishes and real change becomes possible.

Families are vital partners in school improvement and innovation. Leaders must reach out intentionally, recognize diverse backgrounds, and ensure parents feel included and valued. This means schools provide accessible communication through newsletters, social media, and personal outreach; remove language barriers by offering translation and support services; and invite parents to participate on decision-making committees and in classroom activities. Communicating through the use of technology can expand access and engagement. When parents are treated as empowered partners rather than passive recipients, they become advocates for their children, supporters of the school, and allies of the change process. When diverse voices of parents share lived experiences and students display projects, they reinforce a sense of community. Inclusive dialogue among teachers, students, parents, and the broader community builds a sense of belonging and shared ownership in collaborative problem-solving and improving student learning. Celebrating these efforts reinforces that change is not the work of one, but of many working together and that many hands make light work.

Darling-Hammond (1997) maintains that "Innovation does not happen in isolation. It emerges from shared learning, co-creation, and deep collaboration." A spirit of trust and collaboration facilitates innovation. Relational trust and collaboration are the bridge between vision and action. Without it, improvement efforts stall. With it, schools become dynamic communities of learning, growth, and innovation. In order to establish and maintain relational trust, educational leaders, teacher teams, and faculty, with parents and other community members, must regularly revisit the school's values, vision, and goals. When the gap between stated values and actual behavior widens, trust erodes. A culture of shared purpose, communication, and consistency reduces toxicity and boosts engagement.

When just about any kind of change is suggested, expect resistance. As Einstein astutely noted, "Great spirits have always encountered violent opposition from mediocre minds." However, with trust established and maintained, leaders can turn opposition into opportunity and schools into places of lasting, transformative change and innovation where all children from all families can learn at high levels.

▶ REVISITING SELF-REFLECTION, VALUES, LEADERSHIP IDENTITY, AND VISION

Self-reflection on values, leadership identity, and vision directly influence how educational leaders shape the culture of their schools and shape their approach to collaborative school improvement efforts. When leaders communicate values and leadership identity, they exhibit the moral clarity so essential to cultivating trust and building a sense of community.

Values and beliefs guide leadership behavior and decision-making. For example, when school leaders and faculty truly believe that all students, regardless of background, can learn at high levels when provided with adaptive learning environments, they commit to creating the conditions for every student to thrive. These convictions guide how educators interact with students, structure classrooms, allocate resources, and approach professional collaboration. Mindsets and commitments, when aligned with inclusive values, ensure that leaders do not give up on students or colleagues, even in the face of challenge or resistance.

Leadership identity emerges from this reflective foundation. It encompasses how leaders perceive their roles within a democratic society, their purposes as educators, and the actions they take to support teaching and learning. As discussed in the previous chapter, leadership identity is not fixed. Instead, it evolves over time through cycles of reflection, experience, and feedback. A leader's identity embodies the values they hold most dear and is made visible through their everyday decisions and interpersonal interactions. It signals to others what kind of leadership they can expect and depend on.

Crucially, the enactment of these elements of values, identity, and vision is what creates the conditions for relational trust. As Bryk and Schneider (2002) write,

> Relational trust is forged in daily social exchanges. The social respect that school participants display toward one another is key to building trust. When individuals perceive that others are acting in their best interests, trust deepens and a sense of community emerges.

In other words, trust is not built solely through declarations or policy; it is created through the everyday enactment of a leader's beliefs and commitments. When teachers, staff, students, and families experience consistency between what leaders say and what they do, trust and mutual respect grow.

Ultimately, leadership that is grounded in reflective practice, shaped by shared values, stimulated by a strong identity, and guided by a compelling vision fosters not just organizational coherence but also relational integrity. It invites collaboration, sustains morale, and nurtures the deep sense of community that is essential for meaningful and lasting school improvement.

▶ COLLABORATIVELY DEVELOP A SHARED VISION

The leader's vision may influence the collaboratively developed shared vision, but it should not become the school's vision. Wheatley (1999) asserts that "People only support what they create. We can't impose a vision; we must invite people to co-create it with us." It is the collaboratively developed shared vision statement that inspires a commitment to actualizing it. Since faculty are the ones who are expected to live by it, rather than developed in isolation by the leader based on his or her values, the collaboratively developed shared vision should be based on faculty and community shared values. When leaders avoid imposing their vision on faculty and community and instead work with their communities to develop a shared vision that resonates, it reinforces the idea of relational trust and a sense of community and helps motivate all members of the school community to engage and take action.

True collaboration begins with shared purpose. Every school should have a shared vision of a preferred future to keep the faculty and school community focused on what is important. Creating a shared vision helps begin the process of determining what a school hopes to become if it is true to the purposes of schools. Developing a shared vision collaboratively helps design the kind of school or district the community would like their children to go to. It gives direction, creates a context for all decisions, establishes standards, and shapes an agenda for action. It should be easy to communicate.

The process of collaboratively developing a vision begins by inviting faculty, families, and community members into the process. In a faculty meeting, the principal or superintendent models this reflective practice by posing questions similar to those they asked themselves. Together, the faculty and community members embark on a journey to uncover and articulate a vision that captures the heart of their collective purpose. This collaborative process thrives on inclusivity, striving to engage as many stakeholders as possible. It draws from the rich tapestry of the community's shared values, aligning the emerging vision with what truly matters to those they serve. Grounded in data and shared experiences, the vision becomes not only aspirational but also practical and deeply resonant.

To guide this exploration, a leader might pose thoughtful questions designed to spark meaningful dialogue and foster connection. These questions could include: Who are we as a community, and what are our shared values and beliefs? What do we stand for, both in principle and in practice? What is most important to us in our work and relationships, and what is our true purpose? Finally, leaders might encourage reflection on the fundamental question: what business are we really in? An educational leader might use the following prompts:

- I want our school to be a place where . . .
- The kind of school we would like our children to attend would . . .
- The kind of school I would like to teach in would . . .

Through these inquiries, a clearer picture and a deeper understanding begin to emerge of the community's values, vision, identity, priorities, and goals, not imposed but co-created. It becomes a reflection of the community's identity, a compass pointing toward a shared future, and a rallying cry for transformation and innovation. In replicating the process of reflecting, writing, and communicating a vision statement, and inviting participation in developing a shared vision statement, the leader is also serving as a role model for reflection, communication, collaboration, and transparency. Educational leaders should constantly reflect on how to be a role model for other effective leadership practices.

A final draft of the vision statement, in all likelihood, will not be completed, presented, and consensus reached in one session. A teacher team should be formed to 'polish the stone' and present the proposed final draft of the vision statement for feedback from the faculty, principal, or superintendent. The next step would be to engage parents in providing input and feedback on the vision. This creates a natural pathway to discuss with faculty, families, and other community members the disparity between the vision and the current reality of teaching, learning, and leading and the conditions in which they occur. After consensus is reached by the principal, faculty, and community on the vision, there should be a celebration of the vision and its collaborative development. Via newsletter or other forms of media, the vision should be communicated to the community at large.

Example: A Collaboratively Developed Shared Vision Statement

This no frills, shared vision statement was collaboratively developed by faculty and families in consultation with the principal.

> We envision a school community where every individual feels valued, connected, and inspired to achieve their fullest potential. Together, we foster a culture of excellence in teaching, learning, and leadership, driven by a shared commitment to relational trust, innovation, and continuous improvement.

▶ COMMUNICATE FREQUENTLY

Another factor contributing to relational trust and a sense of community is frequent communication. Discussion and communication communicate transparency and openness and reinforce trust in the educational leader. By fostering a culture of trust, respect, and collaboration, and regularly communicating with faculty and families, schools can transform challenges into opportunities, ensuring that every student has the support they need to reach their full potential. Kouzes and Posner (2017) argue that the ability to inspire a shared vision is central to exemplary leadership and begins with communication. As Fullan (2001) asserts, "If moral purpose is job one, relationships are job two, as you can't get anywhere without them. And you can't build relationships without communication." Leaders who clearly communicate their values ensure that all decisions are anchored in their leadership identity and minimize confusion within the school.

Whether you are new to your role or a seasoned professional, whether or not you hold formal authority, communicating is essential. Who you are and what you stand for should not remain internal. It must be clearly expressed to your colleagues, students, and community. For example, at the start of each school year, consider communicating your values, beliefs, mindset, commitments, leadership identity, or shared vision through a brief face-to-face speech or written message. This communication can set the tone for how you hope to work with others and what you aim to accomplish collaboratively. It serves as a source of clarity during times of challenge or distraction, a compass for decision-making, and touchstone for accountability. When communicated authentically, leadership identity becomes more than a personal statement; it becomes a catalyst for change, improvement, transformation, and innovation. Communicating values and commitments help to build an environment where all students, regardless of background, can succeed and thrive. Leaders grounded in values of equity, access, and social justice are better equipped to challenge systemic barriers and advocate for policies that promote fairness. Hargreaves and Shirley (2009) maintain that meaningful, focused communication is essential for ongoing improvement and cultural change.

Communicating with clarity is kindness because it eliminates the anxiety of not knowing and eliminates second guessing. It helps mobilize buy-in for student learning improvement. Barth (1990) positions communication as the mechanism through which relational trust and collaboration are maintained and sustained. Argyris (1993) underscores transparent communication as a key leadership skill in surfacing and challenging assumptions during transformational change. Strong communication skills allow leaders to navigate conflict and resolve disputes. Cultivating a positive workplace culture, leading change and innovation, and admitting when you're wrong are all important to communication and engendering loyal followers.

In an increasingly diverse educational landscape, school leaders must be able to articulate their commitment to equity, access, and social justice. Reflecting on and expressing beliefs related to fairness, inclusion, and the needs of marginalized students ensure that these values are embedded in all aspects of school leadership.

Fundamentally, schools move forward when families and educators join forces to create a supportive, collaborative learning community. Education leaders must embrace the vital role parents play by promoting change, improvement, transformation, and innovation in our schools. By inviting meaningful parent engagement, educational leaders can cultivate relational trust and build a supportive school community where every voice matters and every contribution counts. Educational leaders should be willing to discuss and adjust their views to incorporate new information from research and input from faculty and community. By embedding communication skills into their practice, educational leaders are better equipped to foster meaningful relationships, make informed decisions, and lead schools toward continuous improvement.

Interacting, while crafting a shared vision with parents alongside teachers and school leaders, ensures that the vision is aligned with the community's values and beliefs. The process fosters mutual understanding and identifies common ground, makes sure that every voice is heard, and creates a unified approach to supporting students. By communicating and eliciting families' perceptions of systemic barriers, schools can address equity and access and other challenges that prevent participation.

The promise of parent engagement is a commitment to building bridges and achieving excellence together. Keeping families informed about student progress by sharing formative and summative data, displaying student work and progress in a parent center, and empowering parents with actionable ways to support learning at home builds trust. Education is not the work of schools alone. Parents should be invited to actively engage in the school improvement process by offering a menu of participation options. Using Joyce Epstein's six types of parent involvement, we empower families to create supportive learning environments at home, engage in two-way communication, volunteer in classrooms, participate in decision-making, and collaborate with community organizations to strengthen school programs. These avenues of participation enrich the school experience for everyone involved. A school–parent compact developed by a team of teachers and parents working together clearly outlining the roles of school and home further strengthens this bond by clarifying shared responsibilities in advancing student achievement.

Creating open channels of communication, regular office hours providing families a direct line to share their feedback, raise concerns, and ask questions further builds relational trust and a sense of belonging. Inviting parents to join discussions about curriculum, assessment, and teaching practices ensures that their insights inform efforts to improve student learning. Providing refreshments and interpreters at meetings are sure to communicate that all families feel welcomed and valued. Informal gatherings like breakfast meetings or evening neighborhood coffees provide additional opportunities to share values, gather input, and build trust in a relaxed setting.

Example: A Collaboratively Developed and Communicated Vision for a High School

> Our school envisions a community where every student discovers their unique potential and thrives in an inclusive, equitable, and dynamic environment. Guided by our unwavering belief in the transformative power of education, we

commit to fostering a culture of respect, collaboration, and innovation. We believe in

- Equity and opportunity and ensuring every student has the resources, support, and encouragement to succeed, regardless of their background or circumstances.
- Lifelong learning and cultivating curiosity, critical thinking, and resilience to prepare students for a rapidly changing world.
- Community and collaboration and partnering with families, educators, and the wider community to create a supportive network that empowers every learner.
- Democratic ideals and teaching empathy, active citizenship, and the skills necessary to contribute meaningfully to a just and inclusive society.

As educational leaders in our community, we the faculty are committed to embracing diverse perspectives, modeling integrity, and advocating for policies and practices that uphold our shared values. We nurture relationships that build trust, spark innovation, and inspire action. Together, we pledge to

- Champion the voices of all students, teachers, and families.
- Celebrate the unique strengths of each individual.
- Ignite a passion for learning that transcends the classroom.
- Shape a generation of compassionate, engaged citizens who lead with purpose and courage.

Our vision is to inspire every mind, empower every voice, and build a better tomorrow.

▶ IMPLEMENT A PROFESSIONAL LEARNING COMMUNITY

A professional learning community (PLC) plays a vital role in building and sustaining relational trust and a strong sense of community within a school. More than just a routine gathering of colleagues, a PLC is a collaborative, dynamic structure where educators unite around a shared commitment to improving teaching practices and advancing student learning (DuFour, 1998). It fosters a culture of collective inquiry, reflective dialogue, and continuous professional growth. At the core of a PLC is the belief that collaboration drives improvement. Educators work together to set clear goals, analyze data to uncover student needs, and develop responsive strategies to address those needs. This collaborative process not only strengthens trust and collegiality but also promotes alignment in curriculum, assessment, and instruction across classrooms and departments, ensuring consistency, coherence, and equity in student learning experiences.

PLCs also promote innovation by creating a space where educators can reflect, take risks, and refine their practice. Regular engagement in data analysis and shared reflection encourages experimentation with new instructional methods and supports informed decision-making. Teachers are better equipped to differentiate instruction, providing targeted support for students who are struggling while offering enrichment opportunities for those ready to go further. Ultimately, a PLC is not simply a professional development initiative; it is a transformative approach to school improvement. By nurturing a culture of shared responsibility, collaboration, and continuous learning, PLCs create the conditions for both educator growth and student success, ensuring that schools evolve into communities of intentional practice, sustained excellence, and meaningful collaboration.

▶ ESTABLISHING AND MAINTAINING NORMS

In collaboration with faculty colleagues, educational leaders should guide and facilitate the development of guidelines for respectful and productive interactions. This process takes the form of establishing norms and structures for collaboration. Norms promote a culture of relational trust, a sense of community, openness, and collegiality and make sure that all voices are valued and respected. This step-by-step approach of collaboratively establishing norms ensures transparency, collaboration, and a sustained commitment to relational trust and community building. Norms should include agreements on respectful communication, active listening, conflict resolution, and the manner in which decisions are made. Members of a team meeting should hold each other accountable for adhering to the consensus agreed upon norms. Prior to the end of the meeting members should reflect and comment on the degree to which the norms were followed. For all meetings in a school, whether it be for a faculty or a team of teachers working together to problem-solve student learning problems, snacks and refreshments create a welcoming, comfortable sense of community and belonging atmosphere and should be provided.

▶ CELEBRATING GAINS

Creating a recognition system to publicly acknowledge students who exemplify school values; teacher teams contributing to the collective attainment of specific goals; parents who actively support the school's vision, mission, and goals; and local agencies contributing to the well-being of students is another way to help establish relational trust, a sense of community, and a supportive school culture where every parent feels empowered to contribute to the success of our students (Peterson & Deal, 2009). School assemblies should be scheduled during the day and families and other community members should be invited to recognize the accomplishments of students, teacher teams, parents and community members in achieving the vision and goals of the school. Newsletters and social media should also be used to communicate to the community at large. Celebrating values, vision, and the gains made in accomplishing shared goals will be discussed in more detail in Chapter Seven.

▶ WRITING AND COMMUNICATING A LEADERSHIP PLATFORM

In preparation for writing your leadership platform a preliminary plan should be developed. This plan should be written as a series of short, direct statements, without full sentences, that clearly communicate what *you*, as the educational leader, will do. It is important that the plan reflects your leadership role and avoids describing what others should do or using third-person language. Each preliminary plan created serves as a foundation for the next, contributing to a coherent and connected sequence that ultimately supports the development of an innovation plan in Chapter Eight.

A leadership platform further deepens the communication of leadership identity. Your one- to two-page leadership platform should be a touchstone inspiring dialogue, uniting faculty and community, and guiding the transformative work ahead (Frei, 2023). It can be communicated in writing, but in person would be much better. A leadership platform is a foundational communication device for leaders at all levels. A leadership platform is more than a personal statement. It is a public declaration of your purpose, values, and vision. It answers fundamental questions like, "Who are you as a leader? What do you stand for? Where do you want to lead your school? What do you want your leadership to be remembered for?" It should reflect not only who you are, but also who you are becoming in guiding the inclusive, empowered community you are committed to creating. A leadership platform anchors your leadership in clarity and purpose. It sets expectations and fosters a shared culture. It aligns with your personal and shared vision. A leadership platform builds trust through transparency and authenticity. It helps navigate dilemmas and leads through change. It serves as a living document, not a one-time exercise. It invites dialogue, guides action, and holds leaders accountable to their stated values.

Your leadership platform should share the specific conditions of your school context, incorporate key details, and cite relevant sources that support your leadership approach and align with the ideas presented. Your leadership platform should provide direction for teaching, learning, and decision-making. It should promote relational trust, equity, collaboration, and a shared commitment to improvement. While each leadership platform will be unique, based on context and your leadership position with or without formal authority, it should be thoughtfully aligned with the Six-Point Conceptual Framework.

To create a compelling leadership platform, begin by reflecting on experiences that shaped your leadership. Consider your journey, beliefs, values, and mindset. Share how qualities like empathy, equity, collaboration, and transparency guide your daily decisions and relationships. Define your leadership identity and describe the culture you strive to create. Next, if the faculty has developed a shared vision, describe it and how it informs your leadership. If not, offer an aspirational vision grounded in equity, access, and well-being for all students, and then invite the faculty and community to collaboratively create a shared vision. Emphasize how relational trust enables collaboration, risk-taking, sustained improvement, and innovation.

Be honest about strengths and challenges. Acknowledge what's working and recognize the dedication of faculty, staff, and families. At the same time, name the challenges that affect teaching and learning. Mention that your purpose in stating challenges is not to assign blame but to build shared understanding and urgency. Be clear about what you hope to accomplish and what's needed from others to help improve student learning. Stress the importance of collaboration and shared responsibility. Explain that improvement is not the job of a single leader but instead is a collective effort. Describe how you will create space for working together, hold yourself accountable, and support others in staying focused on making schools better for students, teachers, and families. Affirm your commitment to lead with integrity, humility, and persistence.

Once drafted, pause to reflect and ask yourself, "Will this resonate with students, staff, and families? Will it inspire and motivate?" Then share it. A high school leader, for example, introduced himself on day one of his new position by emailing his leadership platform to all faculty and inviting feedback. He followed up with a meeting to discuss it, demonstrating openness, transparency, and a commitment to collaboration. Your platform should remain active, referenced in meetings, shared in planning sessions, and used to ground tough decisions. As Maxwell (2019) notes, a leadership platform can refocus attention on what truly matters, especially when distractions arise.

Examples of Leadership Platforms

One of the most powerful leadership platforms is, the Singapore Minister of Education's "Work Plan" (Shanmugaratam, 2003). The transcribed leadership platform of Singapore's interim minister of education, while long, is a wonderful example to emulate. It paints a picture of the current reality. It begins by accentuating the positive by acknowledging past successes and the good work of teachers. It goes on to describe the urgent need for change and the imperative for the collaborative improvement, transformation, and innovation journey that lies ahead. All this said in a manner that does not shut people down! Instead, his leadership platform invites participation and concludes with an inspirational call to action.

The following four examples may be delivered to the designated audiences separately or together.

You are free to adapt, combine, and present the following examples of leadership platforms developed and used in the past. It is recommended that educational leaders present their leadership platform face-to-face or, if that is not possible, in an email.

Example 1: The Journey Ahead

Good evening, faculty, families, and members of our school community,

Thank you for taking the time to be here tonight. Let me begin by sharing a little bit about my background . . . . (select some highlights) . . . .

I am filled with gratitude and a deep sense of purpose as we come together to shape the future of our school. I want to describe where I'm coming from and to give you a sense of where I think we need to be going. Our collective journey begins with a shared vision of a school community where every individual feels valued, connected, and inspired to achieve their fullest potential. We aim to foster a culture of excellence in teaching, learning, and leadership, built on a foundation of relational trust, a commitment to continuous improvement, and innovation. This vision is a promise to every student, teacher, and family who call this school their own.

Relational trust is our foundation. It is more than a belief. In our daily interactions, we bring the practice of honesty, transparency, and consistency. Equity and inclusion are at the center of our values, vision, and mission. We are dedicated to ensuring that every student, regardless of their background and challenging circumstances, has the opportunities and support they need to succeed.

A sense of community and collaboration is our strength. When we unite as a community of students, families, educators, and leaders, we create something far greater than the sum of our parts. Growth and innovation are values we embrace wholeheartedly. We possess the courage and persistence to step beyond the ordinary and reimagine what's possible. To achieve this, we must embody key dispositions such as empathy to understand one another, resilience to persevere through challenges, integrity to guide our decisions, and adaptability to meet the evolving needs of our community. Together, these dispositions define how we lead and learn.

As your principal, I commit to celebrating the remarkable work of our teachers and students. We will acknowledge both our strengths and areas for improvement, developing a blueprint for meaningful change, improvement, transformation, and innovation. Together, we will foster a sense of community where everyone feels supported and valued.

There is urgency in our work. Education is both a privilege and a responsibility, and we cannot afford to wait to address the areas where we can and must do better. I invite each of you to join me in building a collective commitment to this vision. Our priorities are to enhance teaching and learning by providing professional development and embracing innovative approaches; to strengthen leadership through shared decision-making; to improve the conditions that enable every student and teacher to flourish; and to transform and innovate by leveraging creativity and technology to reimagine the learning experience we provide. This is our moment. Together, we can build stronger connections that inspire trust and collaboration. We can celebrate our successes while addressing our challenges with honesty and determination. We can ignite a passion for innovation that drives us forward into a brighter, more inclusive future.

Tonight, I invite each of you to be part of this journey. Your voice matters. Your ideas matter. Your energy matters. Let us commit to a shared journey of growth, excellence, and innovation, making sure that our school is a place where everyone has a sense of belonging, grows, and succeeds.

Let us move forward together with hope, determination, and a shared vision for what we can make happen.

Thank you.

Example 2: Communicating a Sense of Urgency

Faculty and Parents,

Thank you for gathering here today. I want to start by acknowledging the dedication and passion each of you brings to our school. We are here because we share a common goal to provide the best possible education and opportunities for our students. However, I stand before you today with a sense of urgency and a call to action that cannot be ignored.

Our students deserve more from us. They deserve an education that not only meets but exceeds their needs, preparing them not just for today, but also for the challenges and opportunities of tomorrow's world. Yet, despite our best efforts, we are facing significant challenges. Our formative and summative assessments, standardized test scores, student engagement levels, and feedback from both parents and the community indicate where we are falling short. They all point to a clear need for change. It's evident that the status quo is no longer acceptable.

We cannot afford to wait. Every day that passes without meaningful change is a missed opportunity for our students. We owe it to them to provide an environment where they can thrive academically, socially, and emotionally. Therefore, I propose a series of immediate actions that we must consider as a school community.

Curriculum review is first. We need to critically evaluate our current curriculum to ensure it aligns with the latest educational standards and best practices. This includes integrating more hands-on learning experiences and real-world applications into our lessons. Second, professional development. Our teachers are our greatest asset. We must invest in their ongoing professional development based on their specific areas of need, equipping them with the instructional approaches needed to engage and inspire our students. Third, student support services. Many of our students require additional support beyond the classroom. We must strengthen our student support services, ensuring that every student has access to the resources they need to succeed. Fourth, community engagement. Building stronger ties with parents, local businesses, and community organizations is crucial. We need their support and involvement to create a holistic learning environment for our students. And finally, data-driven decision making. We must utilize data more effectively to track student progress, identify areas of improvement, and measure the impact of our initiatives.

These actions are for your consideration. The future of our students, our school, and our community depends on the choices we make today. Let us not underestimate the power we have to make a difference in the lives of our students. Let us embrace this sense of urgency as a catalyst for positive change. Our students are counting on us, and we cannot afford to let them down. Change will not be easy, and it will require commitment and perseverance from each of us. But I am confident that together we can rise to the challenge and take action because We Care, We Share, We Dare!

Example 3: Time for Transformation Is Now

Good morning faculty colleagues, parents, and community members,

Thank you for joining me today. We gather to discuss a matter of utmost importance, not just to us as individuals connected to this school, but as a collective force with the power to shape the future of our students and, by extension, our society.

Imagine a school where every student feels supported, challenged, and inspired. A place where innovative teaching methods and cutting-edge technology are seamlessly integrated into the learning experience. Picture a community where parents, teachers, and stakeholders work hand in hand, creating a vibrant ecosystem that nurtures the intellectual and emotional growth of every child. Our school, like many others, faces significant challenges. Despite our best efforts, we have seen stagnation in standardized testing results, widening achievement gaps, and a growing disconnect between the skills our students acquire and the demands of the real world. These issues are not merely statistics; they represent real children whose futures are at stake.

The time for transformation is now. We cannot afford to wait. The world is changing at an unprecedented pace, and our students must be equipped with the skills and knowledge to thrive in this new reality. The consequences of inaction are dire. Every year we delay necessary changes, we risk leaving more students behind, diminishing their potential and, ultimately, weakening our community. Our students deserve better, and it is our duty to provide them with an education that prepares them for a rapidly evolving world. This requires bold, immediate action on the following several fronts: integrity and transparency; empathy and compassion; collaboration; the power of self-agency; adaptability and resiliency; continuous improvement, lifelong learning, and *curriculum and instruction*. We need to ensure that our curriculum is relevant, rigorous, and responsive to the needs of the 21st century. This means integrating STEM education; integrating technology; promoting critical thinking; and encouraging collaboration, creativity, and innovation. We must invest in continuous *professional development*, providing teachers with the resources and training they need to engage every student and be creative and innovative. *Technology integration* is a gateway to limitless possibilities. We must embrace digital learning platforms, utilize data analytics to tailor instruction, and ensure every student has access to the necessary devices and connectivity. *Community engagement* means education is a shared responsibility. We must strengthen our partnerships with parents, local businesses, and community organizations to create a supportive network for our students. *Equity and inclusion.* is about every student deserving an equal opportunity to succeed. We must address disparities in resources, provide targeted support to underserved populations, and create an inclusive environment where every child feels valued and empowered.

Today, I am asking each of you to join me in committing to working together. This is not the responsibility of a few but the collective duty of all who care about the future of our children. We need your support, your ideas, and your passion. Together, we can turn urgency into action and action into the improvement of student learning and our organization.

The challenges before us are great, but so too is our resolve. Let us seize this moment to make a lasting impact. The time for change is now, and with your commitment, we can create a brighter, more promising future for our students and our community.

Thank you.

It is often a good strategy to follow up your leadership platform communication by posting a shorter version in teacher team meeting rooms, parent centers, or school hallways. The following example is a condensed version of the main ideas presented to the school community in the previous leadership platform example, "The Time for Transformation Is Now."

Example 4: Posted Follow-up communication for The Time for Transformation is Now

I want to first acknowledge the knowledge, skills, dedication, and passion our teachers bring to our school. Despite our best efforts our school, like many others, faces significant challenges. The world is changing at an unprecedented pace, and our students must be equipped with the knowledge, skills, dispositions, and commitments to flourish in this new reality. The time for transformation is now. We cannot afford to wait. For the remainder of the school year, we will be meeting during faculty meetings and professional development days to determine by consensus what we as a school community need to pay attention to and then working together to implement what we have prioritized from the following topics: integrity and transparency; empathy and compassion; adaptability and resiliency; equity, access, inclusion, and justice; collaboration; self-agency; continuous improvement; lifelong learning; curriculum and instruction; formative and summative data-driven, decision-making; student-centered teaching and learning; differentiated instruction; support services; professional development; technology integration; and community engagement.

For additional speeches regarding establishing and maintaining relational trust and a sense of community refer to the Appendices.

▶ DEVELOP A BULLETED PRELIMINARY PLAN TO ESTABLISH AND MAINTAIN RELATIONAL TRUST AND A SENSE OF COMMUNITY

A preliminary plan should use bullets to describe the step-by-step leadership actions that will be taken as an educational leader to advance school improvement. The preliminary plan should avoid generic or third-person descriptions and make clear the actions taken by you as the educational leader have been taken to facilitate collaborative discussions aligned with the purpose of schools. Include relevant citations to reinforce the content, process, and rationale behind your approach and to communicate that the preliminary plan is grounded in evidence-based practices. Your preliminary plan will differ from the preliminary plans of others due to your unique school context and the degree to which you have a position with or without authority. It will help faculty colleagues collaboratively address persistent factors and conditions needing improvement in classrooms, departments, schools, or districts. In Chapter Eight, the bulleted sentences for each point or subsystem of the Six-Point Conceptual Framework will be expanded into an innovation plan. Developing preliminary plans and an innovation plan prepares educational leaders for when they will be working collaboratively with faculty colleagues to develop preliminary and innovation plans.

▶ CHAPTER SUMMARY

Leadership is becoming a more challenging job every day. The Six-Point Conceptual Framework provides scaffolding and a blueprint for applying systems thinking and strategic planning for the purpose of increasing student learning. Leadership models and new expectations for educational leaders provide insight into what leaders need to know and be able to do. Essential to any improvement effort, the starting points for guiding a collaborative change process are reflecting on self and leadership identity; collaboratively developing a shared vision; building relational trust; and promoting a sense of community, equity, and access. Developing and delivering a leadership platform is a good way to build trust and communicate your leadership identity. Effective leaders instill confidence in their faculties and remain calm, cool, and collected in the face of challenging dilemmas. The key leadership skills they use are built on a solid foundation of 'soft skills' like building trust; being transparent; authentic; agile; resilient; adaptable to change; humble, being able to admit when they're wrong (or saying I don't know but I'll find out); and having great interactive communication skills. If constant, consistent communication is not present, faculty will become disengaged or fill the information vacuum with their own theories.

Trust-building is an ongoing process. By providing examples of leadership communication that emphasize shared values, leaders can create adaptive learning environments where teamwork and innovation flourish. Vision, relational trust, a sense of community, frequent communication, implementing a PLC, establishing norms, distributing leadership, celebrating gains, and building bridges for parent engagement create a vibrant, inclusive learning environment where meaningful change, improvement, transformation, and innovation in teaching, learning, and leadership practices can occur. Effective leadership is also about conflict resolution. With any change effort there will be pushback, and this is where leaders need to be human; draw on the 'soft skills' of emotional intelligence, humility, and empathy; and encourage anxious faculty to relax, be flexible, explore, experiment, and be innovative.

The Six-Point Conceptual Framework reflects this holistic, systems approach. It aligns purpose, values, mindset, and vision to create innovation and transformation. When these elements work in harmony, supported by knowledgeable, emotionally intelligent, courageous leaders, schools, like the Framework, become more than the sum of their parts. They become communities of trust, learning, and transformation. Visionary leadership isn't about being extraordinary; it's about being real. It's about choosing humility over ego, people over power, and purpose over irrelevance. It's about building the kind of community where there is a sense of belonging, happiness, fulfillment, and connection with others.

Leadership Task: *Reflective Journal*

- Respond in writing to the following prompts. This will be your second journal entry. Use the prompts to guide faculty meeting or university classroom discussions:
  - Why is relational trust essential for building community and a sense of belonging in schools?
  - How does a leader's behavior influence trust-building across the school?
  - What are the consequences of neglecting trust, even during stable times?
  - Think of a time when you worked in a trusting school community—how did it affect you?

- What insights did you gain from working in a school where trust was lacking?
- Which leadership qualities are most critical for building trust and fostering belonging?
- How do cultural differences shape the development of trust and community in diverse schools?
- How do equity, diversity, inclusion, and justice shape school culture, relationships, and student success?
- How can leaders recognize and use cultural differences to build stronger, more inclusive communities?
- What specific actions can leaders take to ensure everyone in the school feels they belong?
- What barriers to trust have you seen in schools, and how might they be addressed?
- How can leaders rebuild trust after it has been damaged within a team or school?
- What strategies help sustain trust and belonging during times of change or challenge?

Leadership Task: *Provide a Rationale for the Collaborative Development of a Shared Vision*

- If you are a principal, special education director, or superintendent, schedule a community meeting. Explain the significance of a collaboratively developed shared vision of a preferred future and facilitate the process.

Leadership Task: *Develop a Leadership Platform*

- Based on your unique school context, develop a leadership platform to deliver to faculty, parents, and other community members. Please feel free to adapt, combine, and use the examples of leadership platforms presented previously or create your own.

Leadership Task: *Develop a Bulleted Preliminary Plan to Establish and Maintain Relational Trust and a Sense of Community*

- Develop a preliminary plan that outlines the concrete actions you will take to establish and maintain relational trust and a sense of community.

References

Argyris, C. (1993). *Knowledge for action: A guide to overcoming barriers to organizational change.* Jossey-Bass.

Barth, R. S. (1990). *Improving schools from within: Teachers, parents, and principals can make the difference.* Jossey-Bass.

Bryk, A. S., & Schneider, B. (2002). *Trust in schools: A core resource for improvement.* Russell Sage Foundation.

Darling-Hammond, L. (1997). *The right to learn: A blueprint for creating schools that work.* Jossey-Bass.

Deal, T. E. (1996). *The field of educational administration: School- and district-level leadership.* Routledge.

Di Pietro, G., Biagi, F., Costa, P., Karpiński, Z., & Mazza, J. (2020). The likely impact of COVID--19 on education: Reflections based on the existing literature and recent international datasets-. *European Journal of Education, 55*(4), 385–391.

DuFour R., & Eaker, R.E. (1998). *Professional Learning Communities at Work.* National Education Service.

DuFour, R. (2010). *Leadership for learning: How to help teachers succeed.* Solution Tree.

Frei, F. (2023). *How to build (and rebuild) trust.* TED Talk.

Fullan, M. (2001). *Leading in a culture of change.* Jossey-Bass.

Heifetz, R. (1994). *Leadership Without easy Answers.* Harvard University Press.

Hargreaves, A., & Shirley, D. (2009). *The Fourth Way: The inspiring future for educational change.* Corwin Press.

Kouzes, J. M., & Posner, B. Z. (2017). *The Leadership Challenge.* Wiley & Sons.

Kuhfeld, M., Soland, J., Tarasawa, B., Johson, A., Ruzek, E., & Jing, L. (2020). The COVID-19 slide: What summer learning loss can tell us about the potential impact of school closures on student academic achievement. *Northwest Evaluation Association.* Retrieved from https://www.nwea.org/content/uploads/2020/05/Collaborative-Brief_Covid19-Slide-APR20.pdf

Loades, M., & Chatburn, E. (2020). Rapid systematic review: The impact of social isolation and loneliness on the mental health of children and adolescents in the context of COVID--19-. *Journal of the American Academy of Child & Adolescent Psychiatry, 59*(11), 1218–1239.e3.

Maxwell, J. (2019). *Leadershift: The 11 essentials changes every leader must embrace*, New York, NY: Harper Collins.

Peterson, K. D., & Deal, T. E. (2009). *The shaping school culture fieldbook* (2nd ed.). Jossey-Bass.

Shanmugaratam, T. (2003, October 2). *Singapore minister of education work plan seminar at Ngee Ann Polytechnic.* Archives Online.

Wheatley, M. J. (1999). *Leadership and the new science: Discovering order in a chaotic world* (2nd ed.). Berrett-Koehler Publishers.

Additional Resources

The following books, articles, and websites, although not cited in the text, influenced and contributed to my overall educational leadership knowledge, skills, and practice. They contribute valuable perspectives regarding building relational trust and the development and completion of leadership tasks. They are provided for educational leaders to share with faculty or other leadership colleagues.

Block, P. (2008). *Community: The structure of belonging.* Berrett-Koehler Publishers.

Bryk, A. S., & Schneider, B. (2002). *Trust in schools: A core resource for improvement.* Russell Sage Foundation.

Celoria, D. (2016). The preparation of inclusive social justice education leaders. *Educational Leadership and Administration: Teaching and Program Development, 27,* 199–219.

Guidelines for writing a leadership philosophy. https://www.ascd.org/blogs/writing-a-personal-leadership-philosophy-will-make-you-a-better-leader

Hattie, J. (2009). *Visible learning: A synthesis of over 800 meta-analyses relating to achievement.* Routledge.

Kovaleski, A. (2003). *How to develop a leadership philosophy statement.* https://www.zippia.com/advice/leadership-philosophy/

Mandinach, E. B., & Gummer, E. S. (2016). *Data-driven decision making in education.* Teachers College Press.

THE 6-POINT CONCEPTUAL FRAMEWORK

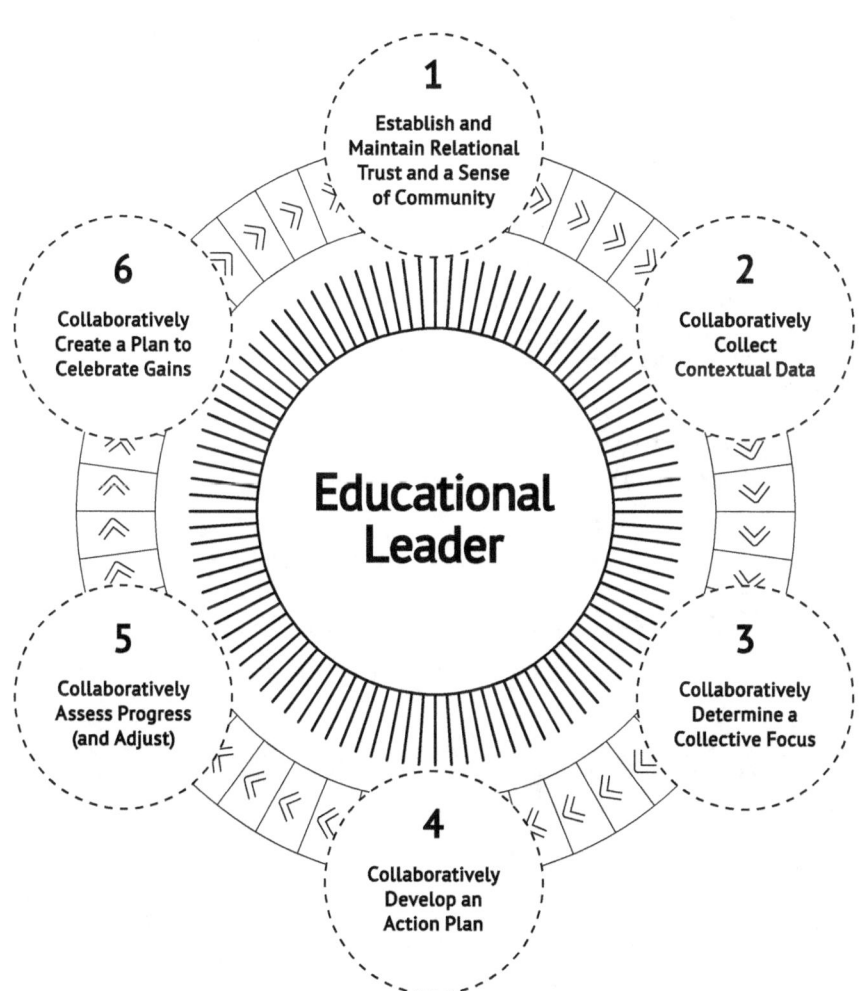

Conceptual Framework design and chapter openers designed by Christian Arichabala.

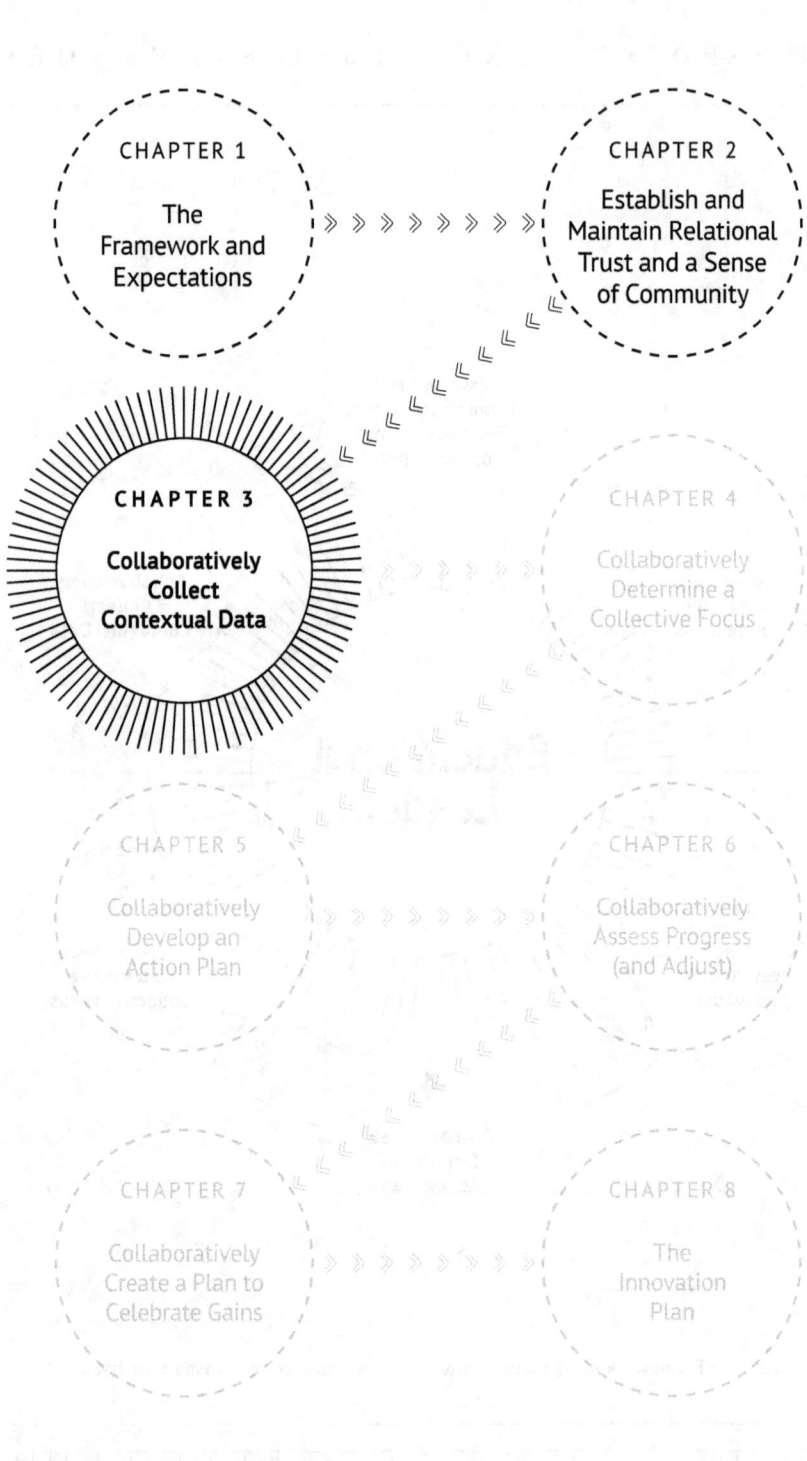

Chapter 3

Collaboratively Collect Contextual Data

▶ INTRODUCTION

Collaboratively Collect Contextual Data is the second subsystem of the Six-Point Conceptual Framework and embodies a systems-thinking approach designed to collaboratively guide the change process to transform PK-12 student learning, teaching and leading. Improving schools is never a one-size-fits-all process. Every school and district are shaped by unique historical, cultural, social, and structural factors. Understanding these contextual factors and conditions is essential for implementing meaningful and sustainable change, improvement, transformation, and innovation.

This chapter presents a structure to help educational leaders identify areas for improvement and engage stakeholders in co-constructing shared goals. As Mandinach and Gummer (2016) postulate, "Data-driven decision making is most powerful when it becomes a collaborative effort. Teachers, administrators, and other stakeholders bring diverse perspectives that enrich interpretation and increase the likelihood of effective decision making and instructional change." By emphasizing collaborative data collection and the use of shared goals and assessment protocols, it aims to promote a culture of transparency and continuous improvement that advances both academic success and social justice.

Collecting data collaboratively is a deliberate and systematic approach that reveals both obstacles and opportunities. This chapter offers practical guidance for using formative, qualitative data to inform decisions at the grade, department, school, and district levels. By involving teacher teams in data collection and analysis and listening to the lived experiences of educators and families, leaders gain a richer, more human-centered understanding of what needs to change. This inclusive process builds relational trust, transparency, and a sense of community. The resulting data helps identify specific areas needing attention. Working in partnership with faculty, leaders can begin to chart actionable pathways for meaningful change. As John Dewey noted, "A problem well stated is a problem half solved," and collaboratively collecting data to identify the problem is the first step.

By the end of the chapter, educational leaders, whether in formal roles or acting as change agents, will be prepared to

- Collaboratively identify contextual factors and conditions impacting learning for many students.
- Use inclusive approaches to collect data.
- Adjust or design tools to assess local contextual factors.
- Pinpoint key conditions that drive school improvement and innovation.
- Explore applying Bryk's essential supports and Gould's systems alignment protocol.
- Draft a preliminary plan for collaborative data gathering and analysis.

These processes lay the groundwork for improvement efforts that are both evidence-based and equity driven, ensuring that actions align with the values and priorities of each unique school community.

▶ STARTING WITH HUNCHES

Before engaging in collaborative data collection, educational leaders should first reflect on their own *hunches*, i.e., the assumptions about what may be hindering student progress. For example, a leader may suspect that collaboration between general and special education teachers is limited or that the school culture does not support differentiated instruction. Other possible concerns may include inconsistent use of formative assessments, weak alignment of lessons with standards, insufficient tracking of student progress, or lack of clarity in communicating expectations to students and families. These hunches, grounded in experience and observation, can be introduced as part of communicating values and beliefs prior to or after the educational leader guides a shared vision setting process, depending on whether a shared vision is in place or not. Heifetz and Linsky (2009) urge leaders to "get off the dance floor and go to the balcony," reminding us that stepping back is essential for gaining a broader perspective on complex organizational issues. Listening closely and observing carefully, leaders can begin to form and suggest targeted questions to guide data collection efforts. These questions help ensure that data collection is focused and collaborative and lead to actionable decisions. When explored with teachers, these hunches become starting points for shared inquiry and improvement.

▶ THE PROCESS OF COLLECTING DATA COLLABORATIVELY

The questions leaders pose shape the data collection process. Thoughtfully framed questions uncover critical conditions that affect teaching and learning and inform the selection or development of appropriate assessment tools. For instance, a powerful question such as, "What do we want to be known for?" invites faculty, parents, and other stakeholders into meaningful dialogue about the leader's and school's identity, values, and aspirations. Responses to this question can be as varied as they are inspiring. A school might focus on creating a collective commitment to what truly matters to them and make deliberate choices about what to pursue and what to set aside. Some may wish to be known for its shared vision for the future or possessing a welcoming, inclusive, and engaging culture; one that fosters respectful interaction with families and the community. Others may prioritize empathy, compassion, and nurturing the human spirit; promote excellence in teaching, learning, and leadership; or cultivate a growth mindset that celebrates effort, resilience, persistence, and the courage to take risks. As leaders ask questions, in collaboration with a data collection team of teachers, they are better able to determine the factors and conditions to assess. If the selected focus is curriculum, assessment, and instruction, the questions naturally shift to teachers asking, "What will each grade-level team need to do collaboratively to bring them to life?" The answer to this question provides a pathway for transformative and innovative practices.

Collaborative data collection is a vital step toward meaningful school improvement. Its purpose is to uncover the underlying factors and conditions that persistently pose challenges and inhibit improvement. When approached with care and intentionality, collaborative data collection identifies barriers to progress and areas for improvement, while also strengthening relationships and fostering a culture of transparency. Engaging teachers and stakeholders in this process builds trust, transparency, buy-in, and shared ownership of the work ahead. It supports distributed leadership and grounds decision-making in a shared understanding of what's working and what needs to change. This inclusive and credible process challenges the status quo, encourages urgency, and inspires innovation rooted in the school's unique context. Just as importantly, it surfaces the stories, experiences, and systemic realities that cannot be captured by quantitative data alone. As Fullan (2003a) reminds us, effective leaders are system thinkers and organizational developers who facilitate improvement through collaboration and inquiry. Leaders must adopt a systems-thinking approach, recognizing the interconnectedness of curriculum, assessment, and instruction and ultimately all six points of the conceptual framework.

The process of collaboratively collecting data begins with a review of what students should know and be able to do at each grade level and in each subject. Teams then unpack content and performance standards to identify high-leverage "power standards" that guide instruction. Another critical question that might emerge is, "Who will be affected by what our data reveals?" The answer underscores the far-reaching impact of these data collecting efforts. For example, as a result students will take greater ownership of their learning and behavior. Teachers will reconfigure classrooms to meet diverse needs, embrace differentiated instruction, or collaborate to align the subsystems of the Six-Point Conceptual Framework. Parents, families, and community members will experience stronger ties to the school as it actively engages them in its vision, mission, and goals. The next step is for educational leaders to distribute a list of factors and conditions for faculty to review, discuss, and select the process for data collection and analysis. The school community is then invited to provide additions based on their hunches and present rationales for their suggestions.

▶ INTERNAL FACTORS AND CONDITIONS

Sustainable improvement requires attention to factors and conditions that shape the educational environment. Internally, schools often face challenges such as biased, culturally irrelevant curricula, inconsistent access to quality early education, and low reading and math proficiency by the end of 3rd grade. Overcrowded classrooms, disparities in resources, and inequitable discipline practices, which often lead to the "school-to-prison pipeline," further compound the issue. Many schools offer limited access to advanced placement and gifted programs, while students who are English language learners frequently lack adequate support. Family engagement may be minimal, and mandated high-stakes, statewide testing often narrows instruction and undermines creativity, critical thinking, and social-emotional learning. Professional development, when not job-embedded or tailored to educators' needs, fails to support the continuous growth required for teaching in diverse classrooms.

All these internal factors and conditions hinder the academic progress of students and particularly those of color. Addressing these internal conditions begins with the identification and assessment of key factors and conditions such as school culture, curriculum relevance, and the quality of professional development. Leaders must work to strengthen family and community partnerships, especially in underserved areas, to build the networks of support students need to thrive. By aligning teaching, learning, and leadership efforts, schools can overcome systemic barriers and work toward a shared vision of excellence. Confronting these internal challenges requires culturally responsive leadership that promotes equity in decision-making, discipline, and resource distribution. By collaboratively assessing school culture, curriculum relevance, instructional alignment, and the degree to which general and special education teachers collaborate, leaders and faculty can begin to dismantle systemic barriers and initiate change that benefits all students. These efforts must be inclusive, involving faculty, students, families, and the broader community to make sure there is shared commitment. Presenting data clearly and connecting it to actionable goals fosters a sense of urgency and collective ownership, making progress both achievable and sustainable.

▶ EXTERNAL FACTORS AND CONDITIONS

External factors, although often beyond a school's direct control, significantly influence educational outcomes. State mandates and accountability systems create constant pressure, while shifting community demographics and socioeconomic disparities, especially in low-income areas, present persistent challenges to change, improvement, and innovation. The emphasis on standardized testing often detracts from efforts to promote creativity and social-emotional development. Additionally, teachers often enter the profession without adequate preparation to meet the needs of increasingly diverse classrooms, and school leadership models that lack empathy or relational focus can erode staff morale. In more affluent communities, schools frequently benefit from supplemental resources and robust community support. In contrast, high-poverty areas face limited access to these advantages, hindering both academic and personal growth for students. Public policy decisions, such as restricted funding, inadequate professional development, and rigid mandates, can create systemic obstacles to success. Structural racism, inequality, and social injustice further exacerbate disparities, ensuring that not all students have equal access to opportunity, support, and the realization of their potential.

Through intentional, transparent, and inclusive data-gathering practices, schools can define their priorities, respond effectively to challenges, and articulate a shared vision for the future. Understanding the interconnected systems within schools and aligning efforts across them enables leaders to create environments where all students have the opportunity to succeed. This shared vision, though ambitious, is achievable through the unified commitment of leaders, educators, families, and communities. It represents a bold reimagining of PK–12 education where every student is supported, challenged, and empowered to soar.

Additional details on the specific factors and conditions for assessment are provided next.

▶ EXAMPLES: FACTORS AND CONDITIONS TO ASSESS

School Culture

School culture, often summed up as "the way we do business around here," reflects collective norms and deeply influences teaching and learning. Values, beliefs, and mindsets form the cultural foundation of a school. A shared vision serves as both a foundation and a guidepost, ensuring that decisions are rooted in commonly held values and aligned with long-term goals. When faculty work from a shared vision, they are more likely to engage in meaningful collaboration and stay focused on actions that improve teaching, learning, and leading. There is a strong sense of community and open, transparent communication among all stakeholders. Effective teachers design engaging instruction that promote student ownership of learning, foster collaboration, and model positive behaviors. Cultures that emphasize trust, collaboration, cultural responsiveness, equity, and access support teacher and student engagement.

In such environments, teachers engage in ongoing, job-embedded professional development and work together in high-performing teams. Instruction is differentiated to meet the diverse needs of learners, and leadership is distributed in ways that empower both teachers and students. Class sizes are kept small to foster individualized attention, and student-led parent–teacher conferences encourage student agency and accountability. Parents are meaningfully involved, and meetings follow clearly established norms that encourage productive dialogue and collaboration. These cultural elements profoundly shape instructional and leadership practices and can either enable or hinder improvement efforts. These interconnected practices reflect a shared commitment to continuous growth and equity, and they offer a foundation on which to build a purposeful, collaboratively determined collective focus, which is discussed in the next chapter. Conversely, toxic cultures often perpetuate systemic and structural racism; contribute to student disengagement and teacher burnout; and affect retention.

Curriculum Content and Performance Power Standards

Today's PK–12 students must develop new knowledge, skills, and mindsets for a rapidly changing world. To combat an overcrowded curriculum, which at best can only be covered, a practical solution is to use power standards, i.e., the essential learning goals that students must master in order to be successful in their current grade, the following grades, and in the workplaces of the future (Ainsworth, 2003). By concentrating on power standards, teachers can design instruction that provides in-depth exploration of the content knowledge and performance skills that matter most.

Curriculum continues to remain outdated and overcrowded and usually favors breadth over depth. Due to lack of cultural relevance, curriculum content is often of little interest to students of color. Curriculum should help all students understand their identity and learn about others. The academic curriculum should also include the integration of a "social curriculum" that fosters community and student well-being. Curriculum redesign should emphasize reflection, self-awareness, critical thinking, collaboration, empathy, resilience, adaptability, and social-emotional growth. Early intervention programs such as high-quality Pre-K programs and early intervention reading support enhance long-term academic outcomes. The Responsive Classroom curriculum and project-based learning strengthen academic and personal development. Models such as the Harlem Children's Zone demonstrate how wraparound services offering health care, enrichment, and family support can significantly boost student performance.

Assessment Practices

Overreliance on standardized testing narrows instruction and often fails to capture creativity, social-emotional learning, and critical thinking. These tests disproportionately harm underfunded schools and perpetuate inequity. A balanced approach to assessment practices includes both ongoing formative assessment and summative end-of-unit evaluations. The consistent use of common formative assessments by all teachers within grade level teacher teams or departments ensures all students receive equitable opportunities to learn and grow.

Formative assessments, performance tasks, and student portfolios offer a fuller picture of student learning than state testing. Assessments tied to power standards help measure mastery of critical learning goals and objectives. Exemplary teachers use these formative assessment tools to monitor progress, tailor instruction, and provide actionable feedback. Rubrics with clear performance criteria enhance clarity and fairness. However, there is often inconsistent use of formative assessments.

Teacher Quality

High-quality teaching extends beyond content delivery. Great teachers motivate, guide, and build opportunity through strong content knowledge, instructional skill, adaptability, empathy, and commitment to growth. They establish supportive relationships and inclusive, student-centered environments that promote risk-taking, choice, collaboration, and an environment where students feel valued and supported. There is often weak alignment of lessons with power standards. Adaptability, especially in times of crisis, ensures continuity in student learning (Heifetz, 2006).

Regarding the assessment of student learning, Albert Einstein's quote, "If you judge a fish by its ability to climb a tree, it will live its whole life believing it is stupid," reminds us about the importance of knowing students and addressing their learning needs. Teachers must be equipped to use common formative assessment data, differentiate instruction, co-plan lessons, and create safety-net interventions. Models like Wang's Communities of Learning and strategies like Universal Design for Learning (UDL) and Culturally Responsive Pedagogy (Gay, 2018; Rose & Meyer, 2002) ensure inclusivity and engagement for all students. Teachers often lack the skills, knowledge, mindsets, commitments, and resources to accommodate students with special needs. Insufficient tracking of student progress can also be an issue. Differentiated instruction is a key component of teacher quality and is critical to student success. Failure to differentiate instruction contributes to underachievement. This situation hampers the integration of general and special education and further marginalizes these students.

According to Tomlinson (1992), a one size fits all approach to instruction does *not* work. Differentiated instruction involves creating a flexible and inclusive classroom learning environment. The extent to which teachers differentiate instruction is indicative of the degree to which students learn at high levels. Teachers all using the same assessment instruments, often referred to as 'common' formative assessments, adapting content, processes, and assignments that provide personalized learning practices are all pathways to meeting individual student needs. Great teachers not only deliver essential knowledge and skills, but also combine instructional expertise, empathy, and adaptability to create environments where all students can learn at high levels. The lack of clarity in communicating expectations to students and families can be an inhibiting factor in student success. Differentiated instruction must be assessed as part of teacher effectiveness. In summary, teacher quality and all these exemplary teaching behaviors can and should be observed and evaluated.

Leadership Effectiveness

Strong leadership is essential to school improvement. When leadership is lacking, and does not create an environment where educators feel valued and empowered, and when leadership does not create conditions for shared decision-making and distributed leadership, teacher morale suffers, turnover rises, and schools and districts tend to not be able to increase student learning to a significant degree. The educational leadership behaviors that should be considered for assessment include the following:

- Frequency and what is communicated to all stakeholders (e.g., a big picture perspective, the Six-Point Conceptual Framework, vision, leadership identity, etc.).
- School culture (e.g., establishing and maintaining a collaborative culture and professional learning community).
- The degree to which there is relational trust among faculty and leadership is trusted.
- Using formative assessments to determine student needs.
- Using contextual data to inform decisions.
- Monitoring the implementation of differentiated instruction.

- Involving families in providing input, feedback, and decision-making.

Mastery Learning

Bloom working with his mentor, Ralph Tyler, developed Mastery Learning. Mastery Learning is an instructional strategy where students must achieve at a level of 90% competence in a unit before moving on to the next unit. Students receive feedback and additional instruction if they don't initially achieve mastery. The five steps of Mastery Learning are pre-assessment, instruction, formative assessment, correction or enrichment instruction, and summative grading or assessment.

Adaptive Learning Environments

Safe, inclusive, and student-centered environments support effective teaching and learning. The Adaptive Learning Environments Model (ALEM) reconfigures classrooms so that they support the integration of general and special education students (Wang, 1985). Classrooms support flexible grouping, for whole and small group instruction, one-on-one teacher-led remediation, small group collaboration, student choice, and individual learning. Students take responsibility for their own behavior and learning and rotate between learning centers for learning or remediation with technology or engage in a variety of enrichment, hands-on activities. Posted rubrics guide student self-assessment of learning. Student progress is monitored. Teachers keep records of formative assessment results and learning assignments.

Universal Design for Learning (UDL) ensures all students can access learning through multiple pathways, while dual-language programs support bilingualism and academic achievement (Thomas & Collier, 1997). Additional support and enrichment are often provided in expanded arts and STEM programming, after school, and during the summer (Rabkin & Hedberg, 2011). Schools in underserved communities need access to after-school programs, mental health services, and family engagement programs to address the whole child. Some schools include campus health centers (Pitcock et al., 2013).

Equity, Systemic Racism, Access, and Social Justice

Inequity and systemic racism are deeply embedded in education and must be actively dismantled. Inspired by the work of Darling-Hammond and Drago-Severson, school leaders must engage the school community in reflective processes to define social justice. Leaders might begin by asking what social justice means in our community; what efforts have been made to promote it; and how do we support one another in this work. These questions drive inclusive, systemic change and ensure that all students, regardless of background, have equitable access to high-quality learning experiences. Restorative justice practices are a better alternative to punitive discipline, improve relationships, and reduce suspensions (González, 2012).

Professional Development

Professional development must be responsive to teacher and student needs and be aligned with school values, shared vision, and action plan goals. When this is the case, job-embedded professional development equips educators to implement a forward-looking curriculum, refine instruction, and implement pedagogical approaches that meet the demands of diverse classrooms. Job-embedded, ongoing learning opportunities should build teacher capacity and be based on what is needed to accomplish the goals and outcomes of the action plan. Profession development should be attended by all faculty on the grade level, department, school, or district and be expected to address factors and conditions needing attention as a community. The factors and conditions selected for professional development should be determined by teachers.

Professional learning communities (PLCs) are a powerful source for continuous improvement and innovation. PLCs are rooted in Senge's (1990) concept of the learning organization and refined by DuFour. According to DuFour et al. (2010),

> The PLC process is a continuous, job-embedded method of learning that focuses on results and cultivates a collaborative culture. When educators work in collaborative teams and take collective responsibility for student learning, they

achieve better results than when teachers work in isolation and are evaluated individually.

PLCs offer teachers opportunities to collaboratively develop curriculum, select or design formative assessments, analyze data, and improve instructional practice. PLCs foster shared professional growth and collective efficacy accountability. In addition, as DuFour points out, PLCs result in continuous learning and achieve better results than traditional teacher observation and evaluation.

Lack of Time

Collaboration takes time for teachers to reflect, collaborate, and innovate is a significant and well-documented problem that undermines teaching, learning, and leadership in profound ways. Its effects ripple across the entire educational system, contributing to burnout, stagnant practice, shallow learning, and ineffective school improvement efforts. Teachers are increasingly burdened with administrative tasks, accountability mandates, data reporting, and large class sizes. Research consistently points to time constraints as one of the greatest barriers to teacher effectiveness and school improvement. Darling-Hammond et al. (2017) contends that "Without sufficient time to engage in meaningful professional learning and collaboration, teachers cannot meet the demands of 21st-century teaching." Stagnation of practice results when teachers lack time to reflect on their instruction and are more likely to fall back on routine practices rather than adopt evidence-based, student-centered strategies. Innovation requires time to explore, pilot, and iterate. Without time, promising instructional approaches never move from idea to implementation. Teachers collect formative data but lack time to analyze and act on it collaboratively, undermining personalized instruction. When teachers don't have time to plan deeply engaging, inquiry-based lessons, student learning becomes more rote and less meaningful. Research shows that student achievement improves when teachers collaborate regularly and reflect on student work and outcomes (Hattie, 2009).

Innovation and collaboration are crucial for adapting teaching to diverse learners. Lack of time hampers the ability to meet the needs of all students, particularly those furthest from opportunity. Leaders must protect teacher time as a resource, but many struggle to do so amid competing priorities. The result is increased teacher dissatisfaction, burnout, and turnover and attrition. Without time for teacher teams to engage deeply, professional learning communities become compliance exercises rather than vibrant learning spaces. Informed leadership relies on collective sense-making and shared vision. Without time, leaders face resistance or inertia. According to Fullan (2007), "Time is not a frill—it's a foundation for effective schools. Without it, even the best ideas collapse under the weight of urgency and isolation." When teachers feel overwhelmed and unsupported, trust in leadership and among colleagues erodes. Time to engage in inquiry is essential for continuous school improvement. Without it, schools plateau. Teachers are experts in their craft and context. Without time, their voices and insights are marginalized. Working with faculty colleagues requires educational leaders to make time to meet with faculty. Grade level, department, faculty meetings and professional development days should be devoted to working together to implement the subsystems of the Six Point Conceptual Framework.

Lack of time is not just an operational issue; it's a structural barrier to quality education. Addressing it requires **bold leadership, creative scheduling, policy reform**, and a **culture that values teacher learning as essential to student learning**. When time is prioritized, schools become more innovative, equitable, and effective. Educational leaders should schedule collaborative time during the school day and policymakers must better understand the critical nature of time to collaborate and mandate a transformation of the way the school day is structured.

Technology Integration

Technology plays a key role in reimagining education for the 21st century (Zhao, 2012). The COVID-19 pandemic highlighted the importance of bridging the digital divide (Warschauer & Matuchniak, 2010). Equitable access to digital tools and internet connectivity ensures all students can fully participate in learning, especially in times of disruption.

Parental and Community Engagement

Parental involvement is essential for student success. Engaging families and community stakeholders strengthens support systems and reinforces school goals. When engagement is weak, Epstein's (2001) six types of parent involvement offer a useful framework for building stronger partnerships. Schools must actively seek input from families and community members in planning and decision-making. This topic is further elaborated on in a future chapter.

Essential Supports for Sustained Improvement

Bryk's (2009) five essential supports—coherent instructional guidance, collaborative professional learning, strong family and community ties, a supportive learning environment, and effective leadership—provide a roadmap for sustainable school improvement. These interconnected elements create the foundation for meaningful change. Schools that align systems across curriculum, instruction, and support services are better positioned to advance equity and excellence.

Alignment of Systems in a Standards-Based Environment

Drawing on the work of Elmore and personal experience, it is clear that aligning systems is key to success in standards-based education. This begins with clearly defined power content and performance standards and continues with aligned formative assessments and responsive differentiated instruction. Supporting multi-leveled materials, safety-net support services must be integrated alongside professional development and family engagement (Gould, 2008). When these systems are unified, schools create coherent, equitable, and effective learning environments.

▶ ASSESSMENT INSTRUMENTS

Effective educational leadership today depends on a data-informed approach to improving teaching, learning, and school performance. The faculty should reach consensus on what will be assessed. If the educational leader is the principal, they should assign teacher teams to collect data and select assessment instruments for each selected factor and condition. If the educational leader is one with no authority they should select colleagues for a data collection team. Whether the leader is with or without authority, a leader should be designated, and they should be charged with the responsibility of communicating what will be assessed to faculty, not involved in the selection and data collection process. Families and the broader community should be informed through a newsletter or email.

Using a range of assessment instruments and protocols, schools can gather and analyze both quantitative and qualitative data to drive meaningful improvement. Quantitative data, such as standardized test scores, provides measurable indicators of student achievement. Qualitative data, gathered through formative assessment instruments such as questionnaires, interviews, focus groups, and classroom observations, offer valuable insight into factors and conditions affecting learning.

Common formative assessments are identified or created for assessing factors and conditions that teachers, based on their experience and hunches, select for improvement in concert with the principal. The understanding is that common formative assessments selected by consensus will be used by all faculty in classrooms, grade levels, departments, schools, or districts. Instruction is based on formative assessment results. These common formative assessments help teachers identify the degree to which students understand and have mastered the knowledge and skills presented. Common formative assessments also determine those in need of additional support and those ready for enrichment.

After an improvement need is identified educators collaboratively design differentiated instruction, learning activities, and enrichment extensions. Lessons are continuously revised based on student progress and feedback. This process transforms classrooms into dynamic spaces where all students learn. Summarizing, common assessments are used to inform instruction, monitor student understanding, and track progress. A variety of assessment protocols are provided later in this chapter.

Example: Learning Walk Protocol

Learning walks are a key form of qualitative assessment (Gould, 2004). They involve a collaborative process that provides opportunities for educators to observe, analyze, and reflect on classroom practices with the aim of improving teaching and learning. These observations are non-evaluative and focus on gathering evidence of student learning and instructional strategies. Learning walks are brief, targeted classroom observations by teacher teams with or without the building-based principal. Observers focus on the engagement and curiosity of students, what they say they are learning, and how they take responsibility for their own learning and behavior. Learning walks can uncover barriers to learning, including mental health issues such as trauma and depression. In addition, learning walks help identify important contextual factors that contribute to effective and inclusive learning environments. Examining instructional artifacts, for example, lesson plans, aligned multi-leveled learning tasks and materials; writing samples and projects; access to technology; tracking tools for monitoring student progress; and in-class special education and other academic support services help learning walk teams assess the quality and impact of learning. The observations and insights from teams that collect data inform targeted interventions that support equity and student success.

Instructions

- Form a team of 2–3 faculty members to conduct observations collaboratively.
- Clarify the purpose of the learning walks with the team and participating teachers. The purpose should focus on observing and reflecting on student learning and instructional practices.
- Prior to the learning walk, identify 1–3 classrooms to observe the specific collective focus area for observation and assessment. Schedule times to observe and assess and then meet as immediately as possible after the visit with the classroom teacher(s) to discuss the learning walk teacher-team's observations and assessments regarding the following:

- Grade-level outcomes for the lesson are posted in writing and verbally articulated.
  - Criteria for assessing mastery of the outcomes are clearly articulated.
  - Students can articulate the learning outcomes and their expectations.
  - Students reference rubrics to self-assess and internalize standards and outcomes.
  - Classroom arrangements support whole group, small group, and 1-to-1 instruction.
  - Student work displayed explicitly connects to grade-level standards-based outcomes.
  - Lesson plans outline specific outcomes and include multi-leveled materials.
- Visit classrooms and take detailed notes on the selected, faculty agreed upon collective focus area(s), looking for evidence of student learning and engagement.
- Meet immediately after the classroom visits to review notes, discuss observations, and reflect on the following questions:
  - What did you notice?
  - What are students learning?
  - What is the evidence that students are learning?
  - What could be done to improve teaching and learning?
  - What should we look for next time?
- Immediately after the team has met, meet with the teachers of the observed classroom(s) and share observations, reflections, and insights regarding the questions developed for the learning walk. Provide constructive and actionable corrective feedback in a supportive manner.
- Schedule follow-up learning walks to observe progress, gather additional insights, and adjust focus areas based on feedback and observed needs.
- Encourage ongoing dialogue and collaboration with teachers visited to sustain continuous improvement.

Additional Collective Focus Areas to Select and Observe During Learning Walks

- Relational trust and a sense of community in classrooms.
- Opportunities for student collaboration and peer feedback.
- Student engagement and participation levels.

- Opportunities for higher-order thinking and problem-solving.
- Alignment of classroom learning activities with content and performance standards, the collective focus, and goals of the action plan.
- Reconfigured classrooms for differentiated instruction.
- The degree to which general and special educators work together.

Table 3.1 School Culture Survey (Gould, 2005).

Instructions: Please circle the number beside the indicator that best represents your current experience at our school.

Rating Scale: 1 = Never | 2 = Sometimes | 3 = Often | 4 = Always

Collaborative Practice

Teachers and staff regularly share and discuss teaching strategies and curriculum ideas.	1	2	3	4
Staff members collaborate in building the school schedule.	1	2	3	4
Decisions about materials and resources involve staff input and dialogue.	1	2	3	4
The school's student behavior expectations are shaped through team input and agreement.	1	2	3	4
Common planning time is used for team-based collaboration, not just individual work.	1	2	3	4

Positive Professional Relationships

Staff share stories of successes and events that reinforce school values.	1	2	3	4
Staff members connect socially outside of the work environment.	1	2	3	4
There is a genuine sense of community among faculty and staff.	1	2	3	4
The school's schedule encourages frequent staff communication.	1	2	3	4
Staff feel encouraged to contribute new ideas and innovations.	1	2	3	4
School traditions celebrate important events, goals, and accomplishments.	1	2	3	4

Empowerment and Collective Responsibility	1	2	3	4
Staff members proactively address issues rather than waiting to fix problems after they occur.	1	2	3	4
There is a shared sense of trust and reliance among colleagues.	1	2	3	4
Staff seek out creative solutions to challenges rather than repeating old routines.	1	2	3	4
Staff focus on understanding root causes of issues rather than assigning blame.	1	2	3	4
Educators are trusted and supported to make instructional decisions.	1	2	3	4
People work at this school because they are committed to and believe in its mission.	1	2	3	4

Table 3.2 Professional Learning Communities Survey (Gould, 2008).

This survey assesses the extent to which factors and conditions associated with a professional learning community are currently present in your school.

Instructions: Please circle the number beside the indicator that best represents your current experience at our school.

Rating Scale: 1 = Rarely | 2 = Occasionally | 3 = Frequently | 4 = Consistently

1. Foundational Practices

Open Sharing of Practice

Teachers observe, share, and discuss one another's teaching strategies and philosophies.	1	2	3	4

Thoughtful Dialogue

Faculty/staff members engage in conversations about their contexts and the challenges they face.	1	2	3	4

Collaborative Commitment to Student Success

Teachers believe all students are capable of achieving at high levels and take responsibility for supporting them.	1	2	3	4

Collaborative Development

Teachers co-create lesson plans, formative assessments, and multi-leveled instructional materials	1	2	3	4

2. School Culture

Shared Values, Beliefs, Mindsets, and Commitments

Teachers affirm their common values, shared vision, and meeting norms through words and actions.	1	2	3	4

Mutual Trust and Recognition

Teachers feel respected and valued by colleagues, leadership, families, and the wider community.	1	2	3	4

Growth-Oriented Mindset

Teachers take professional risks, explore new strategies, and engage in continual learning.	1	2	3	4

Shared Expertise

Systems are in place to promote peer learning and support teacher growth, especially for those who need improvement.	1	2	3	4

Supportive Leadership

School leadership maintains focus on shared goals, collaboration, and ongoing improvement.	1	2	3	4

Copyright material from Gould (2026), *School Change is a Collaborative Process*, Routledge

Inclusive Induction

New teachers are integrated into the school community and are viewed as meaningful contributors.	1	2	3	4

3. Organizational Conditions

Communication Pathways

There are opportunities to exchange ideas within and across grade-level teams and subject departments.	1	2	3	4

Time for Professional Dialogue

The school allocates ongoing, structured time for reflection, collaboration, and renewal.	1	2	3	4

Integrated Teaching Practices

Teachers engage in structured collaboration such as lesson planning, lesson study, or team teaching.	1	2	3	4

Shared Physical Spaces

Teachers have grade level or subject specific classrooms grouped together and accessible, common spaces to engage in teaching and learning discussions.	1	2	3	4

Professional Autonomy

Teachers are empowered and trusted to make instructional decisions that are aligned with community values.	1	2	3	4

Table 3.3 Aligned Factors and Conditions in a Standards-Based Instructional System Protocol (Gould, 2008).

Instructions: This protocol provides educational leaders and faculty with a systems-thinking approach that assesses the presence of the essential components of an aligned standards-based system and the degree to which they are present and used by faculty. This protocol is designed to be used during learning walks; grade-level, department, and faculty meeting discussions; classroom observations; and follow-up conversations. Educational leaders with teacher observation and evaluation responsibilities have clear indicators as the basis for observing, assessing, and helping teachers improve instructional practice and aligning the essential component of a standards-based system.

Rating Scale: 1 = Fully Present | 2 = Frequently Present | 3 = Partially Present | 4 = Not Present

Content and Performance Standards Implementation

Curriculum is rigorous and focused on essential knowledge, skills, and mindsets.	1	2	3	4
Content and performance standards for each subject and grade are specified and taught by all teachers on the grade level.	1	2	3	4
Content and performance standards are displayed in classrooms and are the same for all students.	1	2	3	4
Students can articulate the standards they are working toward.	1	2	3	4
A social curriculum is integrated with the academic curriculum.	1	2	3	4
Rubrics are provided to help students understand quality expectations and self-assess.	1	2	3	4
Student work illustrating quality standards is displayed and linked to rubrics.	1	2	3	4
Pacing of topics and standards follows a logical sequence.	1	2	3	4

Assessment Utilization

Common formative assessments are used to by all grade level/department teachers in all subjects.	1	2	3	4
Common formative assessments are used regularly to determine needs and monitor progress.	1	2	3	4
Common formative assessments are used by teachers to adjust instruction.	1	2	3	4
Rubrics aligned with content and performance standards are used for self-assessment by students.	1	2	3	4

Aligned Instruction

Lessons are aligned with content and performance standards.	1	2	3	4
Lessons are planned with standards-based outcomes in mind.	1	2	3	4
Instruction focuses on areas identified by common formative assessments.	1	2	3	4
Differentiated instruction is used to meet the needs of all students.	1	2	3	4
Flexible grouping is used for differentiated instruction.	1	2	3	4
Classroom space is designated for whole group, small group, and one-on-one instruction.	1	2	3	4
Regular, specific positive, and corrective feedback is provided.	1	2	3	4
Student progress is monitored and recorded.	1	2	3	4

Linked Instructional Materials

Instructional materials are multi-leveled for differentiated instruction and aligned with the goals, objectives, and outcomes stated in daily lesson plans.	1	2	3	4

Teachers use learning multi-leveled materials beyond textbooks to support all students.	1	2	3	4
Supplies and multi-leveled materials are labeled for easy student access in the classroom.	1	2	3	4

Connected Safety Nets

Formative assessments identify students needing additional opportunities to learn.	1	2	3	4
Interventions are built into regular classroom structures so that students don't fall through the cracks (e.g., differentiated instruction, special education support personnel).	1	2	3	4
Safety net content is the same content that students not needing extra help are working on.	1	2	3	4
Students not needing extra help go to an enrichment learning center within the classroom.	1	2	3	4

Job-Embedded Staff Development

Staff development is designed to support teachers in curriculum, assessment, and instruction gaps affecting student learning that they self-identify.	1	2	3	4
Grade-level teams have performance goals in self-identified areas that may be part of their observations and evaluations.	1	2	3	4
Faculty have individual professional development plans (IPDPs).	1	2	3	4

Copyright material from Gould (2026), *School Change is a Collaborative Process*, Routledge

Collaboration/Teamwork

Faculty collaborate to develop common assessments aligned with Performance standards.	1	2	3	4
Teachers co-plan lessons and interventions to support all students.	1	2	3	4
Instructional strategies and materials are shared across grade levels.	1	2	3	4

Aligned Parent Outreach/Engagement

Educational leaders and faculty make parents feel welcome and respected.	1	2	3	4
Parents are informed about the many ways the school wants them to be involved.	1	2	3	4
Faculty communicate effectively to engage parents in supporting student achievement.	1	2	3	4

Table 3.4 Parent Engagement Assessment Protocol (Gould, 2008).

This protocol can be used by schools to assess parent involvement practices. It is based on Epstein's Six Types of Involvement.

Instructions: Please circle the number beside the indicator that represents what you think.

Rating Scale: 1 = Fully Present | 2 = Frequently Present | 3 = Partially Present | 4 = Not Present

Type 1: Parenting

Does the school provide families with information about home conditions that support learning?	1	2	3	4
Are workshops or resources available to educate parents on child development and effective parenting?	1	2	3	4
Are family support programs offered for health, nutrition, or other services?	1	2	3	4

Are home visits or neighborhood meetings conducted to bridge understanding between families and schools?	1	2	3	4
Is communication tailored to reach all families, including those unable to attend events?	1	2	3	4

Type 2: Communicating

Are parent–teacher conferences held regularly, with follow-ups as needed?	1	2	3	4
Are communications provided in multiple languages and accessible formats (e.g., large print, digital)?	1	2	3	4
Are there established two-way communication channels for parents and teachers?	1	2	3	4
Are student progress reports clear and actionable for families?	1	2	3	4
Does the school share policies, programs, and transition plans effectively with families?	1	2	3	4

Type 3: Volunteering	1	2	3	4
Are parents actively recruited to volunteer in various roles at school?	1	2	3	4
Are flexible scheduling options available to accommodate working parents?	1	2	3	4
Are volunteers provided with training and recognition for their contributions?	1	2	3	4
Does the school maintain a database of parent talents, skills, and availability?	1	2	3	4
Are there organized efforts (e.g., parent patrols or classroom support) that align with school needs?	1	2	3	4

Type 4: Learning at Home

Is information provided to families about grade-level skills and curriculum requirements?	1	2	3	4
Are homework policies designed to involve parents in supporting learning without requiring direct teaching?	1	2	3	4
Are interactive homework assignments regularly given to encourage family–student discussions?	1	2	3	4
Are resources like calendars or learning packets provided to guide home activities?	1	2	3	4
Does the school involve families in setting goals and planning for students' educational futures?	1	2	3	4

Type 5: Decision-Making

Are parents involved in school decision-making committees or advisory councils?	1	2	3	4
Are parent leaders representative of all racial, ethnic, and socioeconomic groups?	1	2	3	4
Are parents provided training to serve effectively as school representatives?	1	2	3	4
Are there established networks to link families with parent representatives?	1	2	3	4
Are students involved in decision-making processes alongside parents?	1	2	3	4

Type 6: Collaborating With the Community

Does the school provide families with information on community services and programs?	1	2	3	4

Are partnerships established with community organizations to enhance school and family practices?	1	2	3	4
Are community-based activities linked to students' learning and talents?	1	2	3	4
Are alumni or community members involved in supporting school programs?	1	2	3	4
Are efforts made to ensure equity in access to community resources for all families?	1	2	3	4

Table 3.5 Trust in Leadership

The example shows how a 4-point Likert scale can be used by teachers to rate the degree to which teachers or families trust school or district leadership. It can also be used as a self-assessment for special education directors, principals, and superintendents.

Instructions: Use the Likert Scale to rate the degree to which the indicators are in place.

Likert Rating Scale: 1 = Never | 2 = Rarely | 3 = Often | 4 = Always

Acting with integrity (honest, sincere, nonjudgmental, respectful)	1	2	3	4
Avoiding talking behind people's backs	1	2	3	4
Keeping confidences	1	2	3	4
Admitting when wrong	1	2	3	4
Caring about others	1	2	3	4
Listening well	1	2	3	4
Praising efforts	1	2	3	4
Showing interest in others	1	2	3	4
Sharing about myself	1	2	3	4
Working well with others	1	2	3	4
Showing empathy	1	2	3	4
Asking for input	1	2	3	4

Exhibiting reliability	1	2	3	4
Doing what was promised	1	2	3	4
Responding in a timely manner to requests	1	2	3	4
Organizing	1	2	3	4
Being accountable for actions	1	2	3	4
Following through	1	2	3	4
Acting with consistency	1	2	3	4

Table 3.6 Equity, Diversity, Inclusion, and Justice (EDIJ) Assessment.

This protocol may be used for interviews, surveys, or reflective practices to gather meaningful insights from principals, educators, students, and families.

Classroom Observation

The purpose of this protocol (Gould, 2019) is to observe classroom practices and educator behaviors that support equity, diversity, inclusion, and justice (EDIJ).

<u>Instructions</u>: Indicate each practice observed with a ✔ for strengths and an ✘ for areas requiring growth.

☐	Classroom resources and materials reflect a variety of cultures, identities, and lived experiences.
☐	The teacher consistently uses inclusive and respectful language.
☐	Multiple cultural perspectives are embedded within lesson content and discussions.
☐	Students are encouraged to express diverse viewpoints and experiences.
☐	The teacher demonstrates awareness of students' individual learning needs, backgrounds, and identities.
☐	When issues of bias, exclusion, or conflict arise, the teacher responds equitably and constructively.

School Culture

The purpose of this section is to gather perceptions from students, families, faculty, and staff regarding the school's EDIJ practices and climate.

Instructions: Please rate each statement using the following scale.

Rating Scale: 1 = Strongly Disagree | 2 = Disagree | 3 = Agree | 4 = Strongly Agree

Indicators

The school visibly promotes equity, diversity, inclusion, and justice.	1	2	3	4
School policies and practices support fairness and equitable treatment for all.	1	2	3	4
I feel safe, respected, and valued within the school environment.	1	2	3	4
School leadership holds itself accountable for creating an inclusive and equitable culture.	1	2	3	4
Incidents involving bias or exclusion are addressed promptly and effectively.	1	2	3	4
Teachers integrate diverse voices, histories, and perspectives into the instructional process.	1	2	3	4
Faculty foster classrooms that are welcoming and inclusive to all students.	1	2	3	4
Teachers demonstrate cultural awareness in their interactions with students.	1	2	3	4
Learning opportunities are accessible and equitable for every student.	1	2	3	4
My cultural identity and background are acknowledged and respected at school.	1	2	3	4
Teachers treat all students equitably, regardless of identity or background.	1	2	3	4
The school encourages exploration and celebration of diverse cultures.	1	2	3	4

Copyright material from Gould (2026), *School Change is a Collaborative Process,* Routledge

In the Appendices, additional assessment tools and protocols to collaboratively collect data are provided.

▶ EXAMPLE: A RATIONALE FOR THE IMPORTANCE OF COLLABORATIVELY COLLECTING CONTEXTUAL DATA

Colleagues,

Collaboratively collecting contextual data is one of the most impactful steps we can take to understand and address the factors and conditions that shape student learning. When educational leaders work together with faculty colleagues to gather data, we move beyond assumptions to uncover a clear picture of the challenges and opportunities within our school community. This process allows us to focus on areas that truly matter such as curriculum alignment, the types and uses of assessments, equitable access to resources, the integration of social-emotional learning, and the physical and emotional well-being of our students.

By engaging in this collective effort, we ensure that every voice is heard, every perspective considered, and every decision grounded in evidence. Contextual data helps us identify not only where students are excelling but also where they need additional support, whether it's addressing barriers like mental health challenges, attendance issues, or the need for differentiated instruction. Together, we can create targeted approaches that prioritize student success and respond to the unique dynamics of our school.

This shared commitment to gathering and using data fosters transparency, builds trust, and strengthens the partnership between educators and families. It empowers us to work collaboratively toward a common that ensures that every student has the opportunity to learn and grow. Please share your thoughts.

▶ DEVELOPING A BULLETED PRELIMINARY PLAN FOR COLLABORATIVELY COLLECTING CONTEXTUAL DATA

A preliminary plan should focus on key actions you, as an educational leader, will take to guide a teacher team in collecting data and using it to advance school improvement. State whether you have formal authority or operate through influencing others. The plan should avoid generic or third-person descriptions. Instead, it should detail specific, actionable steps highlighting how you will lead discussions, facilitate collaboration, and align data collection and analysis process. Do not describe what you think an educational leader other than yourself would do. Preliminary plans that you develop should make it clear that the step-by-step actions will be taken by you as the educational leader.

When developing your preliminary plan, use bullets that capture the main ideas. Your preliminary plans should include important details and citations to reinforce content and process. Your preliminary plan will differ from the initial plans of others due to your unique school context and the degree to which you have a position with or without authority. Each preliminary plan is foundational to the one that follows. Your preliminary plan will help faculty colleagues collaboratively address persistent factors and conditions needing improvement in classrooms, departments, schools, or districts. Bulleted preliminary plans will be expanded and evolve into an innovation plan in Chapter Eight. The innovation plan narrative will contribute to creating a coherent approach for improving teaching, learning, and leading in classrooms, departments, schools, or districts. Developing preliminary plans and an innovation plan prepares educational leaders for when they will be working collaboratively with faculty colleagues.

▶ CHAPTER SUMMARY

This chapter emphasized the importance of systems thinking, reflective inquiry, and the collection of both qualitative and quantitative data to drive meaningful school improvement. Collaborative data collection offers a comprehensive understanding of a school's context and helps establish a collective focus for change. By engaging diverse stakeholders, schools ensure that data is both relevant and reflective of community needs, leading to strategies that are data-informed and community-driven. This inclusive process builds shared commitment to creating a supportive, equitable, and effective learning environment. Leaders play a vital role in making the data-gathering process transparent and inclusive, while also fostering trust and shared purpose. Working collaboratively with teams, leaders should select or design assessment protocols that identify key factors and conditions affecting student learning and lay the groundwork for sustained improvement and innovation.

Leadership Task: *Reflective Journal*

- Respond in writing to the following prompts. This will be your third journal entry. The prompts may be used to facilitate a faculty meeting or university classroom discussion.
  - What contextual factors do you believe promote or hinder improvement in your school or organization?
  - Which of Bryk's supports have been implemented?
  - How well are curriculum, assessment, and instruction aligned across your grade level, department, school, or district?
  - Which assessment instruments will you use for collaborative data collection?
  - How can leaders and faculty work together to assess equity, access, and social justice?
  - Are assessments meaningfully integrated into the learning process?
  - What are some examples where collaborative data collection led to meaningful change, and why were they effective?

Leadership Task: *The Importance of Collaboratively Collecting Contextual Data*

- Develop a communication to be discussed at a meeting with a teacher team, department, school, or district that describes the importance of "Collaboratively Collect Contextual Focus" and its relation to the school improvement processes and the Six-Point Conceptual Framework.

Leadership Task: *Collaboratively Collect Contextual Data*

- Facilitate a faculty meeting to collaboratively select factors and conditions for assessment.

Leadership Task: *Develop a Preliminary Plan for Collaboratively Collecting Contextual Data*

- Developing a preliminary plan for collecting contextual data, carefully considering the unique characteristics of your school environment, the framing questions that reveal factors and conditions that hinder or support student learning, and the assessments that may be selected or developed.

References

Ainsworth, L. (2003). *Power standards: Identifying the standards that matter the most.* Lead + Learn Press.

Bryk, A. S. (2009). *Organizing schools for improvement: Lessons from Chicago.* University of Chicago Press.

Darling-Hammond, L., Hyler, M. E., & Gardner, M. (2017). *Effective teacher professional development.* Learning Policy Institute. https://learningpolicyinstitute.org/product/teacher-prof-dev

Deal, T. E. (1983). Culture: A new look through old lenses. *Educational Administration Quarterly, 19*(4), 18–30. https://journals.sagepub.com/doi/10.1177/0021886383019000411.

Dewey, J. (1910). *How we think.* D. C. Heath & Co.

DuFour, R., Eaker, R., & Many, T. (2010). *Learning by doing: A handbook for professional learning communities at work* (2nd ed.). Solution Tree Press. https://www.solutiontree.com/learning-by-doing-fourth-edition.html

Fullan, M. (2003a). *Change forces with a vengeance.* Routledge Falmer.

Fullan, M. (2007). *The new meaning of educational change* (4th ed.). Teachers College Press.

Gay, G. (2018). *Culturally responsive teaching: Theory, research, and practice.* Teachers College Press.

González, T. (2012). Restorative justice from the margins to the mainstream: Equity for all students. *Leadership and Policy in Schools, 11*(3), 283–298.

Gould, S. (2004). *Learning walk protocol and form.* [See Appendices].

Gould, S. (2008). *Desired conditions in a standards-based instructional environment protocol.* [See Appendices].

Gould, S. (2019). *Equity, Diversity, Inclusion, and Justice (EDIJ) Assessment Protocol.*

Hattie, J. (2009). *Visible Learning: A synthesis of over 800 meta-analyses relating to achievement.* Routledge.

Heifetz, R. A. (2006). *Leadership without easy answers.* Harvard University Press.

Heifetz, R. A., & Linsky, M. (2009). *The practice of adaptive leadership: Tools and tactics for changing your organization and the world.* Harvard Business Review Press.

Mandinach, E. B., & Gummer, E. S. (2016). *Data-driven decision making in education.* Teachers College Press.

Pitcock, S., Seidel, B., & McCombs, J. S. (2013). *Expanding minds and opportunities: Leveraging the power of afterschool and summer learning for student success.* Collaborative Communications Group.

Rabkin, N., & Hedberg, E. C. (2011). *Arts education in America: What the declines mean for arts participation.* National Endowment for the Arts.

Rose, D. H., & Meyer, A. (2002). *Teaching every student in the digital age: Universal design for learning.* Association for Supervision and Curriculum Development.

Senge, P. (1990). *The fifth discipline.* New York: NY Doubleday.

Thomas, W. P., & Collier, V. P. (1997). *School effectiveness for language minority students.* National Clearinghouse for Bilingual Education.

Tomlinson, C. A. (1992). *Managing a differentiated classroom: A practical guide.* Association for Supervision and Curriculum Development.

Wang, M. C. (1985). *Adaptive learning environments.* McCutchan Publishing.

Warschauer, M., & Matuchniak, T. (2010). New technology and digital worlds: Analyzing evidence of equity in access, use, and outcomes. *Review of Research in Education, 34*(1), 179–225.

Zhao, Y. (2012). *Catching up or leading the way: American education in the age of globalization.* ASCD.

Additional Resources

Banks, J. A. (2009). *Cultural diversity and education: Foundations, curriculum, and teaching.* Pearson.

Blank, R. K., de las Alas, N., & Smith, C. (2012). *Making sense of data-driven decision making in education: Evidence from recent field studies.* The Urban Institute.

Bloom, B. (1956). *Taxonomy of Educational Objectives, Handbook 1: The cognitive domain.* David McKay Co.

Darling-Hammond, L. (2010). *The flat world and education: How America's commitment to equity will determine our future.* Teachers College Press.

Drago-Severson, E., Blum-DeStefano, J., & Brooks Lawrence, D. (2023). *Growing for justice: A developmental continuum of leadership capacities and practices.* Corwin.

Epstein, J. L. (1995). School, family, and community partnerships: Caring for the children we share. *Phi Delta Kappan, 76*(9), 701–712.

Ford, D. Y., Grantham, T. C., & Whiting, G. W. (2008). Culturally responsive gifted education: Recommendations for identifying and serving culturally diverse gifted students. *Roeper Review, 30*(3), 156–165.

Gándara, P., & Hopkins, M. (2010). *Forbidden language: English learners and restrictive language policies.* Teachers College Press.

Kendi, I. X. (2019). *How to be an antiracist.* One World.

Reback, R. (2010). Teaching the teachers: How peer influence affects educational outcomes. *Journal of Public Economics, 94*(7–8), 688–698. https://doi.org/10.1016/j.jpubeco.2010.04.003

Wheatley, M. J. (1999). *Leadership and the new science: Discovering order in a chaotic world* (2nd ed.). Berrett-Koehler.

THE 6-POINT CONCEPTUAL FRAMEWORK

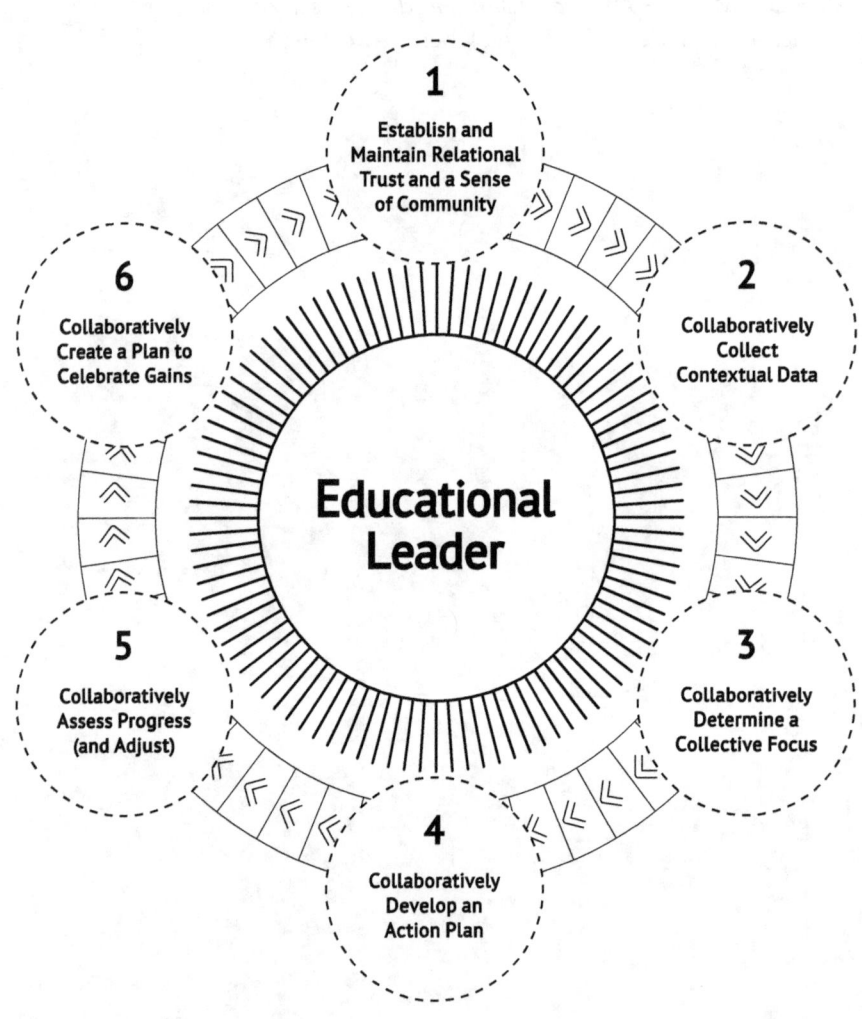

Conceptual Framework design and chapter openers designed by Christian Arichabala.

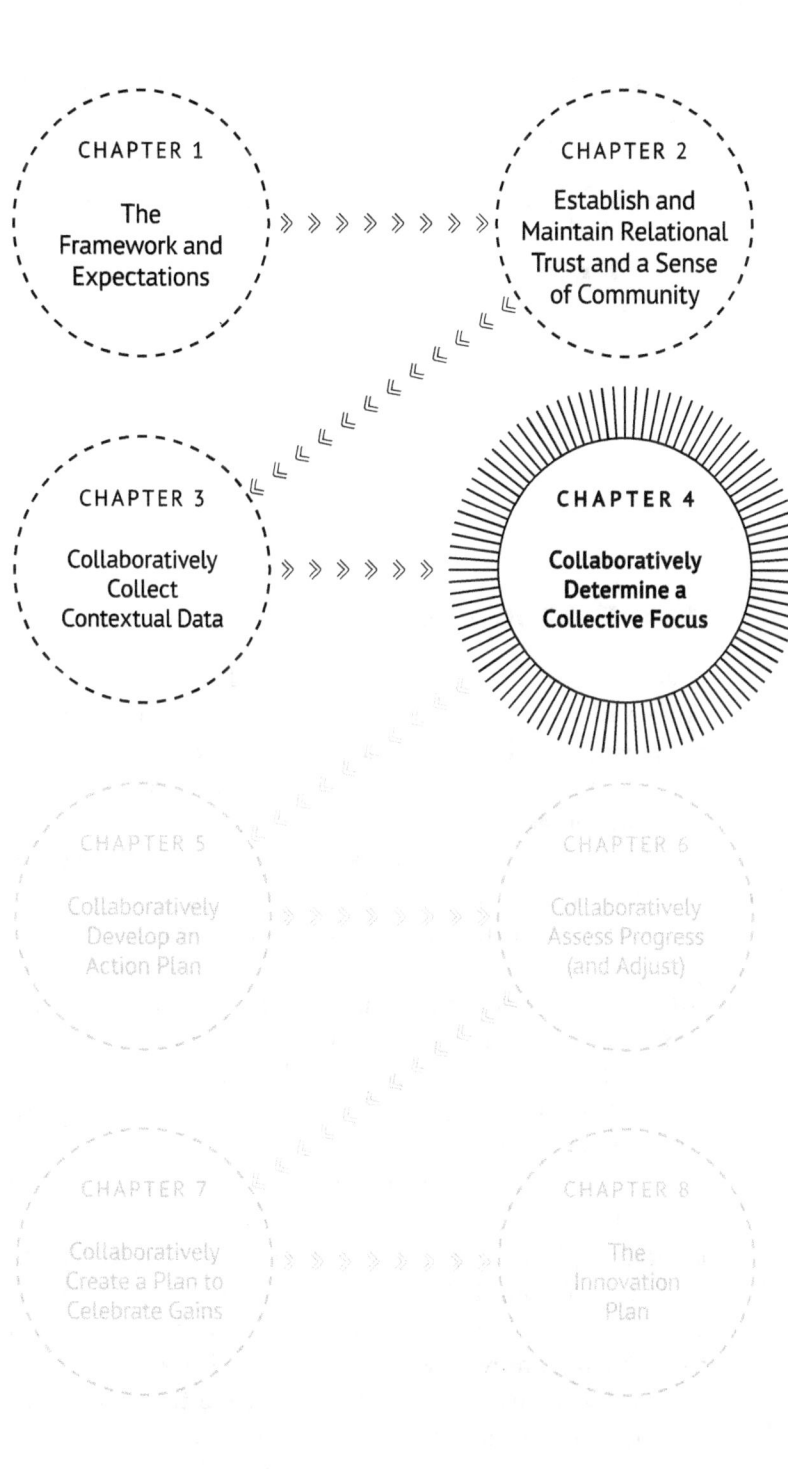

Chapter 4

Collaboratively Determine a Collective Focus

▶ **INTRODUCTION**

Collaboratively Determine a Collective Focus is the third subsystem of the Six-Point Conceptual Framework. A collective focus is the unified attention and purposeful alignment of a teacher team or faculty toward a shared vision, set of goals, or improvement priorities, emphasizing collaboration, mutual accountability, and a consistent commitment to achieving meaningful results. In educational settings, a collective focus often centers on improving student learning, closing equity gaps, and fostering a culture of continuous improvement. It contrasts with isolated or individual efforts by emphasizing coherence, shared responsibility, and team-based problem solving. It also avoids the tyranny of too many initiatives, for as Covey (1989) says, "A school or organization with many priorities has no priorities."

The process of determining a collective focus involves a systems-thinking, strategic-planning approach created to collaboratively lead the transformation of PK-12 student learning, teaching and leading. The foundation of meaningful and sustainable school improvement lies in the ability of educational leaders to work collaboratively with faculty to establish a collective focus. A collective focus is a shared factor or condition that faculty in a grade level, department, school, or district selects by reaching consensus and commits to implementing collaboratively.

There are many possible factors and conditions for a collective focus.

To identify a collective focus, leaders must understand the factors and conditions affecting the learning of a significant number of students. Collaborative data collection and analysis for a number of factors and conditions that the faculty and principal feel should be assessed reveal the degree to which there are gaps or deficiencies needing attention, if student learning is to be increased. Central to determining a priority collective focus is the principle that it must be selected by those responsible for implementing it. Shared responsibility and reaching consensus are key for collaboratively determining a collective focus that everyone will select and implement.

This chapter outlines the process for identifying, prioritizing, and implementing a collective focus. It equips both formal leaders and teacher-leaders with the assessment tools to guide improvement efforts. By facilitating collaboration, collecting and analyzing data, and establishing a system of monitoring progress, leaders can foster meaningful change, improvement, transformation, and innovation.

By the end of this chapter, educational leaders, with or without authority, will be able to

- Identify factors and conditions that support or hinder student learning.
- Examine biases and inequities (e.g., positionality, identity, privilege, power, culture, language, access, race, gender, class, justice).
- Assess potential violations of laws or human rights.
- Revisit essential supports (Bryk) and systems alignment (Gould).
- Create a list of factors and conditions identified by the data-collection teacher team for selection as a collective focus.
- Guide the prioritizing of 1–2 areas for improvement based on collected data and faculty input.
- Build consensus around a collective focus for improvement.
- Create a system to track and sustain progress.
- Hold individual teachers and grade level or department teams accountable for implementing the collective focus.
- Draft a preliminary plan to define and implement the collective focus collaboratively.

▶ FACTORS AND CONDITIONS INFLUENCING TEACHING, LEARNING, AND LEADERSHIP

Reimaging education in PK–12 requires bold, systemic change and innovation. To overcome the deeply rooted challenges in PK–12 education, educational leaders must embrace a systems-thinking approach that addresses the challenges of empowering every student to learn at high levels. This includes implementing inquiry-based, 21st-century curricula that are culturally relevant; using formative assessments to determine what students need to know and be able to do; providing access to skilled educators; fostering inclusive, adaptive learning environments; distributing leadership; advocating for equitable funding; and transforming schools that will better serve all students from all families.

Student success is influenced by a range of internal and external factors and conditions that affect the daily experiences of educators, students, and families. In Chapter Three, factors and conditions were detailed with the intent that leaders form teacher teams to select assessment instruments to determine the degree to which they are inhibiting or promoting student learning. Those internal factors and conditions, previously described in Chapter Three, are especially relevant for identifying a collective focus and are listed next as a reminder:

- School culture.
- Curriculum content and power standards.
- Assessment practices.
- Teacher quality.
- Differentiated instruction.
- Integration of general and special education.
- Mastery Learning.
- Communication.
- Leadership effectiveness.
- Adaptive learning strategies and environments.
- Professional learning communities (PLCs).
- Equity, systemic racism, access, and social justice.
- Professional development.
- Technology integration.
- Time for collaboration scheduled during the school day.

- Parental and community engagement.
- Essential supports for sustained improvement.
- Systems alignment in standards-based environment.

Collaboratively determining a collective focus requires inclusive, data-informed, and ethically grounded decision-making. For this to occur, leaders, teacher teams, departments, and faculties must work from a common set of criteria and shared understandings. To support this, informative materials that will support the decision-making process should be distributed in advance of any meeting where faculty will collaboratively determine a collective focus. Resources such as the Four Lenses of Ethics and the Four Abilities of an Equity Literacy Approach help structure the conversation and guide participants as they assess the values, implications, and potential impacts of their choices on students, families, and staff.

▶ THE FOUR LENSES OF ETHICS

Adapted from Shapiro and Stefkovich, the Four Lenses of Ethics provide multiple perspectives for considering professional decisions.

The "ethic of professionalism" centers on a personal and professional code of ethics. It emphasizes integrity, virtue, sound moral reasoning, and a commitment to values such as honesty, fairness, and responsibility. These principles are embedded in professional leadership standards such as the *Professional Standards for Educational Leaders* and guidelines from the National Policy Board for Educational Administration.

The "ethic of care" emphasizes relationships, empathy, connection, compassion, and belonging. It prioritizes collaboration, listening, cultural awareness, and understanding of lived experiences of others. This lens encourages educators to consider who benefits from decisions, who might be harmed, the long-term implications of their actions, and how their choices contribute to a greater good.

The "ethic of justice" focuses on fairness, individual rights, and the law. It examines how individuals navigate the balance between personal freedoms and the collective good. Schools grounded in this ethic work to promote equity, civic responsibility, and a deeper understanding of justice. It encourages educators to question whether existing laws or policies uphold fairness or need to be challenged or reimagined in pursuit of equity.

The "ethic of critique" challenges systems of power, privilege, and inequality. It raises critical questions about who holds authority; whose voices are heard or silenced; and how race, class, gender, and other identity markers impact educational access and opportunity. This ethic urges educators not only to identify inequities but also to actively dismantle systems that produce oppression and injustice. It encourages the pursuit of democratic ideals and a moral imperative to ensure that all children—regardless of race, gender, or social class—have the opportunity to thrive.

▶ FOUR ABILITIES OF AN EQUITY LITERACY APPROACH

According to Gorski and Pothini, an equity literacy approach empowers educators through four essential abilities that work together to foster just, inclusive schools. The first ability is the capacity to recognize even the most subtle forms of bias and inequity, whether they exist in systems, policies, or interpersonal interactions. The second is the ability to respond to these inequities in real time, using courage and care to intervene constructively when harm is done or exclusion occurs. The third is the ability to redress inequities over the long term, through sustained efforts to change structures, habits, and practices that reinforce injustice. The fourth ability is the capacity to sustain a learning environment where equity and inclusion are ongoing commitments, ensuring that all students feel valued, seen, and supported.

Equity literacy becomes actionable through a deliberate process of analysis and response. This begins with a commitment to identifying inequities and biases, which requires honest reflection and a willingness to confront uncomfortable truths about how schools operate. Educators must then intentionally consider diverse perspectives, especially from voices that have historically been marginalized, in order to expand their understanding of the context and its complexities.

Using established rubrics and/or observation protocols, the team identifies priority areas and frames their findings through ethical and organizational lenses. Summaries of relevant frameworks and guiding materials, like the four lenses, are shared with the faculty in advance of the meeting to set the stage for informed and purposeful discussion.

With a fuller picture of the landscape provided by the Four Lenses of Ethics, the teacher team reflects on the systemic forces influencing student outcomes and envisions equitable and just solutions. They present their findings, highlighting key patterns, strengths, and areas for growth. Faculty then engage in small group discussions using ethical and equity-focused criteria to examine each proposed focus area. These conversations center on the nature of the challenge, whom it impacts, why it hinders learning, and how it aligns with the school's values and vision. Based on feasibility, urgency, and potential impact, the faculty determines whether to adopt the ethical issue as a collective focus. In Chapter Five the process continues as the group collaborates to design an action plan, brainstorms immediate and long-term solutions, and outlines next steps, all grounded in equity, justice, and student success. The result is a clear, actionable plan aimed at transforming the school into a place where fairness and opportunity are realized.

▶ LEADING A DISCUSSION TO COLLABORATIVELY DETERMINE A COLLECTIVE FOCUS

Guiding faculty toward a collective focus requires ethical reflection, inclusive facilitation, and data-informed decision-making. Before the full faculty meeting, a diverse teacher team is assembled to ensure multiple perspectives. This team analyzes both quantitative and qualitative data, especially data reflecting faculty-raised concerns, to surface critical factors influencing student learning. During the faculty meeting, small groups evaluate potential focus areas using ethical and equity-based criteria, considering impact, alignment with school values, and barriers to learning.

Each group identifies and shares recommended priorities, which are then synthesized in a full-group discussion to build consensus around one or two collective focus areas. Final decisions are based on the ability of the chosen factors to address root causes and catalyze meaningful change. The principal or teacher leader communicates the outcome to the wider school community, reinforcing shared ownership of the work. This process strengthens trust, builds organizational capacity, and ensures the focus remains actionable, ethically grounded, and aligned with the school's long-term vision. Regular review and reflection ensure continued responsiveness and relevance over time.

▶ DEVELOPING AN ACCOUNTABILITY SYSTEM

Rooted in transparency and collaboration, this accountability system fosters a professional culture in which feedback is constructive, risk-taking is encouraged, and continuous learning is embraced. This accountability system is designed not to punish, but to deepen reflection, build capacity, and facilitate progress toward shared goals. A collective focus is selected by faculty at the grade-level, department, school, or district in consultation with the school leader. Consensus is reached, and all agree to be held accountable for the collective focus implementation.

The foundation of this system lies in the establishment of clear expectations and school-wide goals aligned with the selected collective focus. Accountability practices may include classroom observations conducted by principals, instructional coaches, or peer teams through learning walks. These observations are followed by timely, specific, and growth-oriented feedback delivered in one-on-one conversations. Rather than focusing solely on deficits, these discussions highlight strengths while addressing areas for growth, cultivating a mindset of reflection and improvement.

Peer collaboration is integral to this process. When a teacher experiences difficulty meeting expectations related to the collective focus, they may be supported through the development of a professional growth improvement plan with targeted objectives and timelines. As part of their professional development, the teacher might maintain a portfolio to document their growth and reflect on their learning. Coaching, modeling, and job-embedded supports should be made available to guide their progress.

Above all, this system is centered on trust and the belief that all educators are capable of growth. By creating space for honest feedback, honoring teacher voice, and aligning accountability with the school's values and goals, the system fosters a professional environment where both teachers and students can thrive. This shift, from compliance-based corrective oversight to professional development driven by an accountability plan, ensures that the collective focus becomes a shared and sustained commitment.

▶ TEAM ACCOUNTABILITY AND INDIVIDUAL ACCOUNTABILITY FOR TEAM MEMBERS

An accountability system that holds teacher teams responsible for implementing a shared goal fosters collaboration, collective ownership, individual responsibility, and genuine buy-in. It reinforces the idea that success relies on both the collective effort of the team and the contributions of each individual. This approach begins with open dialogue among teachers and school leaders about the collective focus, specific goals, and agreed-upon indicators of progress. Regular check-ins, primarily with teams and occasionally with individuals, are scheduled to review progress with the principal, address challenges, and adjust strategies as needed. These meetings include group discussions and individual updates, with each member expected to share evidence of their work, such as lesson plans, student work samples, or data reports. This transparency builds trust and strengthens shared accountability.

Constructive feedback is central to the process. Team members are encouraged to offer feedback to one another, fostering a culture of reflection and continuous improvement. Leaders or facilitators guide these conversations to ensure they remain productive and solutions-oriented. When performance, whether individual or collective, falls short of expectations, timely and supportive interventions are implemented. For individuals, this may include one-on-one coaching, targeted support, or the development of a professional growth portfolio. For the team, it might involve redistributing responsibilities, modifying strategies, or piloting new approaches.

Accountability is further reinforced through regular progress reports shared with the principal. These reports provide honest assessments of challenges, spotlight effective practices, and celebrate accomplishments. Ultimately, this accountability system strikes a balance between individual and team needs by combining transparency, regular communication, and supportive actions. It nurtures a culture of individual and collective responsibility, where educators are empowered to work collaboratively toward shared, meaningful outcomes. This collaborative accountability system also provides an in depth look at curriculum, assessment and instructional practice and an innovative alternative to the current observation and evaluation process that has been shown to be ineffective and extremely difficult for educational leaders to maintain.

▶ EXAMPLE: PRESENTING A RATIONALE FOR DETERMINING A COLLECTIVE FOCUS

Today, I want to talk with you about the importance of collaboratively developing a collective focus and how this process connects to the Six-Point Conceptual Framework that guides much of our work. This is not just about identifying a goal; it's about creating shared ownership of our mission and ensuring that every action we take is aligned with the values and priorities we hold as a community. Collaboratively developing a collective focus starts with understanding why this work matters. It's an opportunity for us to come together, not just as individuals working in silos, but also as a unified team committed to tackling challenges and advancing opportunities in a meaningful way. This process ensures that we are not working at cross-purposes but are moving forward with clarity and intention toward shared goals.

The Six-Point Conceptual Framework serves as our foundation. It gives us a lens through which to examine our priorities and align our focus with key principles like equity, community, and continuous improvement. For example, when we talk about equity, our collective focus should reflect a commitment to ensuring that all students—especially those who may have been underserved—have access to the opportunities and resources they need to succeed. When we think about community, our focus must honor the voices and perspectives of everyone in our school or district, creating a sense of shared responsibility. And when we consider continuous improvement, our focus must include actionable steps that help us grow and evolve over time.

This process starts with dialogue. We need to bring together data, narratives, and observations to understand where we are now and where we want to go. Data is not just numbers—it's a tool for telling a story about our strengths, challenges, and opportunities. By engaging with this story as a team, we begin to identify the most pressing factors or conditions we need to address. The goal here is to cultivate ownership. When everyone has a hand in analyzing the data and setting the direction, the collective focus becomes something we all believe in and work toward.

As our focus takes shape, we'll make explicit connections to the principles of the 6-Point Framework. This isn't just an academic exercise; it's about embedding these principles into the core of our work so that we can see how our efforts in equity, community building, and professional growth are interconnected.

Throughout this process, open communication is critical. We must ensure that all voices are heard, that differing perspectives are valued, and that we build trust through honest dialogue. At the same time, we need to establish clear expectations so that this focus translates into real action. Everyone here will play a role in turning our shared vision into measurable outcomes.

A preliminary plan should focus on key actions you, as an educational leader, will take to guide a teacher team to determine a collective focus. I want to emphasize *collective* focus. That means that all teachers and support personnel on the grade level, department, school, or district will work together to address the collective focus. Key actions should include the data collection team reaching consensus on the collective focus. The plan should avoid generic or third-person descriptions, instead detailing specific, actionable steps you will guide others to implement. Your plan should highlight how you will lead discussions and facilitate collaboration.

This is how we create meaningful change. When we come together to collaboratively develop a collective focus, we strengthen our ability to face challenges, align our actions with our values, and make a lasting impact. I am excited for us to take this journey together, guided by the principles of the Six-Point Conceptual Framework. I look forward to working together to identify and determine 1–2 areas for collective focus for improving student learning and seeing the results of our shared commitment.

▶ **EXAMPLE: A COLLECTIVE FOCUS STATEMENT**

Our collective focus is values, beliefs, and mindsets. We believe that

- All students from all families can master the content and performance power standards of the curriculum and essential outcomes when teachers provide students with appropriate learning conditions.
- Good teaching can counterbalance socioeconomic disadvantages and other handicapping conditions.
- Helping all students achieve at a high level can best be accomplished through collaboration and teamwork.
- Formative diagnosis of student learning is critical to developing the capacities of a diverse range of students.
- Student capacity to learn is not innate and fixed.
- Students, teachers, and leaders can get smarter when they reflect on their learning, work hard, and persevere.
- The continual improvement of student learning is a shared responsibility of school leaders, classroom teachers, support personnel students, and parents.
- Educators at the building level have the capacity to identify student learning needs, develop solutions, and report student progress more effectively than those distant from the learner.

▶ **DEVELOPING A BULLETED PRELIMINARY PLAN FOR A COLLECTIVE FOCUS**

This preliminary plan not only unites the school around a collaboratively determined collective focus but also lays the groundwork in the next phase for the development of a comprehensive action plan that will drive meaningful change, increased student learning, transformation, and innovation.

When developing your preliminary plan use bulleted, short, non-sentence statements to capture each main idea regarding how you will lead your faculty or teacher teams. Preliminary plans that you develop should make it clear that the step-by-step actions will be taken by you as the educational leader. Your preliminary plans should include important details and citations to reinforce content and process. Each preliminary plan is foundational to the one that follows. Bulleted preliminary plans will be expanded and evolve into an innovation plan in Chapter Eight. Developing preliminary plans and an innovation plan prepares educational leaders for when they will be working collaboratively with faculty colleagues to develop preliminary and innovation plans for their particular context.

Table 4.1 Factors and Conditions to Determine a Collective Focus (Gould, 2020).

Use this protocol during team discussions to highlight strengths and identify specific areas for improvement. This protocol measures the following critical factors and conditions related to curriculum, assessment, and instruction; culture and learning environment; parent engagement and community support; professional development; observation and evaluation; collaborative leadership; and communication.

Instructions: Circle the number that represents your choice.

Rating Scale: 1 = Never | 2 = Sometimes | 3 = Frequently | 4 = Always

Learning environment is safe, orderly, and equitable.	1	2	3	4
A culture of high academic and behavioral expectations is maintained.	1	2	3	4
Staff are involved in decision-making processes.	1	2	3	4
Sufficient time is allocated to curricular and instructional issues.	1	2	3	4
Instructional time is used effectively.	1	2	3	4
School vision, mission, and beliefs guide planning.	1	2	3	4
Leadership communicates a shared vision effectively.	1	2	3	4
Team planning is supported.	1	2	3	4
Resources are allocated to facilitate school improvement.	1	2	3	4

Copyright material from Gould (2026), *School Change is a Collaborative Process*, Routledge

Resources are clearly defined and directed by need assessments.	1	2	3	4
Resources are allocated to maximize student access to the curriculum.	1	2	3	4
Resources support professional development initiatives.	1	2	3	4
Long-term professional growth needs are addressed.	1	2	3	4
Professional development aligns with school improvement goals.	1	2	3	4
Professional development is ongoing, and job embedded.	1	2	3	4
Clearly defined observation and evaluation processes are in place for staff.	1	2	3	4
Evaluation processes are connected to professional growth plans.	1	2	3	4
Teachers understand their role in student success.	1	2	3	4
Teachers are assigned to maximize opportunities for students.	1	2	3	4
Clear goals and action steps are defined for school improvement.	1	2	3	4
Data collection informs strategic planning.	1	2	3	4
Planning reflects unique learning needs and desired results.	1	2	3	4
Curriculum is aligned with content and performance power standards.	1	2	3	4
Clearly articulated content and performance standards guide teaching and learning.	1	2	3	4
Content and performance standards are clearly communicated to students and families.	1	2	3	4
Students are aware of academic and behavior expectations.	1	2	3	4
Integration of social-emotional learning (SEL) in curriculum.	1	2	3	4

Development of critical thinking skills is prioritized.	1	2	3	4
Curriculum promotes equity and inclusivity.	1	2	3	4
Curriculum gaps are identified and addressed.	1	2	3	4
Lesson plans are informed by formative assessments.	1	2	3	4
Multiple formative classroom assessments are used.	1	2	3	4
Assessment tasks are diverse and comprehensive.	1	2	3	4
Continuous analysis of assessment results informs improvement in teaching, curriculum, and policies.	1	2	3	4
Barriers to learning are identified and reduced.	1	2	3	4
Students participate in self-assessment process.	1	2	3	4
Assessments provide meaningful feedback to students and teachers.	1	2	3	4
Leadership uses formative assessment and disaggregated data for school planning.	1	2	3	4
Implementation of assessment and accountability is consistent.	1	2	3	4
Student sample work is utilized to enhance learning.	1	2	3	4
Assessment processes for school improvement plans are established.	1	2	3	4
Teachers create clear, well-structured lesson plans.	1	2	3	4
A variety of instructional strategies are effectively used in all classrooms.	1	2	3	4
Instructional strategies and activities align with curriculum goals.	1	2	3	4
Differentiated instruction meets diverse student needs.	1	2	3	4

Copyright material from Gould (2026), *School Change is a Collaborative Process*, Routledge

Instructional strategies and activities are regularly monitored.	1	2	3	4
Teachers demonstrate cultural responsiveness in their methods.	1	2	3	4
Student-centered approaches are prioritized.	1	2	3	4
Teachers effectively manage instruction and behavior.	1	2	3	4
Teachers use a system to monitor and record student progress.	1	2	3	4
Students collaborate during learning activities.	1	2	3	4
Teachers provide timely and constructive feedback.	1	2	3	4
Technology and instructional resources are effectively integrated.	1	2	3	4
School provides for the needs of all students from all families.	1	2	3	4
Special education programs and interventions are effective.	1	2	3	4
Support beyond the classroom is available for students.	1	2	3	4
Homework supports instructional goals.	1	2	3	4
Students actively participate in class and demonstrate interest in learning.	1	2	3	4
Stakeholders are included in collaborative decision-making.	1	2	3	4
Stakeholders receive regular information about school activities.	1	2	3	4
Student achievement is publicly celebrated.	1	2	3	4
Families and the community are actively involved in using and promoting programs and services.	1	2	3	4

▶ CHAPTER SUMMARY

Establishing a collective focus within a school is essential for guiding effective and sustainable improvement. By narrowing priorities to just one or two key areas, schools can avoid initiative overload and foster shared purpose among faculty. This process must be collaborative with teachers and leaders engaging together in data collection, analysis, and decision-making. When those closest to the learners identify the priorities, the goals become more relevant, actionable, and understood, and teachers are more likely to commit to them. Teachers, by and large, do not sabotage their own projects.

The aim of a collective focus is to target the few critical factors and conditions that significantly affect a large number of students. This creates a foundation for strategic action planning that enhances teaching, learning, and leadership across grade levels, departments, schools, or districts. A clearly defined collective focus ensures that educational leaders and teachers align their efforts resulting in equitable learning outcomes for all students.

Accountability systems play a key role in supporting this process. When designed to build teacher capacity and reinforce commitments made through consensus, these systems help sustain focus and momentum. Regular check-ins emphasize shared responsibility and ensure that teams remain aligned and responsive.

This chapter also underscored the importance of examining broader contextual factors and conditions such as school culture, equity and access, and support systems. Educational leaders, regardless of formal title, must engage in reflective practice and open dialogue with faculty to determine which factors or conditions must shift to enable transformation. What should by now be obvious, although not explicitly said, is that this kind of collaboration takes time and thoughtful planning so that faculty meetings and professional development days are spent on the tasks necessary to address each step in a preliminary plan, in this case, to Collaboratively Determine a Collective Focus. This means that these meetings should no longer be spent on administrivia messages that could be better delivered by email. By working collaboratively to select and implement a collective focus grounded in student needs and building school capacity, leaders and teachers lay the groundwork for developing the fifth system of the Six-Point Conceptual Framework, *Collaboratively Developing an Action Plan*, and lasting and impactful school improvement.

Leadership Task: *Reflective Journal*

- Respond in writing to the following prompts. This will be your fourth journal entry. These prompts may be used to facilitate a faculty meeting or a university classroom discussion.
  - Why is it essential for schools to collaboratively determine a collective focus?
  - How can educational leaders navigate disagreements or conflicts that may surface during discussions or while implementing a collective focus?
  - What approaches can be used to reach consensus without compromising the integrity of diverse viewpoints?
  - What will you do to promote equity and inclusion throughout this collaborative process?
  - What challenges arise when teachers try to balance teacher autonomy with implementing a mutually agreed upon collective focus?
  - How does the process of collaboratively determining a focus build ownership, buy-in, and commitment among team members?
  - What tools or methods have you found effective for facilitating collaborative discussions about determining a collective focus?
  - Once a collective focus is determined, what steps can be taken to maintain alignment and sustain momentum?
  - How will this chapter influence you to lead the collaborative development of a collective focus in your own context?

Leadership Task: *Develop a Rationale to Introduce the Importance of a Collective Focus*

- Develop a description to be used at a meeting with a teacher grade-level team, department, school, or district that describes the importance of *Collaboratively Developing a* Collective *Focus* and its relation to the school improvement processes and the Six-Point Conceptual Framework.

Leadership Task: *Develop a Bulleted Preliminary Plan for Determining a Collective Focus*

- Taking into consideration the reflective questions posed, resources shared, the uniqueness of your context, develop a bulleted preliminary plan (no sentences, just a series of sound bites that capture the main ideas) for determining a collective focus on the instructions in Table 4.1.

Reference

Covey, S. R. (1989). *The 7 habits of highly effective people: Powerful lessons in personal change.* Free Press.

Additional Resources

Alderfer, C. P. (1976). Consulting to under-bounded systems. In D. A. Kolb, I. M. Rubin, & J. M. McIntyre (Eds.), *Organizational psychology: A book of readings* (2nd ed., pp. 429–438). Prentice-Hall.

Gay, G. (2000). *Culturally responsive teaching: Theory, research, and practice.* Teachers College Press.

Heifetz, R. A., Grashow, A., & Linsky, M. (2009). *The practice of adaptive leadership: Tools and tactics for changing your organization and the world.* Harvard Business Press.

Kotter, J. P. (1996). *Leading change.* Harvard Business Review Press.

Margaret C. Wang (1991). *Adaptive Education Strategies: Building on diversity.* Paul H. Brookes Pub Co.

National Policy Board for Educational Administration. (2008). *Educational leadership policy standards: ISLLC 2008.* Authors. https://www.npbea.org/

National Policy Board for Educational Administration. (2015). *Professional standards for educational leaders.* Authors. https://www.npbea.org/

THE 6-POINT CONCEPTUAL FRAMEWORK

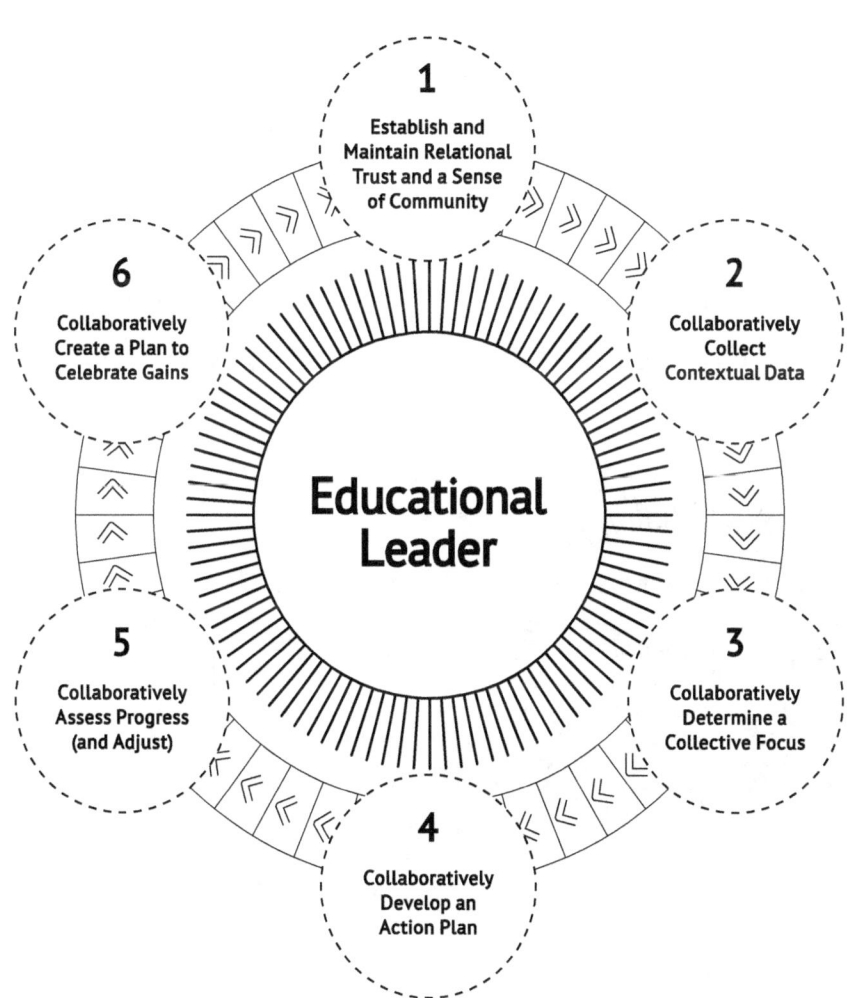

Conceptual Framework design and chapter openers designed by Christian Arichabala.

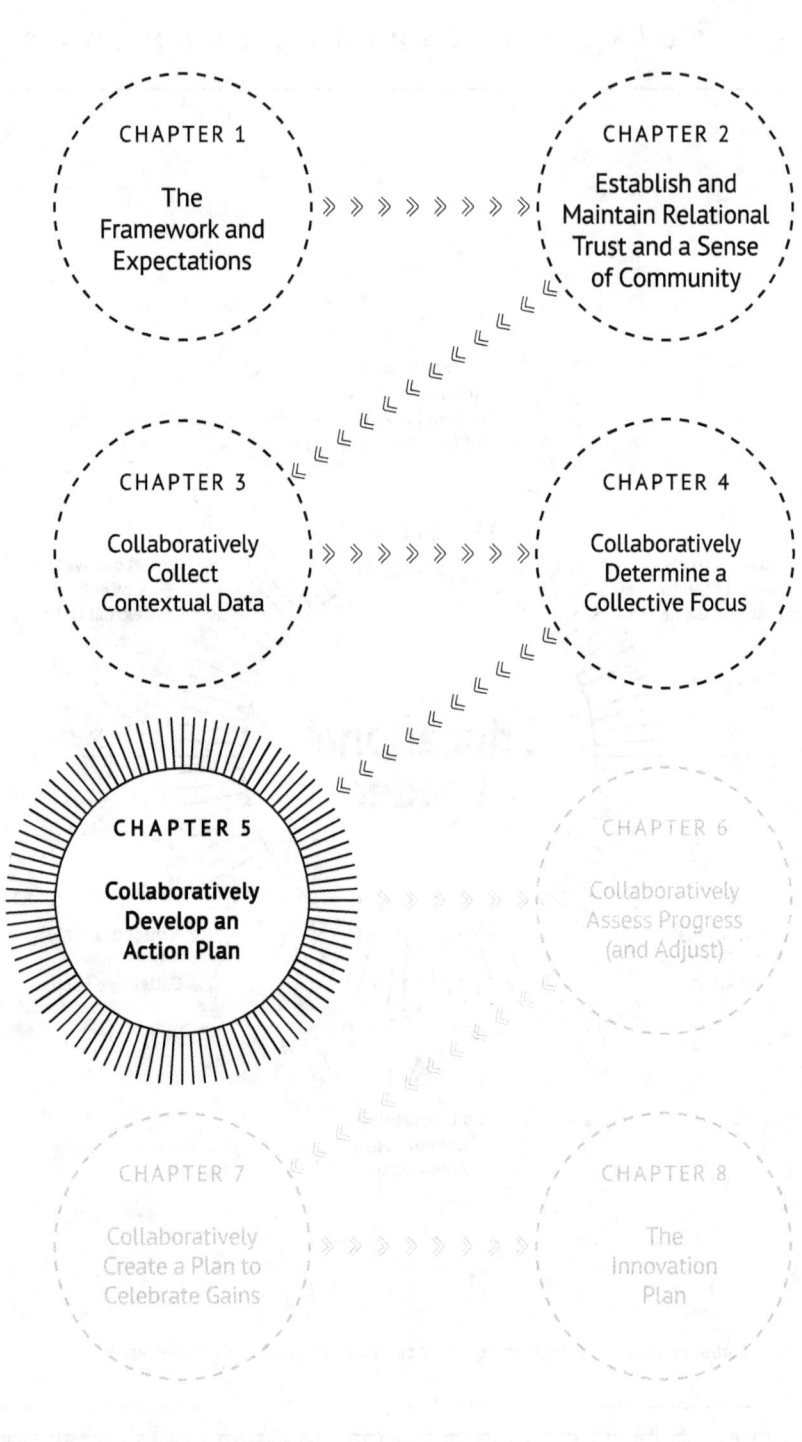

Chapter 5

Collaboratively Develop an Action Plan

▶ INTRODUCTION

Collaboratively Develop an Action Plan is the fourth subsystem of the Six-Point Conceptual Framework. This systems-thinking, strategic-planning approach is dependent on collaborative leadership and relies on shared responsibility regarding its development and implementation. This chapter underscores the vital role of action planning and addresses the faculty-selected collective focus, derived from collecting and analyzing data, for factors and conditions needing improvement, into actionable goals. The collaboratively developed action plan reflects the essential balance between thoughtful planning and effective implementation. It prepares educational leaders with the knowledge, skills, mindsets, and commitment to collaboratively design an action plan and guide its implementation, for as Fullan (2007) eloquently says, "Planning without action is futile, but action without planning is fatal."

A well-crafted action plan strengthens trust, promotes shared purpose, stimulates collaboration, and builds cohesion within the school community. It provides clarity, direction, and focus for daily decision-making and progress monitoring. The action plan is a unifying subsystem that aligns the school's shared values, vision, aspirations, and collective focus into short-term (2–10 months) and long-term (6 months–3 years) actionable SMART goals and objectives that describe steps for achieving the collective focus, goals, and intended outcomes. The plan also allocates necessary resources, sets timelines, and assigns responsibilities for specific tasks.

By the end of this chapter, educational leaders will be able to

- Guide a teacher team to craft an action plan.
- Translate the collective focus into SMART goals.
- Select short-term and long-term goals aligned with the school's vision, values, and collective focus.
- Develop specific objectives or action steps to achieve the collective focus goals.
- Identify outcomes that are observable and measurable.
- Facilitate consensus on action plan goals.
- Determine the resources needed to accomplish each goal.
- Assign responsibilities to individuals or teams to implement portions of the action plan.
- Create implementation timelines.
- Communicate the action plan with clarity and transparency to all stakeholders.
- Use the action plan to guide daily operations and ongoing school improvement efforts.
- Reflect on leadership steps taken in guiding the plan's development.
- Anticipate and address potential challenges.
- Identify job-embedded professional development to support implementation.
- Establish accountability systems for individuals and teacher teams.
- Monitor implementation faculty and community commitment to the goals of the action plan.

▶ THE PROCESS OF COLLABORATIVELY DEVELOPING AN ACTION PLAN

A clearly articulated action plan serves as a comprehensive guide for informing day-to-day leadership decisions and instructional practices. It outlines clear goals, measurable objectives, specific action steps, designated roles for accountability, and supporting resources to enhance school improvement efforts. The collective focus of an action plan is typically informed by factors and conditions identified by the designated data collection teacher team, faculty, and principal, referencing the data collected and analyzed. Depending on the school context and identified needs, this shared collective focus can give rise to a variety of goals. While the format of an action plan may vary slightly by school or district, it generally includes the following core components: a clearly stated collective focus; articulated goals and objectives with clearly articulated action steps; anticipated outcomes or indicators of success; a timeline; necessary supporting resources; and identification of persons responsible for each action.

The development of an action plan is not a top-down mandate but a collaborative process. When developed collaboratively, an action plan becomes a practical and strategic structure through which educational leaders and faculty can implement change and improvement with shared commitment. The teacher team, previously selected in partnership with the faculty and principal to collect and analyze the data, or a new team becomes responsible for determining the specific goals, objectives, and indicators of success; coordinates the collaborative drafting of the action plan; and solicits feedback from the principal, faculty, and families. The principal plays a central leadership role by shaping a school-wide vision, guiding the development of a positive school culture, selecting a collective focus, facilitating the team in developing an action plan, and allocating resources. While principals may not work directly with every student, their leadership directly influences the conditions for teaching and learning, the development of faculty capacity, and the cultivation of strong home–school connections.

Through this process of inclusive input and revision, a revised plan is created and presented to the broader faculty and community for review and consensus. This shared ownership is key to ensuring both meaningful implementation and long-term sustainability. Faculty are then charged with implementing the agreed-upon collective focus, goals, and action steps, along with the principal. The principal and teacher teams regularly review implementation efforts across grade levels, departments, schools, or districts and monitor progress. To support this continuous improvement process, feedback loops must be established and maintained with staff, students, and families. In turn, families and community members are expected to actively support both teachers and students by championing the goals of the action plan and celebrating milestones at scheduled events throughout the year. Through this collaborative, data-informed, and inclusive process, the action plan becomes a living document that drives purposeful action and fosters a culture of shared responsibility for improving student learning and innovation. In the next chapter, "Collaboratively Assess Progress," goals, objectives, and outcomes are assessed and refined as needed.

The following are factors and conditions for a collective focus; also provided, for your consideration, are options for accompanying action plan goals.

School Culture

Goals may include

- Building relational trust.
- Fostering a sense of community.
- Establishing shared values and vision.
- Promoting collaboration.
- Advancing equity, diversity, inclusion, and justice.
- Strengthening communication with families.
- Creating professional learning communities.

Curriculum

Goals may include

- Ensuring culturally responsive content.
- Integrating critical thinking and social-emotional learning.
- Aligning curriculum with performance standards and assessment systems.
- Incorporating multi-leveled materials and supports.

Assessment to Inform Instruction

Goals may include

- Implementing formative, non-disruptive assessments.

- Using data to inform differentiated instruction. Developing common assessments for power content and performance standards in each subject.

Teaching, Learning, and Leading

Goals may include

- Differentiated and culturally responsive instruction.
- Technology integration.
- Alignment with professional teaching and leadership standards.
- Integration of general and special education.
- Mastery Learning.

Learning Environment

Goals may include

- Designing adaptive learning environments.
- Establishing effective behavior management systems. Establishing effective innstructional management systems.
- Creating learning centers.

Instructional Resources

Goals may include

- Using technology effectively. Aligning instructional materials with content and performance goals and objectives in a particular subject.
- Providing equitable access to instructional materials.

Job-Embedded Professional Development

Goals may include

- Subject-specific professional learning opportunities.
- Ongoing coaching aligned with action plan goals.

Meeting Time

- Collaboratively restructure the school day.
- Collaboratively develop creative scheduling for each grade level or department.
- Collaboratively set agendas for grade level or department meetings, faculty meetings and professional development days.
- Budget for substitute teachers to take classes while grade level or department teachers meet.
- Budget for workshop presenters and instructional and leadership coaching.
- Reduce paperwork for teachers.
- Seek parent volunteers to provide enrichment activities while teacher teams meet.

Parent Engagement Practices

Goals may include

- Applying Epstein's six types of parent involvement.
- Strengthening school-family partnerships.

Alignment of Systems

Goals may include

- Applying Gould's critical factors and conditions in a standards-based instructional system to align systems.
- Integrating Bryk's essential supports.
- Advancing equity and eliminating systemic racism (Darling-Hammond, 2010).

General and Special Education Collaboration

Goals may include

- Assessing student learning needs.
- Co-planning and developing lesson plans.
- Reconfiguring classrooms for differentiated instruction.
- Using Wang's Adaptive Learning Environments Model (ALEM).

Once goals are identified, teacher teams define specific objectives (the actionable steps required to achieve each goal). These objectives should be measurable and linked to a goal and clear outcomes. The teacher team determines the instruments that will be used to assess the outcomes. The action plans developed for the aforementioned collective focus areas include timelines outlining the sequence of tasks and a list of resources required (e.g., materials, technology, professional development) and identify individuals or teams responsible for implementation.

▶ EXAMPLE: AN ACTION PLAN FOR INCREASING STUDENT LEARNING IN FOURTH-GRADE READING

Collective Focus: Power Standards for Reading in Grade 4
Goal: To improve student learning outcomes in 4th-grade reading by increasing the percentage of Grade 4 students meeting or exceeding proficiency by 15% by the end of the school year.
Objectives:

- Identify the power standards in reading for Grade 4 students.
- Conduct an initial review of assessment data to identify areas of strength and weakness in reading.
- Design or select and implement common formative assessments aligned with the power standards.
- Collaboratively identify gaps in student mastery of reading.
- Create differentiated lesson plans tailored to address student needs.
- Establish small reading groups for targeted support and differentiated instruction.
- Target the gaps by for all learners, particularly struggling readers.
- Introduce engaging and culturally relevant texts to build comprehension and interest.
- Provide regular feedback to students and adjust instruction based on results.
- Schedule regular biweekly collaborative meetings for Grade 4 teachers to review progress, discuss strategies, and refine approaches.

- Provide job embedded professional development for Grade 4 teachers on effective reading instruction strategies.
- Host information sessions for parents regarding the reading curriculum and provide resources for supporting reading at home.

<u>Outcomes/indicators of success</u>:

- Increased engagement reading growth and development.
- At least 85% of students demonstrate improvement on formative and summative assessments aligned with reading power standards.
- Teacher collaboration is increased as evidenced in shared lesson plans, reflections, and best practices.
- Positive feedback from students and parents regarding the reading curriculum and instructional practices.
- Active parent participation in reading-related activities at home.

<u>Timeline</u>:

- Weeks 1–3: Finalize formative assessments and conduct data analysis and review.
- Weeks 4–6: Develop lesson plans and initiate small group interventions.
- Week 7: Launch instructional strategies and student reading groups.
- Week 8: Provide professional development sessions based on a breakdown of power standards.
- Monitor progress continuously at grade-level teacher team meetings (biweekly).
- Provide progress to students and parents.
- Evaluate overall progress at the end of the academic year, reflect on challenges, and make adjustments for the following year.

<u>Supporting resources</u>:

- Grade 4 power standards and reading association documents describing reading standards.
- Culturally relevant curriculum and engaging reading materials.

- Assessment tools for formative and summative evaluation.
- Technology tools for tracking progress and providing differentiated instruction.
- Materials necessary for differentiated instruction.
- Learning stations.
- Professional development workshops on release days.
- Resources for parent workshops (e.g., guides, take-home reading materials).

Persons responsible:

- Grade 4 teachers implement differentiated instructional strategies, participate in collaborative meetings, conduct assessments, and track student progress.
- Instructional coaches provide ongoing support and facilitate professional development workshops.
- School leadership team oversees the action plan and, with the principal, provides necessary resources and monitors progress.
- Parents/guardians support reading initiatives and development at home and engage in parent workshops.

▶ EXAMPLE: AN ABBREVIATED ACTION PLAN FOR INCREASING STUDENT LEARNING IN MATHEMATICS

In this expanded version the outcomes immediately follow each objective.

Collective Focus: Improvement of Teaching and Learning in Grade 4 Mathematics
Goal #1: Differentiate instruction.
Objective #1: Implement an instructional management system.
Outcomes: Successful adoption across classrooms by teachers.

Increased student engagement.

Objective #2: Identify and utilize grade-level power standards in ELA and mathematics.
Outcome: Power standards integrated into instruction.

Objective #3: Utilize ongoing assessment to design instruction.
Outcome: Data-driven instruction plans in use.
Objective #4: Increase teacher collaboration.
Outcome: Regular interdisciplinary team meetings.
Goal #2: Help students take responsibility for learning and behavior.
Objective #1: Implement a learning management and a behavior management system.
Outcomes: Students take more responsibility for their learning.

Reduction in disciplinary incidents.

Students take more responsibility for their behavior.

Objective #2: Implement an instructional management system.
Outcomes: Learning centers and an instructional monitoring system is in place.

Students take more responsibility for their learning.

Objective #3: Create a student learning and behavior compact.
Outcomes: Signed compacts by all students and families.
Students take more responsibility for their learning and behavior.
Goal #3: Improve the connection between home and school.
Objective #1: Increase communication between home and school.
Outcomes: Regular newsletters; increased parent–teacher meeting attendance.
Objective #2: Promote and support parenting skills.
Outcomes: Parent workshops held.

Parent satisfaction surveys show increased satisfaction with the school's outreach program.

Objective #3: Help parents assist student learning at home.
Outcome: Parents utilize homework packets provided by the school.
Objective #4: Welcome parents and seek their support and assistance.
Outcome: Scheduled parent meetings and activities with interpreters provided.
Objective #5: Involve parents in the decisions that affect their children.
Outcome: Parents provide input regarding development of a vision and an action plan.

Objective #6: Use community resources to strengthen school, families, and student learning.
Outcome: Partnerships in place that provide mental health and social services.

To access the fully developed action plan example, see the Appendices.

▶ DEVELOPING A PRELIMINARY PLAN FOR AN ACTION PLAN

This preliminary plan lays the groundwork for the next preliminary plan. A preliminary plan should focus on key actions you, as an educational leader, will take to guide a teacher team to develop and action plan. Begin by creating bullets that describe the key steps you will take to select and engage a teacher team to develop the action plan and reach consensus. Your preliminary plans should include important details and citations to reinforce the steps when appropriate.

▶ CHAPTER SUMMARY

Collaboratively developed action plans are essential for actualizing shared vision, values, and goals and addressing factors and conditions that both inhibit and promote student learning. By creating clear goals, objectives, and outcomes; fostering participation; and ensuring accountability, educational leaders can authentically maintain and sustain change, improvement, transformation, and innovation in teaching, learning, and leading. When grounded in a shared vision and guided by a collective focus, these plans empower teachers, teacher teams, and educational leaders to lead collaborative change efforts that address persistent school challenges.

This process also strengthens school culture, builds faculty capacity, fosters collective ownership, and deepens community engagement.

Leadership Task: *Reflective Journal*

- Respond in writing to the following prompts. This will be your fifth journal entry. Prompts regarding the collaborative development of an action plan are designed to encourage reflection and meaningful dialogue, uncover

potential challenges, and build consensus around the development and implementation of a collaborative action plan. The following are useful in facilitating discussions during faculty meetings or in university classrooms.
- What is the primary purpose of an action plan?
- Why is it important for us to develop an action plan collaboratively?
- What specific goals should we address to actualize our collective focus?
- To what degree should the selected goals of your action plan actualize the values and vision of your school community?
- Are Bryk's essential supports a part of your action plan?
- What common challenges arise when creating a collaborative action plan?
- What factors or conditions in our school would support the successful implementation of an action plan?
- What obstacles might hinder the implementation of an action plan in our school?
- How can we work together to overcome these challenges?
- How can leaders ensure that differing priorities or perspectives do not derail the planning process?
- How do you think involving diverse perspectives in the development of the action plan can strengthen its impact?
- What strategies have worked well in the past to promote faculty collaboration and engagement in school-wide initiatives?
- What role should students, parents, and other stakeholders play in the development and implementation of the action plan?
- How can we design the action plan to be flexible and responsive to changing circumstances while still staying focused on our objectives?
- What methods of accountability would help ensure that all faculty members actively contribute to the success of the action plan?

- What role does observation and evaluation play in assessing progress of faculty/employee teams toward achieving the goals of the action plan?
- How do you think our school's culture might influence the way we approach the development and execution of the action plan?
- What are your concerns or hopes regarding this process? How can we address these together to ensure a positive experience for everyone involved?
- Does your action plan include capacity building for achieving the goals and outcomes?
- How can organizations ensure that roles, responsibilities, and timelines in the action plan are clearly defined?
- What mechanisms can be put in place to hold individuals and teams accountable for their contributions to the plan?
- How can we communicate the purpose and progress of the action plan to the broader school community to foster support and buy-in?

Leadership Task: *Develop a Rationale to Introduce the Importance of Collaboratively Developing an Action Plan*

- Develop a talking points to be used at a meeting with a teacher team, department, school, or district that describes the importance of *Collaboratively Developing an Action Plan* and its relation to the school improvement processes and the Six-Point Conceptual Framework.

Leadership Task: *Develop a Preliminary Plan for Collaboratively Developing an Action Plan*

- Taking into consideration the prompts, resources shared to date, and the unique conditions of your context, develop a bulleted preliminary plan that captures key actions you will take to guide a teacher team to collaboratively develop an action plan and reach consensus. Reinforce the steps with citations when appropriate.

Reference

Fullan, M. (2007). *The new meaning of educational change* (4th ed.). Teachers College Press.

Additional Resources

Bryk, A. S., Sebring, P. B., Allensworth, E., Luppescu, S., & Easton, J. Q. (2010). *Organizing schools for improvement: Lessons from Chicago*. University of Chicago Press. https://doi.org/10.7208/chicago/9780226078014.001.0001

Darling-Hammond, L. (2010). *The flat world and education: How America's commitment to equity will determine our future*. Teachers College Press.

Doerr, J. (2018). *Measure what matters: How Google, Bono, and the Gates Foundation rock the world with OKRs*. Penguin Publishing.

Duffy, F. M. (2003, Spring). Dancing on ice: Navigating change to create whole-district school improvement. *Organization Development Journal, 21*(1), 36–44.

Elmore, R. F., & City, E. A. (2007, May/June). The road to school improvement: It's hard, it's bumpy, and it takes as long as it takes. *Harvard Education Letter, 23*(3), 1–3.

Fullan, M. (2012) *Drivers of whole systems reform*. https://youtu.be/FLX0NwaFaQQ

THE 6-POINT CONCEPTUAL FRAMEWORK

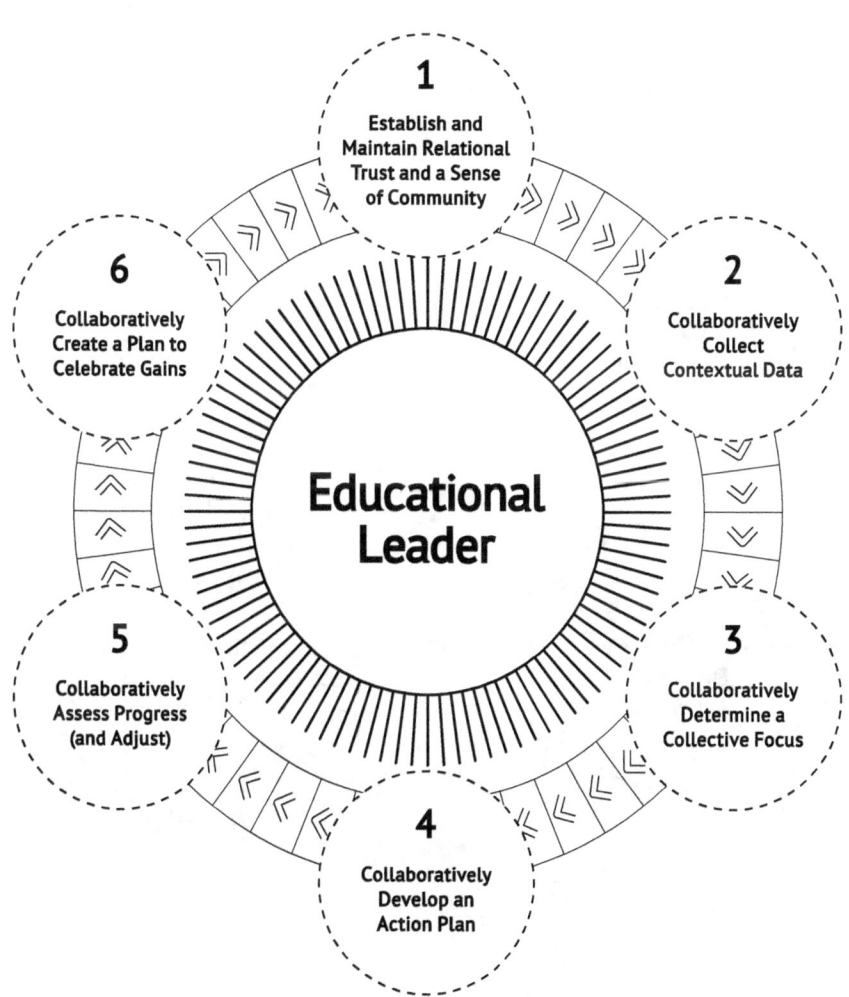

Conceptual Framework design and chapter openers designed by Christian Arichabala.

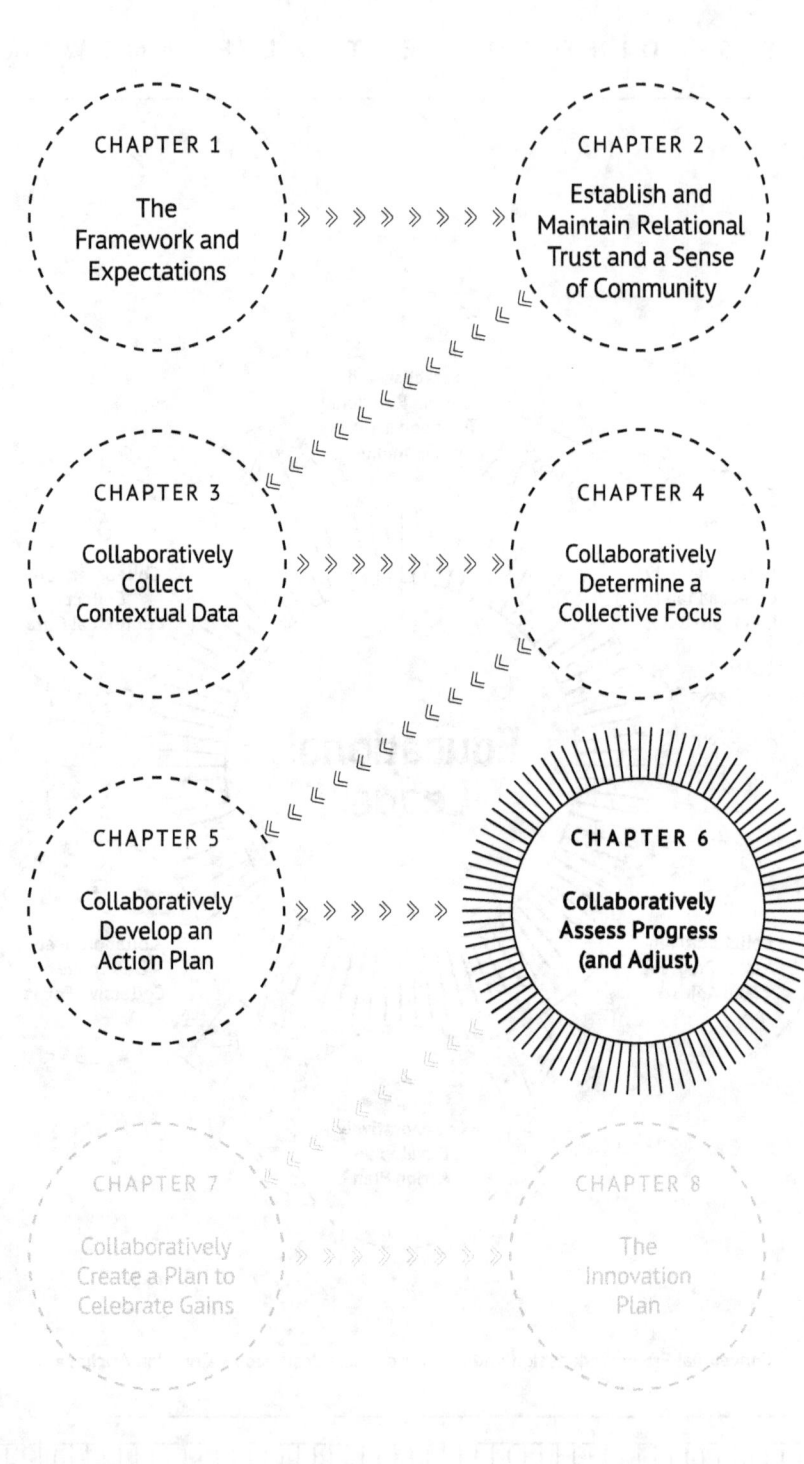

Chapter 6

Collaboratively Assess Progress

▶ INTRODUCTION

Collaboratively Assess Progress is the fifth subsystem of the Six-Point Conceptual Framework, providing a systems-thinking, strategic-planning approach to improving PK–12 student learning. It is a vital leadership responsibility that ensures school improvement efforts remain responsive, data-informed, and aligned with shared goals. Guskey (2003) asserts, "The purpose of assessment is not to prove, but to improve." This chapter explores how educational leaders guide the process of collaboratively assessing progress regarding action plan goals, objectives, and outcomes. It also provides insights on how to identify areas needing adjustment and guides future action. Through this chapter, leaders will also gain a greater understanding of how assessment practices and individual and teacher-team observations not only measure progress but also foster collaboration, reinforce commitment, and hold faculty accountable for achieving the shared vision, values, and action plan goals developed and reached by consensus earlier in the change process.

By integrating thoughtful assessment practices and communicating transparently and authentically, leaders can see to it that improvement efforts remain on track and classroom, department, school, or district goals are achieved. Educational leaders or a teacher team can begin the collaborative assessment process by asking the following guiding questions: "How will we know we are getting there and how do we know we are there?"

By the end of this chapter, educational leaders, with or without formal authority, will be able to

- Guide, facilitate, and lead the development of assessing progress of short-and long-term action plan goals, objectives, and outcomes.
- Use criteria to design, select, or adapt assessments to monitor progress.
- Identify the degree to which action plan goals have been achieved or need to be revised.
- Determine actionable next steps based on the findings of the assessments used.
- Identify job-embedded professional development, meet faculty needs, and build capacity.
- Communicate progress to stakeholders to further build transparency and trust.
- Use individual and team goal achievement as part of the observation and evaluation process.
- Develop a bulleted initial plan to assess progress.

▶ THE PROCESS OF COLLABORATIVELY ASSESSING PROGRESS

Collaborative assessment is critical to effective school improvement. As Wagner (2006) reminds us, even the strongest strategies for increasing student learning must be examined regularly to ensure they are producing the intended results. McTighe and Wiggins (1998) underscore the importance of establishing clearly defined, measurable criteria aligned with action plan goals, objectives, and outcomes. When leaders and teacher teams fully understand these criteria, they can assess progress with consistency and accuracy. Unlike baseline data collection, which simply establishes a starting point, ongoing assessment determines how well the action plan's goals are actually being met. As the familiar saying goes, "What gets monitored gets done." Assessing progress not only keeps improvement efforts on track, but it also reinforces goals, strengthens collaboration, promotes accountability, and builds organizational capacity.

The process begins with leadership. At a faculty meeting, the educational leader should guide the faculty in selecting a teacher-team leader, who in turn will choose team members to collect data, evaluate progress, and adjust goals as necessary. This is the time to reaffirm the collective focus, SMART action plan goals, expected outcomes, and specific timelines including roles and responsibilities regarding who is responsible for specific tasks. Faculty must also be reminded that achieving these goals is part of both the school's evaluation process and its culture of lifelong learning and an effort intended not to add burdens, but to build professional capacity and strengthen collaboration.

The scope and timeline of the action plan will shape what teacher teams assess. Short-term goals are typically designed to be met within weeks or a marking period. For example, a team may decide to monitor numeracy growth over six weeks using common formative assessments, adjusting lessons as needed to boost student understanding. Teams may also observe classrooms to evaluate student engagement and whether students are collaborating, participating in discussions, and solving problems actively.

Long-term goals, in contrast, are broader and summative, typically spanning a semester, a full school year, or longer. These might include raising overall student achievement, with targets such as ensuring at least 80% of students reach proficiency by year's end. They might also focus on equity, for example narrowing performance gaps among English language learners, special education students, and historically underserved groups by 15% or more. Long-term goals may also emphasize professional growth, such as helping every teacher gain greater confidence and skill in using formative data to guide instruction, as measured by peer feedback and learning walks.

Assessing progress on both short-term and long-term goals ensures that improvement efforts remain transparent, data-driven, and broadly shared. When teacher teams working either independently or alongside the principal assess progress several benefits emerge. Collective ownership and accountability deepen as teachers move beyond isolated efforts toward a shared responsibility for student success. Early identification of barriers allows for timely adjustments before small issues grow into systemic challenges. Diverse perspectives among educators improve both data interpretation and instructional decision-making. Keeping long-term outcomes in view also ensures that immediate instructional changes align with broader priorities. And because the process itself builds teacher skill, it doubles as meaningful professional development.

To support these efforts, principals should reaffirm that the tools introduced in Chapter Three such as rubrics, surveys, and observation protocols can be repurposed or adapted to assess progress and that new assessment instruments may be developed as needed. Using multiple measures, including both quantitative data (e.g., test scores) and qualitative insights (e.g., classroom observations, teacher input, student feedback), provides a richer understanding of whether the action plan is producing its intended impact. Once data is collected, teams should reconvene to review not only whether goals and timelines are being met, but also the foundational elements of the school's improvement efforts: relational trust, shared vision, collective efficacy, and core values. These touchstones ensure that the assessment process remains transparent, purposeful, and collaborative.

The principal plays a vital role in facilitating problem-solving conversations about student needs, emerging challenges, unexpected insights, and professional development priorities. This dialogue should remain balanced and inclusive, making sure that no single voice dominates. Teacher teams should also decide how and to whom progress will be reported, whether to faculty, families, and the wider school community, while intentionally seeking feedback from diverse stakeholders. Engaging teachers, students, and families in this process ensures multiple perspectives are represented and promotes equity, fairness, and a fuller understanding of both successes and setbacks.

Acknowledging setbacks openly is as important as celebrating successes. When slow progress is met with resilience rather than frustration, challenges become catalysts for learning, strengthen a culture of improvement, and cultivate innovation. Leaders must clearly communicate this mindset to maintain focus, encourage flexibility, and sustain momentum. Regular recognition of small wins helps keep energy high, sustains morale, and reinforces the sense that collective efforts are paying off.

Ultimately, this cycle of review, communication, refinement, and revision ensures that the action plan remains relevant, responsive, and aligned with the school's shared goals. By collaboratively assessing progress on both short- and long-term goals, schools build professional practice, advance equity, and drive sustained improvement in teaching, learning, leadership, and the conditions that support them.

▶ EXAMPLES OF ASSESSING PROGRESS FOR SHORT- AND LONG-TERM GOALS

Assessing both short- and long-term goals is essential to maintaining momentum in any school improvement plan. This process is illustrated through examples from 4th-grade mathematics, 7th-grade language arts, and 11th-grade algebra. In every case, assessment begins with clear criteria for examining student work and classroom artifacts, supplemented by observations, conversations with teachers and students, and reflection on teaching approaches that provide both immediate and lasting solutions. Job-embedded professional development builds the capacity of teachers and principals with the knowledge, skills, and mindsets needed to increase student learning.

When teacher teams, working independently or with the principal, assess action plan goals, the benefits are substantial. Collaborative assessment promotes collective ownership and accountability, helps teachers break free from working in isolation, and ensures that responsibility for student success is shared across classrooms. This process sharpens data interpretation, allows teams to identify and address barriers early, and ensures that instructional adjustments remain aligned with broader improvement priorities and are made before small challenges grow into systemic problems. It also doubles as professional development, building educators' capacity to analyze evidence and refine instructional practice.

Short-term goals, typically spanning weeks or a marking period, focus on targeted outcomes, such as strengthening numeracy over six weeks as measured by common formative assessments, and adjust lessons accordingly. Teachers may also observe classrooms to determine whether students are collaborating and actively participating in problem-solving discussions.

Long-term goals extend over a semester or school year, measuring broader outcomes such as raising overall achievement so that at least 80% of students reach proficiency; narrowing performance gaps among English learners, students with disabilities, and historically underserved groups by 15%; or increasing teachers' confidence and skill in using formative assessment data to guide instruction.

By collaboratively assessing progress on both short- and long-term goals, teacher teams ensure that daily instructional decisions translate into sustained improvement, greater equity, and stronger professional practice.

▶ GOAL ASSESSMENT IN 4TH-GRADE MATHEMATICS

Short-Term Goal Assessment

The 4th-grade teacher team, with or without the principal, examines student work and classroom artifacts to determine how well students compute accurately in all four operations, use multiple strategies flexibly, and demonstrate conceptual understanding by explaining *why* procedures work rather than simply performing them. Teachers look for evidence that students represent mathematical ideas with models or symbols, transfer skills to unfamiliar contexts, use precise vocabulary, and persist through challenges by checking and revising their work. This process also uncovers common misconceptions requiring immediate instructional attention.

Long-Term Goal Assessment

Over the course of a semester or school year, the same or another teacher team evaluates whether students have mastered grade-level standards, including operations with whole numbers, fractions, and decimals, and apply reasoning consistently to complex problems. They look for clear communication using the language of mathematics; measurable growth in skills and confidence; and students' ability to self-assess, reflect on their learning, and identify persistent gaps that signal areas for ongoing instructional focus.

▶ APPROACHES TO TEACHING MATHEMATICS IN 4TH GRADE

Short-Term Approaches

After reviewing student work, the team documents findings, identifying students who have met goals, those making progress but needing support, and those requiring intervention or enrichment. Instructional actions may include targeted mini-lessons, differentiated activities, flexible grouping, and additional formative assessments to monitor progress. Reinforcing number sense daily, through quick "number talks," concrete materials such as base-ten blocks and fraction strips, and visual tools like number lines or arrays, helps students move beyond memorization toward deeper understanding. Scaffolded instruction, small-group work, peer tutoring, and real-world connections make content more accessible and engaging. Adaptive technology platforms such as Khan Academy, Freckle, or Prodigy can provide personalized practice while allowing teachers to focus on direct support. Students should regularly articulate their reasoning aloud, helping teachers diagnose misconceptions and reinforcing a mindset that mistakes are natural steps in learning. Frequent, specific feedback builds confidence, motivation, and persistence.

Long-Term Approaches

Lasting improvement requires building strong conceptual foundations, consistent instructional practices, and a classroom culture that values mathematical thinking. Teachers should integrate hands-on exploration and visual models throughout the year to strengthen understanding alongside procedural fluency. Collaborative curriculum planning ensures key concepts are revisited and connected, while spiraling reviews prevent gaps and reinforce prior learning. A classroom climate that treats mistakes as opportunities fosters resilience, curiosity, and deeper engagement with content. Regular teacher collaboration through analysis of student work, sharing strategies, and adjusting instruction builds coherent practices across classrooms. Sustained family engagement, with tools and strategies for supporting math learning at home, further extends progress.

Finally, targeted professional development deepens teachers' mathematical knowledge and pedagogy, ensuring continuous growth in instructional skills.

▶ TOPICS FOR PROFESSIONAL DEVELOPMENT

Professional development for 4th-grade teachers, especially those who find teaching mathematics to diverse learners challenging, should focus on building both deep mathematical understanding and versatile instructional skills. A key priority is strengthening teachers' own conceptual grasp of the mathematics they teach. When teachers understand the structure of arithmetic, fractions, and early algebraic thinking at a deep level, they can explain ideas in multiple ways, adapt to student questions, and help students move beyond rote procedures.

Equally important is learning how to design lessons that meet the needs of all learners. Training in differentiated instruction and UDL equips teachers to provide multiple entry points for students with varied readiness levels, language proficiency, or learning differences. Teachers also benefit from strategies that support English learners and students with learning differences through visuals, manipulatives, and structured mathematical discussion.

Formative assessment deserves sustained attention. Professional development should help teachers use quick checks, and work analysis to identify misconceptions early, before they take root, and adjust instruction accordingly. Rather than focusing solely on whether answers are correct, teachers can learn to analyze how the students reason, gaining insight into both strengths and misunderstandings.

Culturally responsive mathematics instruction is another powerful area for growth. By connecting math problems to students' cultures, experiences, and communities, teachers can make mathematics more relevant and inclusive. Alongside this, sessions on fostering positive mathematical mindsets can give teachers strategies for reducing math anxiety, normalizing productive struggle, and encouraging perseverance.

Technology integration should also be explored. Interactive tools, adaptive software, and virtual manipulatives can personalize learning while enhancing whole-class instruction. Equally valuable is professional collaboration: co-planning lessons, participating in lesson study, and working in professional learning communities where teachers share strategies, analyze student work, and refine practice together.

Finally, teachers need a clear view of how mathematical ideas progress across grades. Professional development that emphasizes instructional coherence and alignment with standards helps teachers address learning gaps without losing sight of future expectations.

This comprehensive approach, combining content knowledge, formative assessment, differentiated instruction, cultural responsiveness, technology integration, and professional collaboration, builds teacher confidence and directly supports stronger, more equitable outcomes for all students.

▶ COLLABORATIVELY ASSESSING PROGRESS IN GRADE 7 ENGLISH LANGUAGE ARTS

In order to keep both teachers and students motivated and maintain momentum, Kotter suggests pairing long-term action plan goals with short-term wins that can be achieved within a few weeks, a semester, or a marking period. To measure progress toward these goals, 7th-grade teacher teams can collaboratively review student work and classroom artifacts, sometimes with the principal's involvement, to evaluate the degree to which students demonstrate growth.

Short-Term Wins

In 7th-grade English language arts, short-term wins might include mastering specific reading and writing skills within a unit, such as analyzing character development in a short story, improving paragraph structure in an essay, or strengthening introductions and conclusions. The assessment process also may focus on whether students can accurately summarize chapters from novels, identify an author's purpose, analyze figurative language, compare and contrast perspectives, structure paragraphs effectively, support claims with textual evidence, refine essays through editing and revision, participate thoughtfully in class discussions, and communicate clearly both orally and in writing.

Long-Term Wins

Long-term wins, in contrast, focus on broader competencies, such as developing stronger research skills, cultivating confidence in public speaking, and improving overall literacy. Teacher teams examine evidence of students becoming more proficient and independent readers capable of analyzing complex texts with critical insight, producing well-developed writing across genres, using technology skillfully for research, and building confidence as communicators and thinkers. They also assess whether students are developing strong presentation skills, demonstrating active listening, expanding vocabulary, conducting effective research, evaluating source credibility, synthesizing information from multiple texts, and applying critical thinking to analyze information and ideas.

▶ APPROACHES TO TEACHING LANGUAGE ARTS IN GRADE SEVEN

Short-Term Approaches

Supporting 7th graders in language arts requires both immediate strategies and sustained instructional approaches. In the short term, teachers can personalize instruction by scaffolding tasks, providing timely feedback, and fostering a positive classroom climate. Lessons become more engaging when connected to students' interests, enriched with games, interactive materials, and varied texts including audiobooks or tactile resources for learners with specific needs. Teachers may pair students for shared reading, introduce longer works through audio versions, and use visual aids such as graphic organizers to help structure thoughts. Complex tasks can be broken into smaller steps, with explicit vocabulary instruction offered through multisensory methods. Collaborative planning among teachers ensures consistent support, while celebrating small successes builds confidence and nurtures a growth mindset. Daily reading practice, guided discussions about books, and focused mini-lessons on targeted skills create a rhythm of steady improvement.

Long-Term Approaches

True literacy development is not built on quick fixes. Long-term solutions focus on cultivating habits of mind and ways of thinking that help students grow as readers, writers, and communicators over time. Teachers model comprehension strategies such as summarizing, questioning, and making inferences showing not just how these strategies work, but why they matter so students internalize them and apply them independently. Writing instruction prioritizes planning, revising, and reflecting rather than simply producing final drafts. Core concepts like theme, argument, evidence, and structure are revisited throughout the year with increasing depth, creating a cumulative understanding rather than treating skills as isolated units. Students engage with inquiry-based questions such as "What makes a hero?" or "How does language shape power?" and apply reading and writing as tools for meaningful exploration through research projects, multimedia presentations, or podcasts.

Independent reading and writing time, anchored by mini-lessons on craft and structure, helps students develop voice and agency. Personalized conferences allow teachers to set individual goals, while offering students choices in texts and topics ensures that rigor is balanced with relevance. Vocabulary and grammar are learned in context, through authentic reading and writing, where punctuation, syntax, and word choice are seen as tools for shaping meaning and tone. Professional texts are analyzed as models, and students reflect on their own progress through journals or portfolios that turn learning into a habit rather than a checklist.

Culturally relevant and diverse literature fosters engagement and helps students see themselves in their learning. Structured discussions such as Socratic seminars, debates, and peer reviews deepen comprehension and sharpen communication skills. Reading and writing become collaborative processes, supported by frequent, low-stakes assessments that track growth without creating fear of failure. Feedback emphasizes strategies and process over simple correctness, reinforcing the idea that literacy is a journey, not a destination.

By combining collaborative assessment with both immediate instructional adjustments and long-term skill building, teachers equip students to become confident, thoughtful readers and writers prepared for the challenges ahead. Over time, this dual focus—celebrating short-term achievements while nurturing enduring habits—creates a strong foundation for academic success and lifelong learning.

▶ TOPICS FOR PROFESSIONAL DEVELOPMENT IN GRADE 7 LANGUAGE ARTS

When selecting professional development opportunities, department heads, principals, and teachers should begin by identifying the specific challenges teachers face and then provide a range of options to meet these needs. Effective professional development can take many forms, including in-person workshops and seminars, online courses and webinars, mentoring relationships between new and experienced teachers, and instructional coaching that includes classroom observation with targeted feedback and strategies. Collaboration within professional learning communities; attendance at conferences; and engagement with professional books, articles, websites, and podcasts further enrich teachers' growth. Peer observation followed by reflective discussion offers another powerful way to sharpen instructional skills.

Grade 7 language arts teachers who are struggling can significantly strengthen their practice by choosing professional development that aligns closely with their needs and preferred learning formats. One critical area is behavior management, where teachers learn to establish clear expectations, build positive relationships with students, and address challenging behaviors in ways that maintain a productive learning environment. Equally important is differentiated instruction, enabling teachers to address the diverse learning styles, readiness levels, and cultural backgrounds that characterize middle school classrooms.

Professional development should also focus on formative assessment as an essential tool for monitoring student learning and adjusting instructional strategies in real time. Teachers benefit from training that helps them use assessments not merely to evaluate students, but also to guide lesson planning and provide timely support. In addition, developing strategies to create a captivating and interactive learning environment can help teachers address issues with student motivation and participation.

Deepening understanding of the curriculum and exploring innovative ways to present material ensures that instruction remains rigorous and engaging. Building skills in social-emotional learning is equally valuable, as it equips teachers to foster supportive, empathetic classroom communities where both students and teachers thrive. Finally, exploring how technology tools can enhance instruction, support classroom management, and engage students provides teachers with practical strategies that reflect the realities of 21st-century learning.

Through a thoughtful combination of these professional development opportunities, Grade 7 language arts teachers can refine their instructional approaches, meet the needs of all learners, and create classrooms where students feel both challenged and supported.

▶ AN INNOVATIVE APPROACH TO THE OBSERVATION AND EVALUATION PROCESS

Individual and teacher team observations are a means to hold people accountable to the shared vision, values, and action plan goals developed and reached by consensus. Individual and teacher-team observations provide distinct yet complementary insights into teaching practice. Individual observation offers a focused view of how each educator applies instructional strategies, manages the classroom environment, and engages students in alignment with the school's shared vision, values, and action plan goals. It affirms each teacher's responsibility for providing equitable, high-quality learning opportunities while enabling leaders to identify strengths, address specific needs, and provide tailored feedback.

Teacher-team observation, by contrast, highlights the collaborative dimension of teaching, showing how faculty members design curriculum, analyze data, and make joint decisions to improve student learning. By examining group processes, leaders can assess how teams build relational trust, maintain consistency of practice, collaborate, and share responsibility for advancing equity and access. Together, these approaches provide a balanced understanding of instructional practice, capturing both personal accountability and collective efficacy. Integrating both perspectives enables leaders to support educators as individuals and as members of a professional learning community, ensuring that teaching is not an isolated endeavor but a coordinated effort to meet the diverse needs of all students.

Given the almost impossible range of responsibilities assigned to educational leaders today, ranging from managing daily operations to leading school improvement initiatives, the time required to individually observe and evaluate 20 or more faculty members can be overwhelming. One of the major benefits of incorporating teacher-team observations and evaluations is that it provides a practical and accurate way to evaluate how educators collaboratively address diverse student needs. It frees educational leaders to dedicate more time to their essential work of guiding, facilitating, and sustaining school-wide improvement, organizational transformation, and innovation.

Rather than being consumed by scheduling and conducting dozens of individual observations, with this added capacity, leaders can focus on cultivating a collaborative culture, maintaining and sustaining the deeper processes of organizational change, transformation, and innovation. They can more effectively plan and schedule job-embedded professional development and ensure that systemic initiatives, designed to raise student achievement and close opportunity gaps, are successfully implemented. In this way, teacher-team observation and evaluation not only supports an accurate understanding of instructional practice but also strengthens the leader's ability to serve as a catalyst for continuous improvement.

Relational trust is the foundation of this process. Ethical and compassionate leaders approach observation and evaluation as opportunities to empower rather than simply evaluate. Evidence is gathered from classroom visits, instructional artifacts are examined, and attended teacher-team meetings provide insight into alignment with the school's vision, values, action plan goals, social curriculum, equity, access, and collaboration. Prior to an observation, each individual teacher meets with the leader to discuss and select one growth goal, while two additional goals, aligned with shared action plan goals, common to the entire team, are assigned. Teachers receive private feedback on their selected individual goal, while team members receive collective feedback on the two shared goals assigned.

Feedback sessions are respectful, reflective, and dialogic where teachers feel heard, valued, and supported. Leaders actively listen, affirm individual and collective strengths, and demonstrate confidence in educators' capacity to grow. Supportive feedback links progress to student impact and encourages teachers to share their insights, fostering partnership in identifying approaches to close instructional gaps or address barriers to equity and access. Individual teachers meet with the educational leader responsible for observation and evaluation prior to being observed to determine and select one mutually agreed upon goal of their choice. The other two goals, related to shared vision, values, action plan goals, social curriculum content, equity, and access, and collaboration are common to all members of the teacher team. Individual teachers get feedback privately on the degree to which they achieved their goal, and teacher-team members get feedback together on the two goals common to their group. The leader harnesses the power of prompts to promote reflection and discussion throughout the process.

When significant concerns arise, and improvement is needed, corrective feedback is delivered with clarity and compassion. Leaders set explicit expectations, explain the necessity of change for student growth, and co-create improvement plans that balance accountability with encouragement. Leaders often provide targeted supports such as coaching, resource sharing, or peer observation.

The combined approach of individual and teacher-team observation and evaluation with feedback reinforces shared purpose; strengthens relational trust, a sense of belonging, and respect; supports instructional coherence; creates a culture where improvement is continuous and student-centered; and models ethical, compassionate leadership that is consistent and equitable. By integrating individual and teacher-team evaluation with feedback, leaders inspire faculty to meet the diverse characteristics and needs of all students and bring the school's vision, values, goals, change, improvement, transformation, and innovation to life in daily practice.

▶ DEVELOPING A PRELIMINARY PLAN FOR COLLABORATIVELY ASSESSING PROGRESS

A preliminary plan should focus on key actions you, as an educational leader, will take to guide collaborative and transparent process to assess progress. Your preliminary plan should build on the previous subsystem and set the stage for the one that follows. As part of a larger systems-thinking approach, developing a preliminary plan prepares educational leaders to engage in deeper collaboration with faculty. The plan should avoid the use of third-person and instead detail the specific, step-by-step actions you will take as the educational leader to lead discussions and facilitate collaboration.

When developing your preliminary plan, use bulleted sound bites to capture the main ideas. No sentences are necessary. Your preliminary plan should include some citations to reinforce content and process. Developing preliminary plans prepare educational leaders to use the same process when they will be working collaboratively with faculty colleagues to develop preliminary plans based on their assessed needs as well as a create a comprehensive innovation plan for their context.

▶ CHAPTER SUMMARY

Collaboratively assessing progress is a vital component of the Six-Point Conceptual Framework. Progress assessment is a cycle of collecting data, reflecting, adjusting, and building capacity. Using multi-measure systems, such as learning walks, formative assessment protocols, and summative state testing and reflections, leaders can align efforts across individuals and groups, making sure improvement remains dynamic and inclusive. The collaborative assessment of progress empowers leaders and teacher teams to evaluate the impact of action plan goals and make meaningful improvements to student learning and school conditions. More than just measuring progress, this process yields actionable data and feedback that reinforces transparency, accountability, and collective effort. Its long-term value lies in informing planning and cultivating a culture of continuous improvement. Ultimately, this work builds a culture of trust and shared responsibility. It supports leaders in adapting to challenges, celebrating successes, and sustaining momentum.

This chapter has outlined the criteria and processes essential for collaboratively assessing progress and fostering the continuous improvement of teaching and learning. By evaluating both short-term and long-term action plan goals using established protocols and clear criteria, educational leaders can more effectively guide schools in ways that respond to the diverse needs of students, teachers, and families. Such collaborative assessment helps schools realize a shared vision in which all students have the opportunity to learn at high levels when provided equitable access to supportive learning conditions, ultimately preparing them to be informed, engaged, and productive members of a democratic society.

Leadership Task: *Reflective Journal*

- Respond in writing to the following prompts. This will be your sixth journal entry.
    - What approaches will ensure collaboration and optimize results?
    - What tools and processes will be most effective for collaboratively assessing progress?
    - Who will assess and monitor progress?
    - What changes and adjustments could enhance the action plan's effectiveness and optimize outcomes?
    - What effect do you think observation and evaluation by the principal will have in assessing team progress?
    - What are the various ways leaders can inspire ongoing improvement and maintain and sustain momentum?
    - How will progress be reported to the community?

Leadership Task: *Introduce the Importance of Collaboratively Assessing Progress*

- Develop a communication to be used at a meeting with a teacher team, department, school, or district that describes the importance of *Collaboratively Assess Progress* and its relation to the Six-Point Conceptual Framework and school improvement.

 **Leadership Task:** *Develop a Preliminary Plan to Collaboratively Assess Progress*

- Taking into consideration the reflective questions posed, resources shared, the uniqueness of your context, develop a bulleted preliminary plan for collaboratively assessing progress.

References

Guskey, T. R. (2003). What makes professional development effective? *Phi Delta Kappan, 84*(10), 748–750. https://doi.org/10.1177/003172170308401007

McTighe, J., & Wiggins, G. (1998). *Understanding by design.* Alexandria, VA: Association for Supervision and Curriculum Development (ASCD).

Wagner, T. (2006). The ecology of change. In T. Wagner, R. Kegan, L. Lahey, R. Lemons, J. Garnier, D. Helsing, A. Howell, & M. Rasmussen (Eds.), *Change leadership: A practical guide to transforming our schools* (pp. 133–166). Harvard Education Press.

Additional Resources

Dewey, J. (1933). *Experience and education.* New York, NY: Macmillan.

Tyler, R. W. (1949). *Basic principles of curriculum and instruction.* Chicago, IL: University of Chicago Press.

THE 6-POINT CONCEPTUAL FRAMEWORK

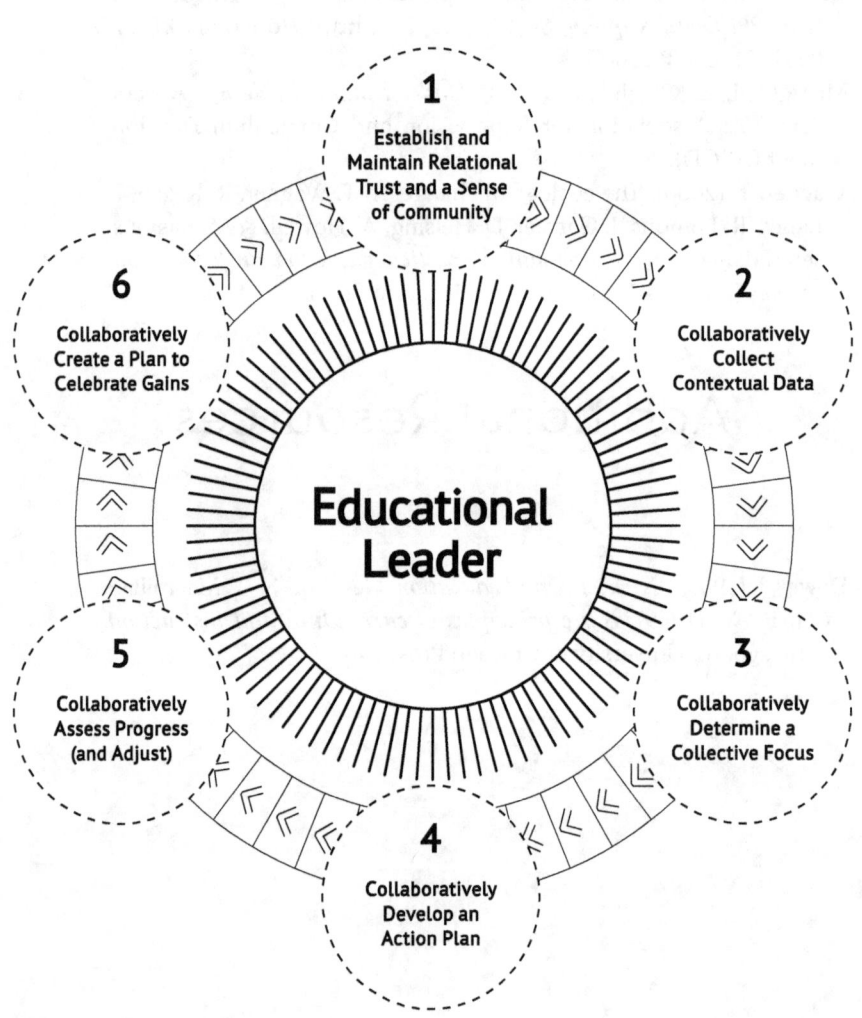

Conceptual Framework design and chapter openers designed by Christian Arichabala.

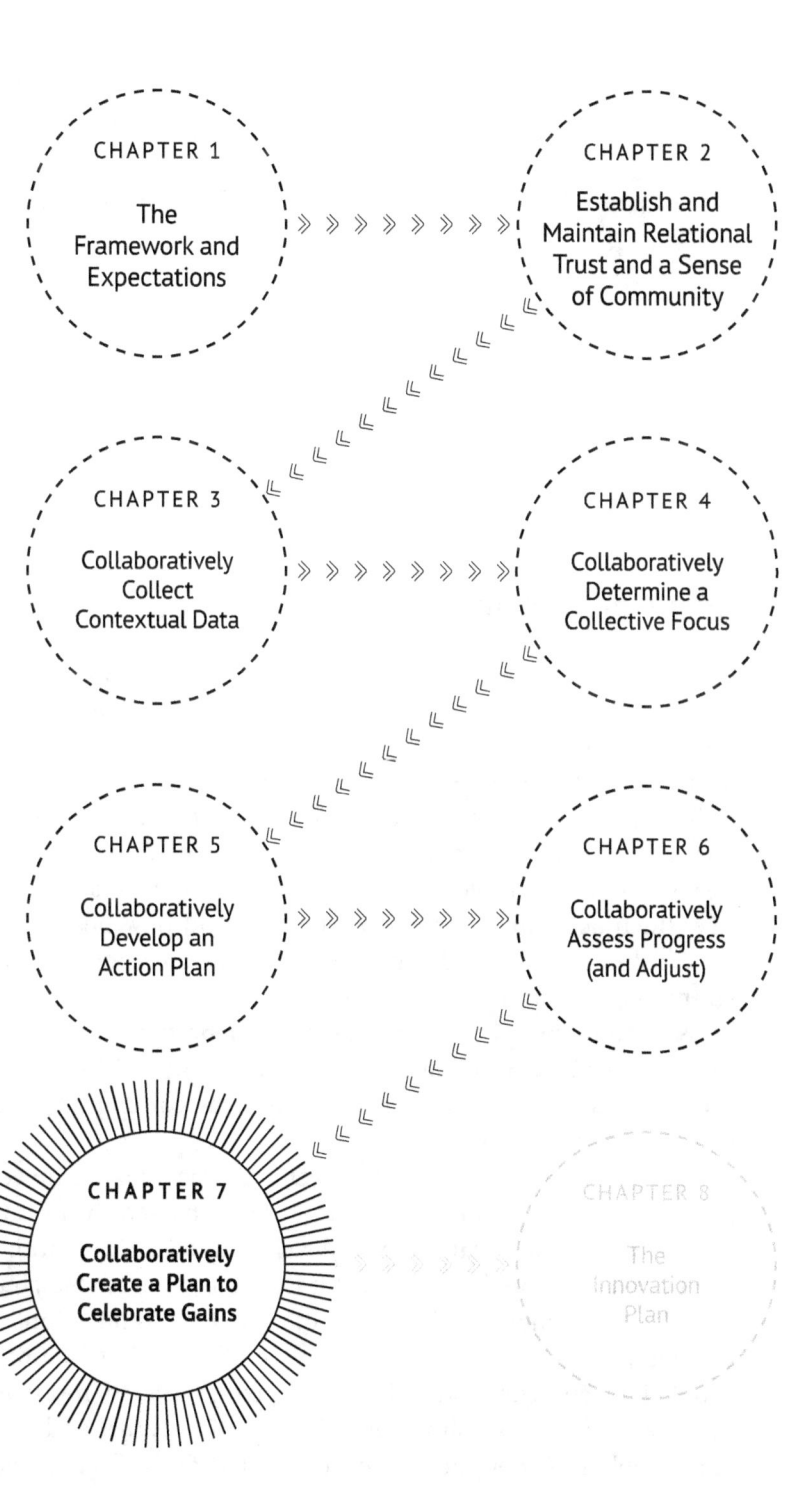

Chapter 7

Collaboratively Develop a Plan to Celebrate Gains

▶ INTRODUCTION

Celebrating gains should not be an afterthought. As the sixth subsystem of the Six-Point Conceptual Framework, *Collaboratively Develop a Plan to Celebrate Gains* emphasizes the power of intentional recognition to reinforce relational trust, a sense of belonging, shared vision, and values; strengthen action plan goals; and maintain and sustain momentum for improvement. Leaders play a vital role in working with teacher teams to identify which accomplishments to recognize and how best to do so. Celebrating is a leadership practice that fuels motivation, strengthens relationships, and sustains school improvement. As Nell Noddings (1992) reminds us, "Celebration of achievement is not a luxury; it is an essential component of the learning process that nurtures motivation, reinforces community, and sustains commitment."

Although many schools hold events to recognize achievement, such celebrations often feel disconnected from the school's vision and collaboratively developed goals. Celebrations should not be framed as rewards for isolated achievements, but as acknowledgment of learning, ethical and compassionate behavior, persistence, and collaborative efficacy. Celebrations should be seen as opportunities to energize continued improvement. According to Bolman and Deal (1995), "Ritual and ceremony help us experience the unseen webs of significance that tie a community together." Effective educational leaders should make sure that celebrations are aligned with the school vision, shared values, and improvement efforts. Rather than waiting to fully accomplish goals and outcomes, these leaders recognize incremental gains along the way.

Leaders committed to equity and transformation-embed celebrations within the continuous improvement cycle, co-constructing a culture of reflection and appreciation. As action plans are implemented and data analyzed, leaders invite students, staff, and families to pause, reflect, and acknowledge what is working. These celebrations center not only on outcomes, but also on the effort, collaboration, and improvement that mark the journey, particularly in communities where progress may have long gone unrecognized.

Effective celebrations are embedded in school culture through ceremonies, rituals, traditions, symbols, and storytelling. As Deal (1994a) remarks, rituals and symbols that reflect a school's values and goals serve to strengthen its culture and identity. Celebrations are framed not as rewards for isolated achievements but as acknowledgments of learning, persistence, and collaboration. They become opportunities to strengthen shared values and commitments; share effective teaching, learning, and leading approaches; and renew energy for the ongoing work ahead.

Meaningful celebrations are inclusive, participatory, and deeply rooted in the school community. Leaders work with a teacher or a teacher team to identify accomplishments worth celebrating and design events and rituals that are culturally responsive and affirming. They invite diverse voices to share stories of transformation, connect gains to shared values and goals, and institutionalize practices of gratitude. These moments highlight the factors and conditions that support effective teaching, learning, and leadership and recognize the contributions of students, educators, families, and community partners. Celebrations can also be used to promote values, mindsets, and behaviors and support academic and social growth still in development.

As celebrations unfold, leaders help institutionalize them as part of the school's culture, embedding regular opportunities for reflection and recognition into the rhythms of school life. These celebrations, whether simple or elaborate, become symbolic markers of growth and belonging. After each celebration, the planning teacher team engages in thoughtful reflection, considering what the celebration revealed about their collective efforts and what it suggests about next steps. These reflections often surface insights about what should be sustained, where adjustments are needed, and how to strengthen the work moving forward.

Ultimately, leading a school in collaboratively celebrating gains is affirmation of learning, teaching, compassion, courage, persistence, resilience, and an act of renewal. It honors the work of students and the labor of educators, elevates student voice, recognizes contributions made by parents and other community members, and reinforces the power of working. In doing so, the leader not only acknowledges gains in academic pursuits and students taking responsibility for their learning, behavior, and positive mindsets, but the leader also cultivates trust and stimulates energy and hope, essential ingredients for change, improvement, transformation, and innovation.

By the end of this chapter, educational leaders, formal or informal, will be prepared to

- Provide a rationale for celebrating gains and the importance of recognition.
- Identify with faculty the school's shared purpose, vision, values, action plan goals, outcomes, and cultures of underrepresented populations to celebrate.
- Design inclusive celebrations with ceremonies, meaningful traditions, rituals, and symbols that align and embody shared purpose, vision, values, action plan goals, and outcomes.
- Use storytelling to spotlight "heroes" who exemplify the school's vision and mission.
- Honor students, teacher teams, staff, parents, and community members.
- Promote unity, collaboration, and relationships across the school community.
- Schedule regular celebrations and post them in the school calendar, newsletter, and local press.
- Utilize examples of provided celebrations.
- Develop a bulleted preliminary plan that celebrates gains, aligns with the school's improvement efforts, and acknowledges those that contributed.

▶ THE POWER OF CELEBRATIONS

Celebration planning should be collaborative. Teacher teams, with input from the principal, teachers, and parents, design ceremonial events. Planning begins by defining what and who will be celebrated and why. Together, they create traditions and identify symbols and storytelling narratives that align with vision, shared goals, objectives, and outcomes. The team then selects a time, place, and format that will maximize purpose and participation.

Recognition should honor individuals and teams for who they are, what they contributed, and how they made a difference. Honorees' strengths, perspectives, and impacts should be acknowledged to deepen the celebration's meaning. Teacher teams, not individuals, should be celebrated to avoid favoritism and foster collective pride.

Educational leaders can support these efforts by guiding the development and communication of meaningful ways to celebrate. Celebrations should highlight action plan goals, student progress, teacher collaboration, and parental contributions. When thoughtfully executed, they build morale, deepen trust, and energize continued improvement.

Regular assemblies or events, where students and families gather to celebrate achievements, can include activities such as principal/teacher-led storytelling; exhibitions of student work; a 'growing tree' mural of accomplishments; an installation where students dip their hand in paint, 'slap the wall,' and then sign their hand print to acknowledge their empathy and compassion or academic gains; recognition of teacher teams implementing a new curriculum or instruction practice; or an activity honoring parents supporting school vision, values, and goals and working with their children on schoolwork at home. Quarterly celebrations of gains and the contributions of all those involved should then be published in the school newsletter and described in a press release.

▶ EXAMPLE: A CEREMONY TO CELEBRATE DIFFERENTIATED INSTRUCTION IN LITERACY

A 'literacy showcase' event highlights student work and teacher practices aligned with differentiated instruction. Displays of student writing and 'recipe cards' from teachers summarizing successful differentiated instruction approaches are set up prior to the assembly. The principal opens the event by underscoring the importance of literacy and differentiated instruction and then introduces a teacher who further elaborates. The spotlight then shifts to students who share personal growth stories, followed by teacher-team reflections and possibly further recognizing students with gift cards or small tokens of appreciation.

The ceremony ends with a festive community celebration. The school community then enjoys refreshments inspired by beloved books, like *Green Eggs and Ham* sandwiches or *Charlotte's Web* cupcakes, leaving everyone with a sense of accomplishment, connection, and inspiration for continued growth in literacy education.

▶ EXAMPLE: A CEREMONY TO CELEBRATE MATH

This principal, teacher educational leader, or parent tells the story of 6th-grade teachers and parents at Forest Hill Collegiate High School collaborating to bring math adventures into students' daily lives. Through creative events like Family Math Night, real-life problem-solving activities, and take-home "Math Mission" cards, students build curiosity and confidence in math. The celebration ends with parents and teachers honored on stage for their partnership. This story illustrates how celebrations can unify the community and highlight shared efforts toward academic and social improvement.

▶ EXAMPLE: A HOMECOMING CELEBRATION

Another celebration might include asking middle or high school graduates to come back to their school and share a story about a current faculty member who helped them or other students through difficult times. Additional celebrations are described in Appendix 4.

▶ DEVELOPING A BULLETED PRELIMINARY PLAN TO CELEBRATE GAINS

A preliminary plan should focus on key actions you, as an educational leader, will take to guide celebrating gains. Your preliminary plan should build on the previous subsystem and set the stage for the one that follows. As part of a larger systems-thinking approach, developing a preliminary plan prepares educational leaders to engage in deeper collaboration with faculty. The plan should avoid the use of third-person and instead detail the specific, step-by-step actions you will take as the educational leader to lead discussions and facilitate collaboration.

When developing your preliminary plan, use bulleted sound bites to capture the main ideas. No sentences are necessary. Your preliminary plan should include some citations to reinforce content and process. Developing preliminary plans prepare educational leaders to use the same process when they will be working collaboratively with faculty colleagues to develop preliminary plans based on their assessed needs as well as to create a comprehensive innovation plan for their context.

▶ EXAMPLE: A BULLETED PRELIMINARY PLAN FOR PLANNING AND COLLABORATIVELY CELEBRATING GAINS

- Select a respected teacher, in consultation with faculty, to lead the celebration planning process.
- Revisit the school's shared vision, values, and action plan SMART goals with the teacher team to ground the celebration in collective purpose.
- Have the teacher team gather input from faculty on who should be acknowledged and request evidence of progress.
- Lead reflective discussions with the team to identify which values, goals, mindsets, and practices are worth celebrating.
- Invite students, staff, and families, based on recommendations, to share stories and reflections about their experiences and growth.
- Support the teacher team in designing a celebration aligned with school culture and action plan goals, ensuring it highlights persistence, effort, and teamwork as well as academic achievement.
- Co-develop meaningful ceremonies, exhibitions, rituals, or storytelling events that affirm collaboration and improvement (Deal, 1994a).

- Help the team link recognized gains to shared values, effective practices, and school-wide or system-wide improvement goals.
- Embed celebrations into the school's calendar and routines to create traditions that endure.
- Plan how the event will be documented through photos, videos, and written narratives.
- Determine who will communicate the celebration's outcomes to faculty, families, district administrators, and school committee members, and select appropriate formats (e.g., newsletter, bulletin, assembly, online platform).
- Collect feedback from participants to refine future celebrations.
- Revisit relational trust and shared values with the team to ensure they are evident in both planning and execution.
- Facilitate a debrief after the event to reflect on its impact, identify next steps, and sustain momentum.

▶ A LOOK INTO THE FUTURE

To provide a sense of how educational leaders may translate and expand the bulleted preliminary plan into a narrative for the innovation plan, the following example is presented.

> As an educational leader, I will launch the process of collaboratively celebrating gains by selecting, with faculty input, a respected teacher to serve as the team leader for this work. Together with the teacher team leader and selected members of a teacher team, I will revisit our school's shared vision, core values, and action plan SMART goals to ensure that every celebration remains grounded in our collective purpose and improvement priorities. This alignment will help the team identify what matters most, not only in terms of academic performance, but also in terms of persistence, effort, and collaboration.
>
> The teacher team will gather input from faculty to determine who should be acknowledged and collect evidence of progress, including student work, assessment results, and qualitative reflections. I will guide reflective conversations with the team to surface the values, goals, and mindsets

worth celebrating, and we will invite students, staff, and families to share stories that illustrate how our improvement efforts have influenced their experiences and growth.

Working collaboratively, I will support the team in designing celebrations that reflect our school's culture while reinforcing the practices and conditions that led to our gains. Whether through ceremonies, appreciation rituals, traditions, or storytelling events, we will ensure that these moments affirm both achievement and the collective effort behind it (Deal, 1994b). I will help the team articulate how each recognized gain aligns with our shared vision and connects to broader improvement goals at the grade, school, or system level.

To sustain this culture of recognition, I will assist the team in embedding these celebrations into the school's calendar, making celebrations an ongoing tradition. We will plan how each event will be documented through photos, videos, and written narratives and decide who will share the outcomes with faculty, families, district administrators, and school committee members. Multiple communication channels, such as assemblies, newsletters, local press, and online platforms, will be used to make celebrations visible and transparent.

After each celebration of gains, I will facilitate a structured debrief with the teacher team to evaluate its impact, review participant feedback, and refine future events. Throughout the process, I will revisit the foundational elements of relational trust and shared values, ensuring that they remain central to our planning and execution. By creating celebrations that highlight persistence, teamwork, and authentic growth, we will build traditions that foster shared pride, strengthen collective efficacy, and maintain momentum for continuous school improvement.

This approach to collaboratively celebrate gains builds on the previous subsystems and sets the stage for what follows, anchoring our work in a systems-thinking mindset and prepares me as an educational leader to guide and facilitate the development of a comprehensive innovation plan that supports lasting, equity-driven school transformation and innovation.

▶ CHAPTER SUMMARY

Celebrating gains is a powerful, often overlooked strategy for building a positive and inclusive school culture. Intentional, values-based celebrations reinforce shared goals, foster trust, and sustain improvement efforts. Through ceremonies, rituals, traditions, symbols, and stories, schools can recognize progress, honor contributions, and energize continued work. These events, when tied to vision and action plan goals, become more than moments of recognition. They reflect collaborative purpose, align with the school's vision and goals, and inspire future efforts. By involving teacher teams in the planning and incorporating inclusive practices, celebrations deepen connections across students, staff, families, and community members.

Using the Six-Point Conceptual Framework, school leaders can develop meaningful, recurring celebrations that nurture a thriving, motivated learning community. As you conclude this chapter, consider developing your own plan for celebrating gains. Let celebrating gains become a cornerstone of your school's culture, reinforcing recognition, driving progress, and uniting the community around a shared purpose.

In the next chapter we will learn how to combine all the preliminary plans for each point of the Six-Point Conceptual Framework into an innovation plan to guide, facilitate, maintain, and sustain the improvement of teaching, learning, and leading and the conditions in which they occur.

Leadership Task: *Reflective Journal*

- Respond in writing to the prompts. This will be your seventh journal entry. These prompts encourage readers to reflect on the value of celebrating gains, explore strategies for effective recognition, and consider how celebration can foster sustained growth and connection within their teams or organizations. The prompts may be used to facilitate a faculty meeting or university classroom discussion.
    - What is the leader's role in initiating and facilitating celebrations that are authentic and impactful?
    - How can leaders model the importance of celebrating gains to reinforce its value across the organization?
    - Why is celebrating gains essential for sustaining momentum and morale within an organization?

- How does acknowledging progress, even small wins, contribute to building a positive and productive organizational culture?
- How can leaders ensure that all contributions, both large and small, are recognized during celebrations?
- Why is it important to acknowledge the efforts of individuals and teams, not just the overall outcomes of the action plan?
- What role does gratitude and recognition play in fostering collaboration and trust within an organization?
- How can organizations embed regular recognition of gains into their culture to encourage ongoing effort and innovation?
- What are some creative and meaningful ways organizations can celebrate gains without relying solely on traditional rewards?
- How can celebrations be tailored to align with the organization's values and the preferences of its members?
- How can leaders ensure that celebrations are inclusive and resonate with all stakeholders, regardless of their roles or backgrounds?
- What considerations should be taken into account to avoid unintentional exclusion or favoritism during celebrations?
- How can celebrating gains contribute to sustained motivation for long-term organizational goals?
- What risks might arise if achievements are not acknowledged or celebrated?
- Reflect on a time when you or your organization celebrated an accomplishment. What made the celebration meaningful, and what could have been improved?
- Have you experienced a situation where a lack of acknowledgment for achievements led to diminished motivation? How could that have been addressed?
- How can celebrations serve as a platform to inspire future efforts and refocus on long-term goals?
- What strategies can leaders use to connect past successes with the organization's ongoing efforts to increase student learning?

- While it's important to celebrate, how can organizations ensure they also focus on areas for improvement?
- How can celebrations include moments of reflection to highlight lessons learned alongside achievements?

Leadership Task: *Introduce the Importance of Celebrating Gains*

- Develop a communication to be used at a meeting with a teacher team, department, school, or district that describes the importance of collaboratively celebrating gains and its relation to the school improvement processes and the Six-Point Conceptual Framework.

Leadership Task: *Develop a Preliminary Plan to Collaboratively Celebrate Gains*

- Taking into consideration the reflective questions posed, resources shared, the uniqueness of your context, develop a bulleted preliminary plan (review the previous example) for collaboratively celebrating gains. You may choose to use or adapt the example shared or develop your own bulleted preliminary plan.

References

Bolman, L. G., & Deal, T. E. (1995). *Leading with soul: An uncommon journey of spirit*. Jossey-Bass.
Deal, T. E. (1994a). The culture of schools. In E. S. Marshall & H. J. Sashkin (Eds.), *Educational leadership and school culture* (pp. 23–36). McCutchan Publishing.
Deal, T. E. (1994b). The symbolism of effective schools. In J. Murphy & K. S. Louis (Eds.), *Reshaping the principalship: Insights from transformational reform efforts* (pp. 107–122). Corwin Press.
Noddings, N. (1992). In defense of caring. *Journal of Clinical Ethics*, *3*(1), 15–18. https://doi.org/10.1086/jce199203103

Additional Resources

Bolman, L. G., & Deal, T. E. (1997a). *Reframing organizations: Artistry, choice, and leadership* (2nd ed.). Jossey-Bass Publishers.
Bolman, L. G., & Deal, T. E. (1997b). Organizational culture and symbols. In *Reframing organizations: Artistry, choice, and leadership* (2nd ed., pp. 215–234). Jossey-Bass Publishers.
DuFour, R. (1998). Why celebrate? It sends a vivid message about what is valued. *Journal of Staff Development*, *19*(4). http://www.theartofed.com/wp-content/uploads/2012/09/WhyCelebrate.pdf.
Heifetz, R. A., Grashow, A., & Linsky, M. (2009). *The practice of adaptive leadership: Tools and tactics for changing your organization and the world* (pp. 233–289). Harvard Business Press.
Kotter, J. P. (2012). *Leading change* (Chapter 9, pp. 137–152). Harvard Business School Publishing.
Robbins. M. (2019). *The power of appreciation* (TedTalk). The Power of Appreciation.

THE 6-POINT CONCEPTUAL FRAMEWORK

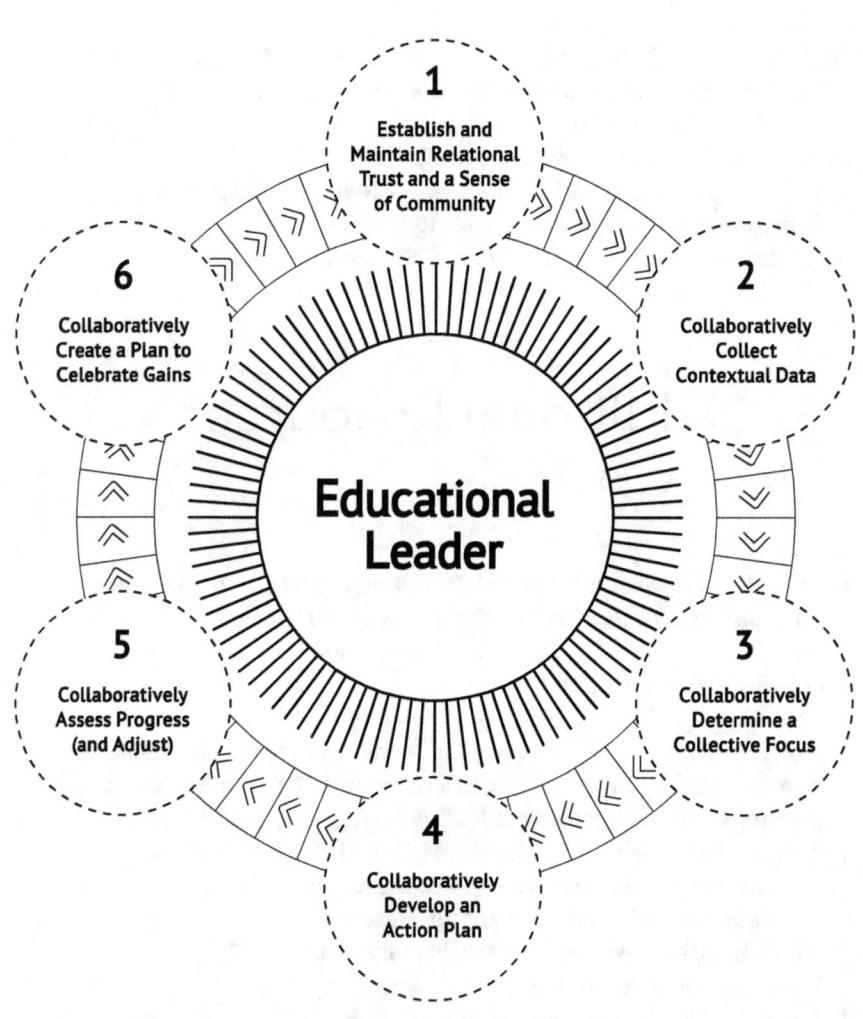

Conceptual Framework design and chapter openers designed by Christian Arichabala.

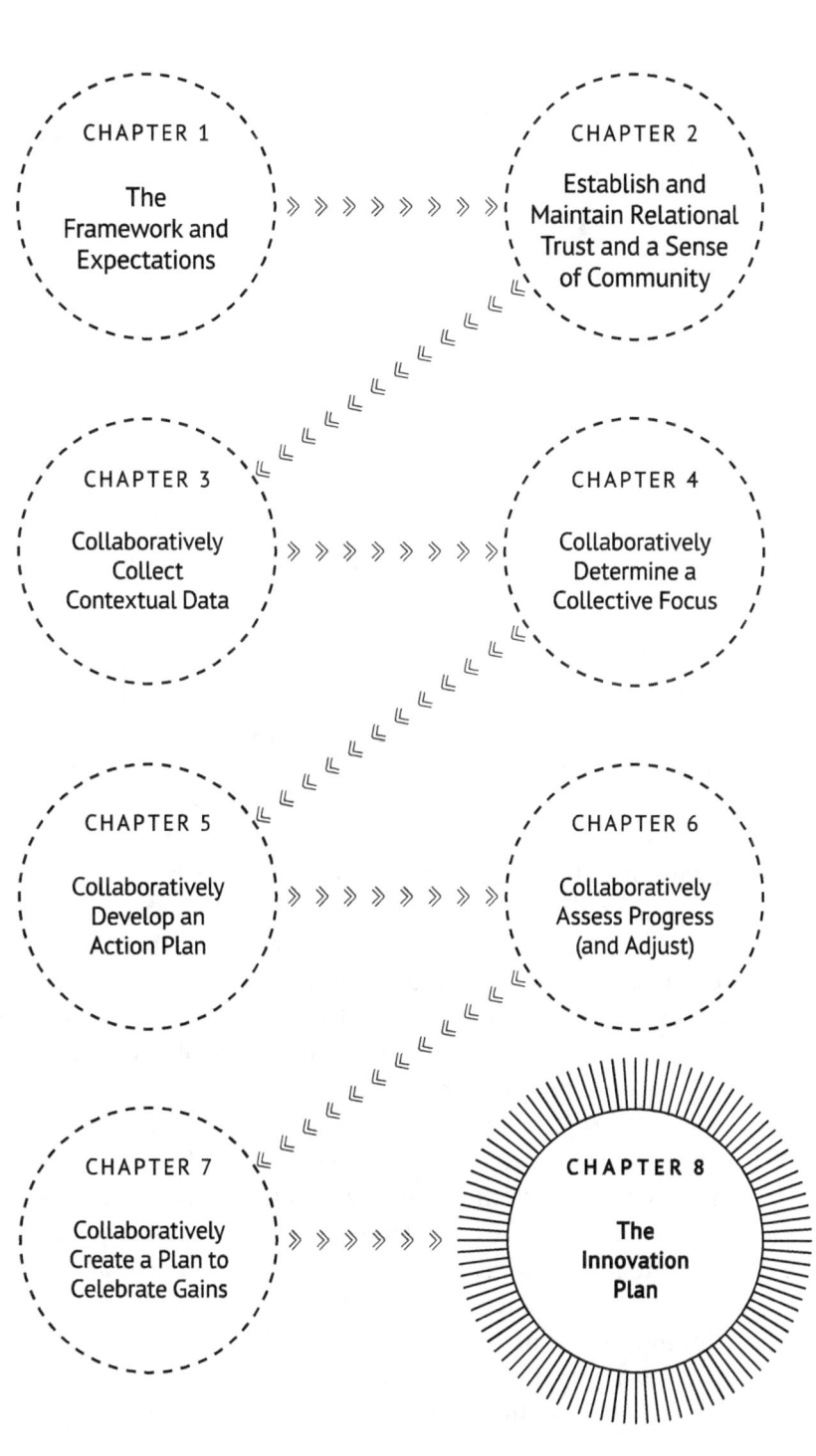

Collaboratively Create a Context-Specific Innovation Plan

Chapter 8

▶ **INTRODUCTION**

Educational leaders today must be reflective practitioners, systems thinkers, and strategic planners who build teamwork and promote consensus to maintain and sustain school improvement. The Six-Point Conceptual Framework provides a structured, collaborative guide for facilitating change, improvement, transformation, and innovation. In an era of profound disruption spanning social, technological, economic, environmental, and psychological domains, school leaders face challenges that cannot be solved through technical fixes or familiar solutions alone. Instead, they must adopt a holistic, adaptive approach that recognizes how each subsystem of the framework interconnects, while tailoring strategies to the unique context of their schools. As Fullan (2014) reminds us, "Successful innovation requires understanding the local context and engaging stakeholders in designing solutions that fit their unique circumstances." This chapter highlights the role of reflection, systems thinking, strategic planning, collaboration, clarity, and coherence in developing a well-organized, context-specific innovation plan. Each preliminary plan introduced in earlier chapters links directly to the next, creating a logical, iterative sequence organized by the six subsystems of the Six-Point Conceptual Framework.

Leaders are guided to transform these interconnected preliminary plans, initially structured as bulleted leadership action steps, into a cohesive, context-specific innovation plan. This process draws on essential leadership capacities to produce a plan that is practical, relevant, and responsive to the needs of students, teachers, parents, and the community. Organizing the innovation plan using the structure of the Six-Point Conceptual Framework ensures alignment with data-informed factors and conditions that are affecting the learning of a significant number of students, identified by data collected by teacher teams and validated by faculty consensus. By expanding each bulleted step into a clear narrative, and then integrating these narratives into one coherent document, leaders and teacher teams create an actionable roadmap to guide and sustain meaningful change, improvement, transformation, and innovation.

Today, educational leaders must be reflective practitioners, systems thinkers, and strategic planners who foster teamwork and build consensus to sustain and maintain school improvement. The Six-Point Conceptual Framework serves as a vital, structured, collaborative guide for improvement and innovation. At this time of incredible disruption across social, technological, economic, environmental, and psychological interrelated domains, to effectively meet the existing complex challenges of school improvement educational leaders must go beyond technical fixes or known solutions and adopt a holistic, adaptive approach recognizing the relationships between each framework point or subsystem and tailoring strategies to their specific context. The following quote by Fullan (2014), "Successful innovation requires understanding the local context and engaging stakeholders in designing solutions that fit their unique circumstances," reinforces the need to collaboratively design a context-specific innovation plan.

This chapter emphasizes the importance of clarity, organizational coherence, and collaboration. Each preliminary plan developed in earlier chapters connects to the previous and following preliminary plans, forming a step-by-step series of bulleted leadership action steps organized according to the titles of the subsystems of the Six-Point Conceptual Framework. Leaders are guided to organize and sequence the integrated bulleted action steps of each preliminary plan into a cohesive, context-specific innovation plan. This process draws on key leadership capacities such as collaboration, systems thinking, strategic planning, and effective communication to develop and deliver an innovation plan that is practical, relevant, and responsive to the unique needs of students and teachers in their schools and districts. Using the Six-Point Framework to organize the innovation plan ensures alignment with the collective focus determined by data collected and analyzed by a teacher team(s) and supported by faculty consensus. By expanding each bullet for each subsystem of the Six-Point Conceptual Framework into a narrative and then integrating each narrative into a much larger clear narrative, leaders, with the teacher team, create an innovation plan that is an actionable roadmap to guide improvement efforts.

By the end of this chapter, educational leaders, with or without formal authority, will be able to

- Provide a rationale for the use of the Six-Point Conceptual Framework to create a tailored innovation plan that incorporates systems thinking and strategic planning.
- Collect the preliminary bulleted plans for the six subsystems of the Six-Point Conceptual Framework previously developed.
- Sequence the preliminary plan bullets into a larger bulleted composite preliminary plan organized and aligned with the Six-Point Conceptual Framework.
- Collaboratively expand the bulleted composite preliminary plans into a clear, cohesive, well-structured, easy to follow, and understandable context-specific innovation plan narrative with relevant citations.
- Go back to the grade level, department, school, or district and, as an educational leader with or without authority, collaboratively develop, with a teacher team, each point of the Six-Point Conceptual Framework, as described in detail in Chapters Two–Seven.

- Collaboratively develop an innovation plan with the teacher team as described in detail in this chapter.
- Collaboratively, with the teacher team, share the final proposed draft with faculty and a representative group of parents and other community members.
- Request input and incorporate feedback into the final innovation plan.
- Present the innovation plan to faculty, families, other district leaders, school committee members, and the broader community.

▶ DEVELOPING AN INNOVATION PLAN

The innovation plan is a strategic, systems-thinking, dynamic blueprint for improvement. It must reflect shared values, a unified vision, leadership identity, and an ethical commitment to equity, access, communication, and collaboration. It should provide a compelling account of how the leader will guide, facilitate, support, and sustain change, improvement, and innovation within a specific context, whether at the PK–6, PK–8, middle school, high school, or district level. By integrating the values, knowledge, skills, and mindsets developed through the content of this book, and by reflecting on professional practice using chapter end prompts, educational leaders are challenged to create a comprehensive, context-specific innovation plan grounded in research-based teaching and leadership practices designed to increase student learning.

In preparing the innovation plan, educational leaders should demonstrate a deep understanding of the Six-Point Conceptual Framework, its systemic design, iterative nature, and potential to drive sustainable innovation. The plan should clearly articulate how the six subsystems are interconnected and how they will be leveraged to foster collective action among faculty, build a culture of relational trust and shared responsibility, and strengthen conditions for teaching, learning, and leadership.

Each section of the plan should describe a step-by-step, collaborative process tailored to the specific needs of the grade level, department, school, or district. Leaders should identify key challenges; reiterate the collaboratively determined collective focus; and reinforce well-developed goals, objectives, and outcomes supported by both qualitative and quantitative data. The plan must detail how leaders and faculty will establish and maintain relational trust, cultivate a sense of community and belonging, assess contextual factors and conditions that inhibit and foster student learning, select a collective focus, design and implement an action plan, measure progress, and celebrate gains.

Ultimately, the innovation plan is a living document that not only diagnoses problems and proposes solutions but also keeps daily decisions aligned with a collaboratively determined collective focus, goals, objectives, and outcomes. To construct such a plan, leaders should first organize each bulleted preliminary plan sequentially according to the six interconnected subsystems of the Six-Point Conceptual Framework. These preliminary plans serve as the foundation for a series of detailed narratives. When expanded and integrated, these narratives form a cohesive, clear, and inspirational innovation plan.

The innovation plan should conclude by summarizing expected outcomes, outlining next steps, and reaffirming the school community's capacity to enact meaningful change, increase student learning, and be innovative. It should close with a message that reinforces shared purpose and inspires confidence and hope.

To help sequence the bulleted preliminary plans for each section of the context-specific innovation plan refer to Appendix 5. To assess the quality, clarity, and coherence of the context-specific innovation plan and your leadership practice, use the provided rubric in Table 8.1.

Once finalized, the innovation plan should be shared with faculty, families, district leadership, and school committee members. During its presentation, the educational leader with a teacher team alongside should highlight the collaborative nature of the school change process, reaffirm a commitment to shared values and innovation, and seek constructive feedback to further strengthen the plan.

Table 8.1 Rubric to Assess a Collaboratively Developed Innovation Plan (Gould, 2023).

Criteria	Emergent Leadership	Developing Leadership	Effective Leadership	Daring Leadership
Introduction	Information presented is unclear and leaves reader with more questions than answers.	Purpose of innovation plan is mentioned but lacks clarity and coherence.	Introduction clearly states the purpose, leadership role, collaborators, and plan organization.	Persuasive narrative highlights context, positionality, and purpose in a compelling way.
Reflective Practice	Plan shows no evidence of reflection or adaptation.	Some shifts are evident, but alignment and reflection are inconsistent.	Plan reflects multiple perspectives and evolving insight.	Deep reflection leads to changes in assumptions, uncovering of bias, and growth in practice.
Establishing and Maintaining Relational Trust	Relational trust is not evident; plan lacks shared decision-making or diverse voices.	Some effort to engage community members, but few perspectives are included.	Stakeholders are identified and included to assess needs and shape goals.	Deep, inclusive collaboration builds urgency, trust, and collective belief in the plan.
Collaboratively Collect Contextual Data	No data collection team formed; unclear methods.	Data protocols are weak or missing; limited data areas explored.	Data collected in 2–3 areas with expectation of shared implementation.	Comprehensive data collected and shared with stakeholders to inform action.
Collaboratively Determine a Collective Focus	No clear collective focus drives the proposed innovation.	A general need is referenced but not well connected to the plan.	Innovation plan is aligned to a collective focus and shows coherence.	Plan responds to a collective focus and a critical need clearly stated.

Copyright material from Gould (2026), *School Change is a Collaborative Process*, Routledge

Collaboratively Develop an Action Plan	Plan is vague and lacks coherence or direction.	Action steps are incomplete or missing key elements of the framework.	Steps toward change are articulated and align with framework elements.	Coherent, timeline-based plan includes specific, strategic actions linked to all framework components.
Collaboratively Assess Progress	No clear data or assessment tied to goals or stakeholder voice.	Data collection is inconsistent or misaligned with goals.	Multiple data sources collected and shared to assess change.	Success indicators are identified, measured, and transparently communicated.
Collaboratively Develop a Plan to Celebrate Gains	No acknowledgment or recognition of progress.	Some improvement noted but not publicly acknowledged.	Public recognition of gains and milestones achieved.	Celebration is embedded in community culture and reinforces vision and values.
Conclusion	Conclusion is disorganized and fails to bring elements of the plan together.	Some outcomes recounted but lack strategic synthesis.	Conclusion summarizes process, key strategies, and outcomes.	Conclusion integrates systems thinking, impact analysis, and next steps in a compelling summary.
References	APA style is missing or incorrect; references not included.	Minimal adherence to APA and limited course readings used.	APA mostly followed and course readings support the plan.	Strong APA use, multiple sources cited, and appendices deepen the plan's impact.

▶ CHAPTER SUMMARY

Our lives are being disrupted by forces that are global, interconnected, and accelerating. These disruptions are not only reshaping how we live, work, and relate to one another, but they are also challenging our assumptions about stability, progress, and what it means to be human in the 21st century. The question now is do we respond with fear and resistance or with adaptability, creativity, innovation, and a renewed sense of collaborative and collective responsibility?

Leadership Task: *Reflective Journal*

- This will be your eighth and final entry. The end of chapter prompts encourage you as an educational leader to reflect on your learning and plan for practical applications. Respond in writing to the prompts. They may also be used to facilitate a faculty meeting or college classroom discussion.
    - Go back and review your initial journal entry in the Preface. Compare your understanding now with your initial entry. Consider how lessons learned might inspire future growth and change.
    - What does the book title *School Change is a Collaborative Process* mean to you now, after completing this book?
    - How has this book influenced your understanding of the complexities of organizational change?
    - What aspect of the Six-Point Conceptual Framework improvement process resonated most with you, and why?
    - What roles do reflection, leadership identity, and collaboration play in leading the change process?
    - If you could share one lesson from this book, what would it be?
    - How has this book reshaped your perspective on the role of leadership in leading change, improvement, transformation, and innovation?
    - What approaches from this book can help you foster a culture of collaboration and shared ownership in your organization?

- How can you ensure that all voices are heard and valued as part of the change process?
- How will you carry forward the insights and approaches from this book into your ongoing personal or professional growth?
- What did you learn about the importance of determining a collective focus and a celebrating gains?
- What challenges do you anticipate in implementing the collaborative practices outlined in this book, and how might you address them?
- What leadership skills or practices do you plan to develop further based on the lessons learned from this book?
- What was the most significant insight, revelation, or biggest takeaway you experienced as a result of this book?
- How do you envision applying the Six-Point Conceptual Framework to your current work?

Leadership Task: *Introduce the Importance of Collaboratively Developing a Context-Specific Innovation Plan*

- Develop a communication to be used at a meeting with a teacher team, department, school, or district that describes the Six-Point Conceptual Framework as a pathway to leading collaborative school change, student learning improvement, transformation of systems, and organizational innovation. Emphasize the purpose and importance of collaboratively developing a context-specific innovation plan.

Leadership Task: *Collaboratively Develop a Context-Specific Innovation Plan*

- Taking into consideration the reflective questions posed, content and resources shared throughout this book, and the previously developed preliminary plans for the Six-Point Conceptual Framework, develop a narrative describing the step-by-step efforts you will take to guide, facilitate, support, maintain, and sustain school change, improvement, transformation, and innovation.

Reference

Fullan, M. (2014). *The principal: Three keys to maximizing impact.* Jossey-Bass.

Additional Resources

Bandura, A. (1997). *Self-efficacy: The exercise of control.* W. H. Freeman.
Bryk, A. S., Sebring, P. B., Allensworth, E., Luppescu, S., & Easton, J. Q. (2010). *Organizing schools for improvement: Lessons from Chicago.* University of Chicago Press.
Deal, T. E. (1994). *The leadership paradox: Balancing logic and artistry in schools.* Jossey-Bass.
Drago-Severson, E. (2023). *Growing for Justice.* Corwin.
DuFour, R., & Fullan, M. (2013). *Cultures built to last: Systemic PLCs at work.* Solution Tree Press.
Fullan, M. (2001). *Leading in a culture of change.* Jossey-Bass.
Heifetz, R. (1994). *Leadership Without Easy Answers.* Harvard University Press.
Noddings, N. (1992). In defense of caring. *Journal of Clinical Ethics, 3*(1), 15–18. https://doi.org/10.1086/jce199203103
Sinclair, R., & Ghory, W. (1997). *Reaching and teaching all children: Grassroots efforts that work.* Corwin.
Tyler, R. W. (1949). *Basic Principles of Curriculum and Instruction.* University of Chicago Press.
Wheatley, M. J. (1999). *Leadership and the new science: Discovering order in a chaotic world* (2nd ed.). Berrett-Koehler.

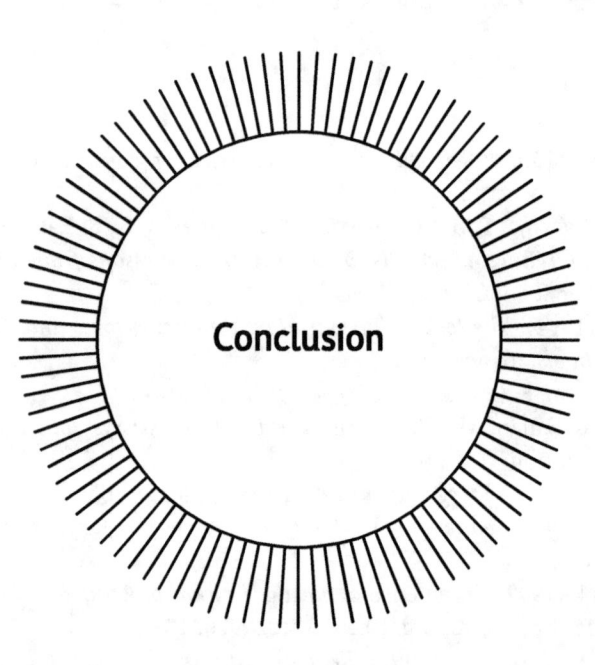

Conclusion

Conclusion

Throughout this book, we have explored how the Six-Point Conceptual Framework, collaborative educational leadership, systems thinking, and strategic planning intersect to support PK–12 school improvement and innovation. From the first pages, *School Change is a Collaborative Process* has made it clear that school improvement is not a series of isolated technical fixes imposed from above. Instead, it is an adaptive, collaborative, living, relational, and deeply humane endeavor, rooted in trust, shared purpose, and local context. At its core, change in schools is about people, their relationships, their courage to ask hard questions, their willingness to listen, and their ability to imagine something better together.

We began our journey with a foundational truth that educational leadership is not a position but a way of thinking. We then examined the shifting landscape of education, increasingly shaped by social inequities, technological disruption, political polarization, a global pandemic, and a growing youth mental health crisis. Against this backdrop, we affirmed the necessity for a new kind of leadership that embraces ambiguity; welcomes complexity; promotes inclusion; fosters a holistic development of each student; and advances a systems-thinking approach to classroom, school, and district improvement. Leadership, in this view, is a shared responsibility among those who care deeply about the purpose and outcomes of schooling.

If you have seen yourself in these pages, it is because this work belongs to you. You are part of the story of educational leadership that is unfolding now in classrooms, in schools, in districts, and in preparation programs. One of the most transformative moments in my career came during my time as a school principal. Leading a building through a major restructuring effort, I resisted the temptation to dictate solutions. Instead, I invited the faculty into sustained inquiry. We built time for reflection into staff meetings, created cross-grade planning teams, and invited families to participate in shaping the school's values, vision, and mission. The results weren't immediate, but they were profound. Trust blossomed. Teacher leadership emerged. And student outcomes improved not just academically, but also emotionally and socially.

As a teacher you are the soul of the school. Let your voice shape the future. Lead from your classroom. Invite your students into the work of change. Hold fast to your vision of what children can become and help others see it too. Principals are the weavers of trust. Build spaces where teachers feel safe to take risks, reflect, and grow. Protect time for collaboration. Listen deeply. Lead with empathy, with humility, and with fire. District leaders are the stewards of systems. See beyond the spreadsheets. Create conditions where schools can thrive, not just survive. Align policy with humanity. Invest in the slow, hard, beautiful work of culture-building. University professors and preparation programs are the cultivators of future leaders. Model inquiry. Prepare leaders who can navigate complexity with clarity and care. Partner with schools. Teach courage and persistence.

At the heart of any meaningful change process is clear, values-based leadership and communication. This foundational work anchors decisions in moral purpose and enables leaders to navigate difficult dilemmas with integrity. The Six-Point Conceptual Framework was introduced and explained as a systems-thinking, strategic-planning scaffold for collaboratively leading a step-by-step, transformative process. The change journey began with reflective practice, the framework, and the cultivation of relational trust. Without them, collaboration becomes performative at best and dysfunctional at worst. With them, collective effort becomes transformative.

From there, we turned to the power of contextual data collection; listening to the voices of students, families, and staff; analyzing contextual data; and identifying patterns of success and inequity. I recall working as an assistant superintendent in a district where one school consistently outperformed others serving similar populations. Rather than standardize their methods, we invited their leadership team to help *teach* and *coach* us. That experience changed how we understood data as an invitation to collaborative learning.

Once a collective focus was determined by consensus, the real work of designing an action plan began. In countless schools I've supported as a consultant, I've watched educators learn to engage in cycles of inquiry, monitor progress, and revise approaches in ways that improve learning and build the capacity of the entire team. Change doesn't come from mandates; it comes from informed, collaborative, and empowered people.

The consistent message throughout this book has been that collaboration is not a soft skill or an optional practice. It is an essential force in school transformation and innovation. But collaboration alone is not enough. To be effective, it must be aligned with reflection, equity, and access and spirited by courage.

We must face the reality that many of our existing educational structures were built for a bygone era that prioritized conformity, control, and competition and often excluded the voices, histories, and identities of marginalized communities. Today's students need schools that nurture curiosity, empathy, agency, resilience, and democracy. They need classrooms that reflect the full diversity of human experience and prepare students not only to succeed, but also to contribute meaningfully to a just and sustainable world.

The civic purpose of public education is to cultivate engaged, self-sustaining, and contributing members of a democratic society. Schools are not merely places to prepare students for the workforce. They are crucibles for civic learning, cultural understanding, ethical development, and democratic action. Every effort to improve schools must be anchored in this broader societal purpose. Intentional, inclusive, sustained collaboration is how we bring that purpose to life.

As a university professor, I've witnessed educators at every level come into their own. Graduate students, often burdened by the limitations of their current work circumstances, rediscover their sense of purpose as they engage in inquiry, write action plans, and lead real change and innovation in their schools. It's in these moments that theory meets practice and hope meets action.

As this book draws to a close, I offer this invitation to carry this work forward to all educational leaders whether you are a teacher, instructional coach, department chair, special education director, principal, superintendent, university professor, student aspiring to lead, or policymaker. Let this guide be a launching point, not a conclusion. Reflect on your values. Build trust. Listen deeply. Focus on what matters most. Act with purpose, urgency, and humility. Organize your school community.

We stand at a crossroads between old models that no longer serve and new possibilities waiting to be built. The future of schooling is not pre-written. It will be co-authored by all of us, together. The stakes are too high for complacency. If change is to be transformative, innovative, and sustainable, it must be collaborative. Trust the process.

Together, we can build schools that not only increase student learning but also prepare students to be thoughtful, self-sustaining, and socially responsible members of a democratic society who contribute to the common, collective, greater good. Let's begin again, with courage. Let's lead with hope. Let's begin today, tomorrow, and every day after that. School change is a collaborative process!

THE 6-POINT CONCEPTUAL FRAMEWORK

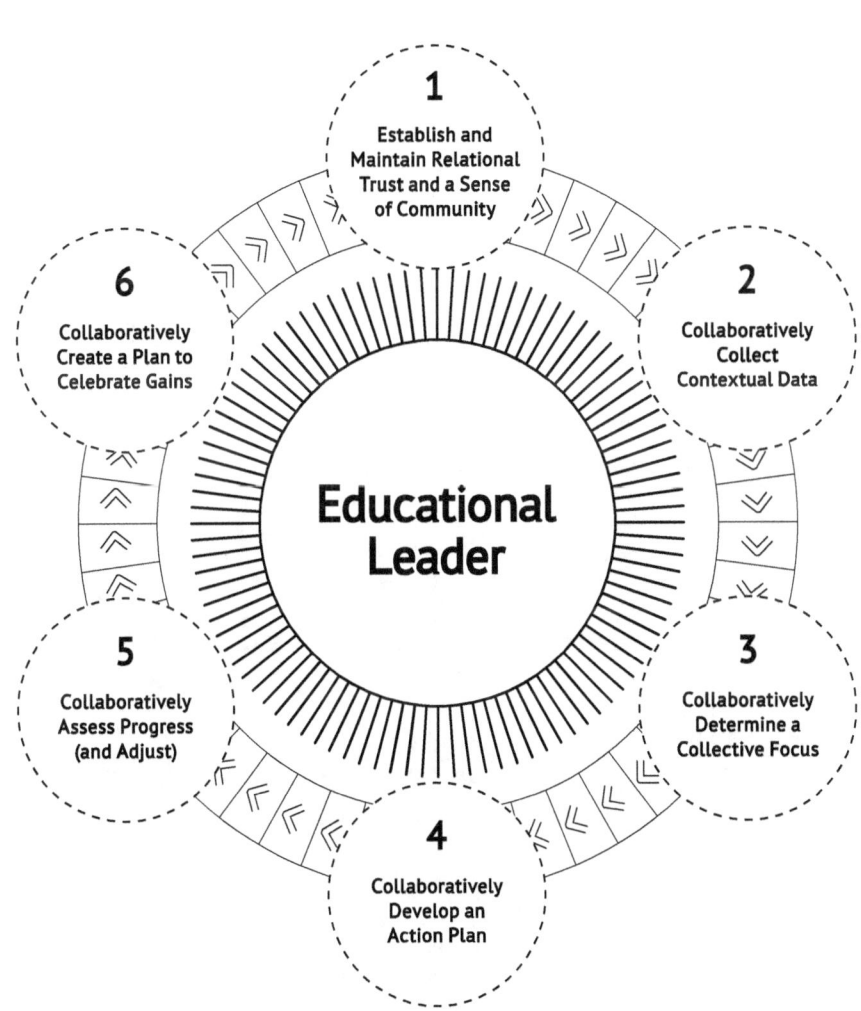

Conceptual Framework design and chapter openers designed by Christian Arichabala.

Appendices

There are six Appendices, some with a number of subsections.

Appendix 1: Four Examples of Communications for Establishing and Maintaining Relational Trust and a Sense of Community

Appendix 2: Three Assessment Instruments to Identify Contextual Factors and Conditions Impacting Teaching, Learning, and Leading

Appendix 3: Two Examples of a Collaboratively Developed Action Plan With a Collective Focus, Goals, Objectives/Action Steps, and Outcomes/Indicators of Success

Appendix 4: Two Examples of Celebrations, Ceremonies, Traditions, Rituals, and Storytelling (for Chapter Seven)

Appendix 5: An Example of End-of-Chapter Bulleted Preliminary Plans to be Expanded Into an Innovation Plan (for Chapter Eight)

Appendix 6: A Rubric for Developing and Self-Assessing a Context-Specific Innovation Plan

Appendix 1: Four Examples of Communications for Establishing and Maintaining Relational Trust and a Sense of Community

▶ 1. INSPIRING SCHOOL IMPROVEMENT

Dear Faculty, Parents, and Community Members,

As a school leader, my approach to school improvement is rooted in collaborative engagement. I believe that the collective power of the community can create meaningful change. I am committed to *Building Trusting Relationships and Inviting Participation*. I enjoy actively engaging teachers, parents, and community members to create strong partnerships. By maintaining regular communication and listening to concerns, scheduling collaborative planning sessions, and using surveys and community forums, I will work to ensure that all stakeholders have a voice in making our school a better place for students, teachers, and families. School improvement efforts must be grounded in a vision that reflects the values and aspirations of the entire school community. I am committed to collaboratively *Create a Shared Vision* (or maintain our previously developed shared vision). I am committed to *Promoting Lifelong Learning and Professional Growth*. Supporting faculty and staff in their professional growth is key to sustained school improvement. I will prioritize teacher identified, job-embedded professional development opportunities that are aligned with school goals and individual needs. I will empower teachers to innovate so that the learning of all students is improved. And finally, I am committed to *Celebrating Gains*. School improvement is a continuous process, and it is important to recognize both small and large gains along the way. By celebrating gains, rather than waiting for complete success, we maintain the momentum of change, improvement, transformation, and innovation and keep the community motivated and engaged in the journey toward excellence.

In summary, this email/speech capturing my leadership approach is a living document that reflects my commitment to leading with purpose, fostering a culture of collaboration, and inspiring all members of this school community to work together for the betterment of our students and future generations.

Thank you for your attention. If you have any questions or concerns or need clarification, don't hesitate to ask.

▶ 2. EMBRACING CHANGE FOR A BETTER FUTURE

Dear Faculty, Family, and Community Members,

The challenges of our time demand a bold reimagining of education and a system that prepares individuals not just for today, but also for the uncertainties and opportunities of tomorrow. The vision, mission, and goals of our school are to empower learners to thrive in a rapidly ever-changing world. We must nurture curious, creative, and resilient minds. Education is no longer about memorizing facts but about cultivating the ability to collaborate, think critically, and innovate. By encouraging exploration and experimentation, we equip students to navigate complexity and seize opportunities with confidence.

Our core values of integrity, empathy, inclusion, adaptability, a sense of responsibility, continuous improvement, and innovation anchor us. They are not optional; they are essential. It is our responsibility to stay ahead of the curve. We must embrace technology and educational research to meet evolving needs. We must prioritize character development and social-emotional learning as highly as academic achievement. We should all feel a sense of urgency. We must prepare students with the knowledge, skills, dispositions, and commitment to contribute meaningfully to our democratic society.

An education that prepares students for the future must

serve every student, regardless of background and challenging circumstances. Students from all families must have the tools and support to succeed. Diverse perspectives enrich learning. Equity, access, and inclusion are a moral imperative and a practical necessity.

Schools, families, and business leaders must join forces with faculties to create opportunities for meaningful engagement through dialogue and lifelong learning. Together, we can bridge gaps and build pathways to success for all.

▶ 3. EMPOWERING SCHOOL COMMUNITIES

Dear Faculty, Students, Parents, and Community Friends,

Thank you for taking the time at the end of a busy day to consider matters of consequence. Let me begin by saying my experience as an educational leader, exploring educational research and so many books about leadership, has influenced my values and beliefs. As a school leader, my primary goal is to foster an inclusive and thriving educational environment where every student and staff member feels valued, supported, and empowered to achieve excellence. The foundation of my leadership is built on the core values of integrity and transparency, empathy and compassion, collaboration, equity, access, inclusion, justice, continuous improvement, and innovation. These values guide my decisions, shape my interactions, and inspire my commitment to improving student teaching, learning, leading, and the conditions in which they occur.

Let me talk a little bit about my abiding commitment to *Integrity and Transparency*. Trust is the cornerstone of any strong school community. I lead with integrity and transparency, ensuring that my actions are aligned with the school's values, beliefs, and vision. Communication is open and honest. Knowing where I'm coming from and what I stand for helps to build trust and contributes to a culture where students, teachers, and families feel valued and respected. My commitment to *Empathy and Compassion* is substantial. I lead with empathy, understanding the unique challenges faced by students, families, and staff. By listening with compassion, I build meaningful relationships that support a positive school climate. Next is *Collaboration*. I believe that a school thrives when it operates as a cohesive community. Collaboration between teachers, staff, students, school leaders, families, and the broader community leads to a shared sense of responsibility for student success and innovative solutions. My goal is to create a culture where open dialogue and teamwork are the norm and there is a strong support network for everyone involved in the educational process. Next are the values of *Equity, Access, Inclusion,* and *Justice*. Every student deserves an equal opportunity to succeed, regardless of their background or circumstances. I am committed to creating policies and practices that address the diverse needs of all students. This includes providing targeted support for historically marginalized groups, removing barriers to access, and ensuring that all voices are heard and respected. In addition, I am consciously aware of how systems of oppression influence leadership and teaching practices. This allows me to make informed decisions that are sensitive to the needs of the entire school community. Finally, to support the values of *Continuous Improvement and Innovation,* schools must continually evolve to meet the challenges of today's world. I value innovative approaches to teaching, learning, and leadership that prepare students for the future. This includes promoting critical thinking, encouraging creative problem-solving among both students and staff, and integrating technology. I am dedicated to fostering a culture of continuous improvement where professional growth and lifelong learning are celebrated.

In addition to my values, I have a strong belief in *Student-Centered Teaching and Leading*. Every decision I make as a leader is centered on what is best for students. I believe that students learn best in environments where they feel safe, supported, and engaged. It is my responsibility to ensure that our school culture nurtures students' academic, social, and emotional development. Another belief is in the *Power of Self-Agency*. I believe in the power of self-agency for both students and staff. When individuals are empowered to take ownership of their learning and growth, they are more motivated and engaged. By promoting self-agency, we create a school culture where students learn to advocate for themselves and staff are empowered to pursue professional development that aligns with their goals. I enthusiastically embrace a belief in *Shared Leadership and Accountability*. Leadership is not confined to a single individual. It is shared across the school community. I believe in distributing leadership responsibilities, giving faculty and staff opportunities to lead and contribute to decision-making processes. With shared leadership comes shared accountability, ensuring that everyone is invested in the school's success and rises to the occasion. Furthermore, I have an enduring commitment to *Resilience and Adaptability*. Education is constantly changing, and a successful leader must be able to navigate uncertainty, learn from setbacks, and adjust strategies when necessary. I model this behavior for staff and students, showing that growth often comes from embracing challenges.

I hope this presentation has given you a good sense of who I am as an educational leader and what I stand for. I want to thank you for your attention. I'm in no hurry to go anywhere, so if you have questions or want to talk, stick around. For those that need to go, keep the faith. Until next time, stay safe and happy trails.

▶ 4. A TEACHER-TEAM COMMUNICATION

This following communication sets expectation for teacher-team meetings and might be shared face-to-face or as an email by the team leader.

- We are committed to fostering a safe, nurturing, respectful, and civil environment that supports productive dialogue and collaboration where all voices are heard and valued.
- We cherish that each team member offers a unique perspective regarding problem-solving or idea generation.
- We treat one another with empathy and compassion, knowing that actions and decisions affect not only our outcomes but also team morale.
- We celebrate diversity—differences in race, ethnicity, culture, socioeconomic status, gender orientation, abilities, and political or religious beliefs—as we strive for a more just and equitable community and world.
- Open and honest communication is fundamental to who we are.
- We are a family where strong relationships, mutual trust, kindness, and respect flourish.

- We confront inequity and injustice.
- We approach our work with curiosity, imagination, creativity, and open minds, asking questions as often as we seek answers.
- We make decisions collaboratively.
- We set ambitious goals and hold ourselves to high standards.
- We hold each other accountable.
- We assess our progress and celebrate our accomplishments.

Appendix 2: Three Assessment Instruments to Identify Contextual Factors and Conditions Impacting Teaching, Learning, and Leading

Depending on the collective focus and goals, the instruments or some of the following indicators may be used to collaboratively assess progress.

▶ 1. SCHOOL CULTURE QUESTIONNAIRE

Instructions: Circle the number that best reflects how often the statement is true in your experience.

Rating Scale: 1 = Never | 2 = Sometimes | 3 = Frequently | 4 = Always

Professional Dialogue

We discuss our teaching strategies in specific, practical ways.	1	2	3	4
We regularly observe and learn from each other's classroom practices.	1	2	3	4
We collaborate on lesson planning and resource development.	1	2	3	4
We share effective teaching techniques with one another.	1	2	3	4
We ask for and offer help with classroom challenges.	1	2	3	4
When I seek help, I know it will come without criticism.	1	2	3	4

Innovation & Risk-Taking

| I am encouraged and supported to try out new instructional approaches. | 1 | 2 | 3 | 4 |

Commitment to Learning

| Our school fosters curiosity and a drive to explore better ways to teach. | 1 | 2 | 3 | 4 |

Recognition & Value

| Strong job performance is acknowledged and appreciated here. | 1 | 2 | 3 | 4 |

Connection & Joy

| We enjoy each other's company and support one another through challenges and celebrations. | 1 | 2 | 3 | 4 |

Shared Traditions

| We have meaningful celebrations, ceremonies, traditions, rituals, and storytelling school events and rituals we look forward to each year. | 1 | 2 | 3 | 4 |

Academic Excellence

| High-quality teaching is expected, and feedback is timely and helpful. | 1 | 2 | 3 | 4 |

Time & Energy Protection

| School leaders shield us from tasks that distract from teaching and planning. | 1 | 2 | 3 | 4 |
| Staff meetings are focused, productive, and worth the time. | 1 | 2 | 3 | 4 |

Resources for Growth

| Funding and time allocations reflect a strong commitment to professional development. | 1 | 2 | 3 | 4 |

Mutual Confidence

| I'm trusted to make instructional choices, and leadership supports my decisions. | 1 | 2 | 3 | 4 |

Inclusive Decision-Making

| Decision-making processes are transparent and fair. | 1 | 2 | 3 | 4 |
| My input is sought out and considered in shaping school policies. | 1 | 2 | 3 | 4 |

Respectful Communication

Honest and respectful dialogue is encouraged—even when we disagree.	1	2	3	4
Conflicts are handled thoughtfully and resolved efficiently.	1	2	3	4
I'm kept in the loop with timely and relevant school information.	1	2	3	4

Creative Contribution

| Staff take initiative to bring new ideas forward and help implement them. | 1 | 2 | 3 | 4 |

▶ 2. THE VARIOUS WAYS EDUCATIONAL LEADERS HELP TEACHERS IMPROVE STUDENT LEARNING

The educational leadership literature identifies several ways in which principals help teachers improve school culture, instructional and leadership practice, and other factors and conditions that support innovation and increase student learning in PK–12 schools and districts. The following examples show how a 4-point Likert scale can be used by teachers to rate a variety of ways principals help teachers improve student learning. It can also be used as a self-assessment for principals.

Instructions: Circle the number that best reflects the degree to which each statement is true in your experience.

Likert Rating Scale: 1 = Never | 2 = Rarely | 3 = Often | 4 = Always

Setting Clear Instructional Goals

The principal clearly articulates instructional goals and aligns resources to achieve them.	1	2	3	4

Encouraging Reflective Practice

The principal promotes self-assessment and reflective practice among teachers.	1	2	3	4

Visiting Classrooms on a Regular Basis

The principal conducts regular classroom observations.	1	2	3	4

Providing Feedback on Instruction

The principal provides supportive and corrective feedback to teachers.	1	2	3	4

Supporting Power Curriculum Content and Performance Development

The principal guides and supports teachers in curriculum design and implementation.	1	2	3	4

Organizing Professional Learning Communities (PLCs)

The principal facilitates professional learning communities to promote teacher collaboration and improvement.	1	2	3	4

Tailoring Professional Development

The principal provides targeted professional development based on teacher needs and student data.	1	2	3	4

Using Student Data

The principal helps teachers analyze student data to inform and adjust their instruction.	1	2	3	4

Implementing Data-Driven Instruction

The principal supports the use of data-driven methods in classroom instruction.	1	2	3	4

Fostering Collaboration

The principal creates structures and opportunities for teachers to collaborate and share best practices.	1	2	3	4

Encouraging Peer Observation

The principal facilitates opportunities for teachers to observe each other's classrooms.	1	2	3	4

Supporting Teacher Leadership

The principal identifies and nurtures teacher leaders who can mentor and guide their peers.	1	2	3	4

Ensuring Access to Resources

The principal provides teachers with the necessary resources, materials, and tools for effective instruction.	1	2	3	4

Allocating Time for Collaboration and Planning

The principal ensures that teachers have adequate time for lesson planning and collaboration.	1	2	3	4

Reducing Non-Instructional Burdens

| The principal minimizes non-instructional tasks to allow teachers to focus on teaching. | 1 | 2 | 3 | 4 |

Creating a Safe and Supportive Environment

| The principal fosters a school climate where teachers feel supported and valued. | 1 | 2 | 3 | 4 |

Promoting High Expectations

| The principal sets and maintains high expectations for both teachers and students. | 1 | 2 | 3 | 4 |

Providing Mentorship

| The principal assigns mentors to new or struggling teachers. | 1 | 2 | 3 | 4 |

Offering Instructional Coaching

| The principal employs or develops instructional coaches to support teacher development. | 1 | 2 | 3 | 4 |

Supporting Experimentation With New Strategies

| The principal encourages teachers to try new instructional methods and supports their efforts. | 1 | 2 | 3 | 4 |

Facilitating Access to Research

| The principal provides teachers with access to current educational research and best practices. | 1 | 2 | 3 | 4 |

Balancing Accountability With Support

| The principal balances holding teachers accountable with providing the support they need to improve. | 1 | 2 | 3 | 4 |

Implementing Performance Appraisal Systems

| The principal uses teacher evaluations as a tool for professional growth. | 1 | 2 | 3 | 4 |

Promoting Family Engagement

| The principal encourages and facilitates communication between teachers and families to support student learning. | 1 | 2 | 3 | 4 |

Leveraging Community Resources

| The principal connects teachers with community organizations for additional student support. | 1 | 2 | 3 | 4 |

Modeling Effective Teaching Practices

| The principal demonstrates or shares exemplary teaching practices with staff. | 1 | 2 | 3 | 4 |

The following are several open-ended *interview* questions designed to prompt principals to identify the various ways and specific behaviors leaders use to gather insights and help teachers improve student learning.

1. Describe specific actions you take to foster a culture of continuous professional growth among your teaching staff?

2. How do you promote collaboration among teachers to share best practices and improve student learning?

3. Can you give an example of how collaborative efforts among teachers led to improved student learning in your school?

4. What specific structures or systems have you put in place to facilitate teacher collaboration?

5. What approaches do you use to support teachers in identifying and addressing student learning gaps?

6. How do you use student performance data to guide teacher instruction and support?

7. What methods do you employ to help teachers analyze and use data to inform their instructional practices?

8. Can you describe a time when your leadership directly influenced a positive change in instructional practice?

9. How do you model effective instructional practices for your teachers?

10. What professional development opportunities do you provide or encourage to help teachers enhance their instructional practices?

11. How do you tailor professional development to meet the specific needs of your teachers and students?

12. Can you share an example of a professional development initiative that had a significant impact on student learning?

13. How do you conduct classroom observations, and what specific feedback do you provide to teachers to help them improve?

14. Can you provide an example of how your feedback led to measurable improvement in student learning?

15. What follow-up actions do you take after providing feedback to ensure that suggested improvements are implemented effectively?

16. What steps do you take to ensure that all teachers, regardless of experience level, are continually improving their practice?

17. What role does mentoring play in your efforts to support teacher growth, and how do you implement it?

18. How do you identify and support teacher leaders or coaches who can assist their peers in improving student learning?

19. Can you share a success story where mentoring or coaching led to a noticeable improvement in student achievement?

20. How do you address resistance or challenges from teachers when introducing new strategies to improve student learning?

21. How do you balance the need for accountability with the need for support in helping teachers improve?

22. How do you ensure that teachers have the resources they need to improve student learning outcomes?

▶ 3. EQUITY, DIVERSITY, INCLUSION, AND JUSTICE (EDIJ) ASSESSMENT

The purpose of these reflective open-ended questions is to gain deeper qualitative insights about experiences and observations related to EDIJ.

<u>Instructions:</u> Respond to the following prompts in the space provided.

- What are the school's current strengths in advancing equity, diversity, inclusion, and justice?
- What opportunities for growth or improvement exist to better support students and faculty from diverse backgrounds?
- Describe a moment or practice you have observed at this school that reflects a commitment to inclusion or equity.
- Have you ever witnessed or experienced a challenge related to diversity, equity, or inclusion in the school setting? Please explain.
- How did you respond?

Next Steps

- Compile responses to identify strengths, areas for growth, common challenges, and suggested improvements.
- Share findings with faculty and relevant stakeholders.
- Facilitate structured dialogue and plan actionable next steps to build a more equitable, inclusive, supportive, reflective, empathetic, compassionate and humane, democratic community.

Appendix 3: Two Examples of a Collaboratively Developed Action Plan With a Collective Focus, Goals, Objectives/Action Steps, and Outcomes/Indicators of Success

▶ **1. AN ABBREVIATED ACTION PLAN WITH A COLLECTIVE FOCUS, GOALS, AND OBJECTIVES WITHOUT ACCOMPANYING ACTION STEPS**

A collective focus may have a variety of goals. Each *goal* has a number of *objectives*. Each objective has a series of *action steps* developed to achieve the accompanying outcomes/indicators of success for the goal. A *timeline, resources* needed to achieve each objective, as well as the *person(s) responsible* for completing action steps listed should be included in the plan. In this example, the faculty, collaboratively with the principal, decided on the following three goals for the collective focus of increasing student learning.

Collective Focus: Increase Student Learning for K–6 Students

Goal #1: Differentiate instruction.
Goal #2: Help students take more responsibility for their behavior.
Goal #3: Improve the home–school connection.

Goal #1: Differentiate instruction has four objectives.

Objective #1: Implement an instructional management system.

Objective #2: Identify and utilize grade-level power standards in ELA and mathematics.

Objective #3: Utilize ongoing assessment to design instruction.

Objective #4: Increase teacher collaboration.

Goal #2: Help students take more responsibility for their behavior and learning has three objectives.

Objective #1: Implement a behavior management system.

Objective #2: Implement an instructional management system.

Objective #3: Create a learning and behavior compact for students.

Goal #3: Improve the home–school connection has six objectives.

Objective #1: Increase communication between home and school.

Objective #2: Promote and support parenting skills.

Objective #3: Help parents assist student learning at home.

Objective #4: Welcome parents and seek their support and assistance.

Objective #5: Involve parents in the decisions that affect their children.

Objective $6: Use community resources to strengthen school, families, and student learning.

▶ 2. AN EXAMPLE OF A COLLABORATIVELY DEVELOPED ACTION PLAN WITH A COLLECTIVE FOCUS, GOALS, OBJECTIVES/ACTION STEPS, AND OUTCOMES/INDICATORS OF SUCCESS

Collective Focus: Increase Student Learning for K–6 Students

Goal #1: Differentiate instruction.

Objective #1: Implement an instructional management system.

- Learning expectations and outcomes are clearly communicated.

- Classrooms are arranged so that there are areas for large group, small group, and individual work.
- "Guided discoveries" are used to introduce the use of centers, equipment, and materials.
- Materials for learning centers are stored closest to the appropriate center.
- Students are provided with academic "choice" time.
- Self-scheduling boards are used to facilitate the use of centers.
- Students assess their own work and the work of others for quality using rubrics.
- Student progress monitoring sheets are developed for each student.

Outcomes/indicators of success

- Students self-schedule their learning activities.
- Students work independently and in flexible groups.
- Teachers respond to students who signal properly for teacher assistance.
- Teachers work with individuals and groups without being interrupted by students.
- Students work independently and in groups without interrupting others.
- During the last 10 minutes of the period students are provided with time to reflect on what and how they learned and record their homework assignments.

Objective #2: Identify and utilize grade-level power standards in ELA and mathematics.

- Teacher teams in each subject with support personnel develop power standards for each subject at each grade level.
- General education and special education teachers work collaboratively to develop learning tasks for the power standards.
- Learning tasks to accommodate different learning levels and rates are developed for each power standard.
- Common assessments are developed for each power standard.

- Multi-level materials are linked to each power standard.
- Learning centers are developed for each power standard.
- Teachers develop a form to monitor and record student progress.

Outcomes/indicators of success

- A list of power standards for each grade in each subject is used by all teachers and support personnel to guide instruction.
- Students work on different tasks to master the power standards.
- Teachers monitor and record student progress using a collaboratively developed form.
- All students master the power standards.

Objective #3: Utilize ongoing assessment to design instruction.

- Rubrics are developed for each power standard in each subject.
- Teachers develop formative assessments to determine the power standards to be taught in each subject and to whom they will be taught.
- Teachers collaboratively develop multi-tiered lessons and activities for each power standard in each subject.
- Teachers develop summative assessments to determine mastery.

Outcomes/indicators of success

- Teachers use formative assessments.
- Teachers flexibly group students according to assessment data.
- Students understand the criteria for mastery along a continuum.
- Teachers use a system of record keeping to monitor the progress of students.

Objective #4: Increase teacher collaboration.

- Teachers and support personnel establish norms for working together.

- Teachers and support personnel co-plan lessons for each power standard for each subject.
- Teachers and support personnel gather multi-leveled materials designed to address different learning needs and rates of students.
- Teachers and support personnel use progress monitoring sheets to focus instruction.

Outcomes/indicators of success

- Teachers and support personnel meet weekly to develop lessons and discuss student progress.
- Instructional practice is de-privatized.
- Monitoring sheets are used to identify the focus of instruction.
- A seamless system is in place rather than two separate systems.
- A program for acculturating new faculty members is in place.

Goal #2: Help students take more responsibility for their behavior and learning.

Objective #1: Implement a behavior management system.

- Teachers create a sense of community and belonging in classrooms.
- Teachers, with the students, develop rules and logical consequences.
- Expectations for behavior are clearly articulated.
- Teachers explain routines and procedures for their class.
- Teachers provide opportunities for students to practice the routines and procedures.
- Teachers conduct "morning advisory" each day.
- Teachers create a sense of community and belonging in classrooms.
- Teachers develop "rules and logical consequences" by engaging students in the process.
- Rules and procedures are explicit.
- Regularly schedule morning advisories.
- All school assemblies are scheduled so that students have opportunities to practice behaviors necessary to

be successful and contributing members of a caring and sharing community.

Outcomes/indicators of success

- Students enter and exit the classroom and the school in an orderly fashion.
- Students follow directions the first time they are given.
- Students move about the classroom freely on task.
- Students are attentive and appropriately responsive.
- Students are engaged in problem-solving their conflicts.
- At the end of the class students reflect and assess their behavior.
- The number of referrals to the principal's office decrease.
- Teachers maintain open and regular communication with families.

Objective #2: Implement an instructional management system.

Outcomes/indicators of success

- See Goal #1, Objective #1.

Objective #3: Create a learning and behavior compact for students.

- Teachers work with students to identify specific behaviors that display that students are taking responsibility for their learning.
- Teachers develop rules and logical consequences by engaging students in the process.
- Teachers consistently apply the rules and logical consequences throughout the school day.
- Teachers create a sense of community and belonging in classrooms.
- Teachers foster responsive interactions such as sharing, caring, listening, and active participation with students.
- Teachers provide students with routines and procedures for being more self-directed.
- The principal works with the school site council to identify specific parent behaviors that will help the school improve the behavior and learning of students.

Outcomes/indicators of success

- Students respect the classroom as a learning environment.
- Students respect the needs and rights of fellow students to freely learn.
- Students seek the assistance of teachers when new information is not clear.
- Students put forth their best effort to produce quality work.
- Students follow rules, procedures, and routines.
- Students enter and exit the building and classrooms quietly.
- Students, when presented with a conflict, use words and tolerance to solve problems.
- Students complete homework assignments on time and with attention to quality.
- Students are more self-directed.
- Parents support the agenda of the school and the behavior code.
- Parents see that children arrive at school on time every day with homework assignments completed.
- Parents provide predictable boundaries, encourage productive use of time, and provide leaning experiences as a regular part of family life.
- Parents establish and monitor a study/homework time and place that is quiet and well lit.
- Parents offer assistance and praise but don't do the assignments for them.
- Parents reinforce the rules and expectations for quality work and behavior established by the teacher and school.
- Parents regularly communicate with teachers to receive behavior and learning progress reports and especially communicate at times when there are changes at home that may influence a student's ability to perform well at school.
- Parents support their children's achievement with interest and praise.
- Parents attend parent–teacher conferences.

Goal #3: Improve the home–school connection.

Objective #1: Increase communication between home and school.
- Parents are provided with information regarding school programs, activities, and student services.
- Parent–teacher conferences are scheduled at times that are convenient for parents.
- Parents are provided with a handbook that clarifies what they can expect from the school, what the school asks of them, and how they can raise concerns or questions.
- Parents are encouraged to contact the school at the first sign of a problem.
- Surveys are used to solicit parent opinions on the operation of the school and areas needing improvement.
- Parents have opportunities to discuss their ideas and concerns with educators.
- Examine existing instruments for reporting progress to students.
- Develop a new reporting instrument that provides a more authentic picture of individual student progress.
- Engage parents in mutual communication regarding student achievement.

Outcomes/indicators of success
- Classroom newsletters and a school newsletter advise parents of events and initiatives at the school.
- Parent breakfasts and neighborhood coffees are scheduled on a regular basis.
- Parents report that they better understand what their child is expected to know and be able to do.
- A system of assessing and reporting student progress to parents is in place.
- Teachers use "3 way" conferences.
- The number and length of parent–teacher conferences are increased.

Objective #2: Promote and support parenting skills.
- The school provides research-based materials on parenting skills.

- The school provides workshops or programs that help parents with parenting issues such as communication, discipline, peer pressure, study habits, and single parenting.
- The school provides transportation and childcare services to encourage parents to attend workshops and programs.
- The school offers parents suggestions for establishing expectations and routines with their children.
- The school links parent programs and resources within the community that provide support services to families.

Outcomes/indicators of success

- Parents have reading materials provided by the school for use at home.
- Parents limit television and video games at home.
- Parents attend parenting skills workshops sponsored by the school on a regular basis.

Objective #3: Help parents assist student learning at home.

- Inform parents of the specific grade-level outcomes or standards for students in each subject.
- Provide parents with school-developed curriculum guides and learning packets for each grade level that suggest how parents can foster learning of particular concepts at home.
- Develop procedures that enable parents to monitor homework, provide appropriate assistance, and give feedback to teachers.
- Establish an email hotline that offers parents reminders of the homework and suggestions for helping students complete the homework.
- Assign homework that will require students to discuss and interact with their parents about what they are learning in class.
- Involve parents in setting student goals each year.
- Ask parents to take an active role in reviewing student portfolios according to standards articulated in a rubric.
- Suggest recommended books that parents might read to their children or encourage their children to read for themselves.

Outcomes/indicators of success

- Parents report that they better understand what their child is expected to know and be able to do.
- Parents report that they are better able to help their children with schoolwork at home.

Objective #4: Welcome parents and seek their support and assistance.

- Survey parents regarding their interests, talents, and availability.
- Develop a program for using volunteers as tutors, mentors for students at risk, translators, chaperones for community service projects, and assistants for clerical support personnel.
- Develop orientation and training programs for all new parent volunteers.
- Create opportunities for parents who may not be available during the day to help the school (e.g., record books on tape).
- Develop a speakers' bureau or pool of parents with particular talents or interests that teachers can use to enhance curriculum development or lead a lesson.
- Use parents to organize and implement special events that further school goals.
- Develop feedback forms that enable volunteers to reflect on their experience, and analyze the results in an effort to make their experience more satisfying.
- Invite parents to morning advisory meetings, muffins for moms, donuts for dads, drop in for lunch, sing-alongs, all school assemblies, and other school events.
- Establish a parent volunteer position.

Outcomes/indicators of success

- Parents report they feel welcome and valued by the school.
- There is an increase in the number of parents who attend events at the school.
- There is an increase in second-language parents who volunteer at the school.
- Parents attend all school assemblies on a regular basis.

Objective #5: Involve parents in the decisions that affect their children.

- Include parents in the process of developing visions, missions, values, and goals.
- Provide the school site council with the necessary information and training to make informed decisions.
- Work with parents to identify the performance data that parents find most relevant and then provide them with the data on a regular basis.
- Provide well-publicized processes that enable parents to raise questions and concerns and propose initiatives.
- Solicit parental input in the evaluation of programs, policies, and procedures that have been made as a result of parental input or involvement.
- Inform parents of local, state, or national issues that impact education.

Outcomes/indicators of success

- The school community is able to articulate the vision, mission, what the school stands for, and what it is trying to achieve.
- The school site council meets every month and are advocates for the school.
- Parents contact the principal to provide input.

Objective #6: Use community resources to strengthen school, families, and student learning.

- Involve the PTO in furthering the vision, mission, values, and goals of the school.
- Coordinate and distribute information regarding cultural, recreational, academic, health, social, and other resources for families in the community.
- Develop partnerships with area businesses.
- Establish "pen pal" or email relationships between students and senior citizens and/or business representatives.
- Create community service opportunities for students.
- Contact schools of social work for placement of students.
- Contact a community organizer to work with the school community at large.

Outcomes/indicators of success

- Events sponsored by the PTO celebrate and reinforce the values of the school.
- Students are engaged in community service projects.
- Students from schools of social work are interns.
- The community at large understands the agenda of the school.
- Senior citizens visit the school.
- There are partnerships with mental health organizations.

A timeline, resources needed to achieve each objective, as well as the person(s) responsible for completing the action steps accompanying the objectives should be included in the plan.

Appendix 4:
Two Examples of Celebrations, Ceremonies, Traditions, Rituals, and Storytelling (for Chapter Seven)

▶ 1. STORYTELLING CELEBRATION: AN ACT OF KINDNESS, COMPASSION, RESILIENCE, AND RESPECT

This ceremony celebrates a 10th grader for an act of kindness that reinforces the values of empathy, community, and leadership for everyone present.

The principal opens with an introduction to the event highlighting the importance of the school's values of compassion, empathy, and leadership and briefly recounts the following story that emphasizes the student's thoughtfulness and courage in helping someone in need despite personal inconvenience.

> Good morning, everyone, and welcome to this very special celebration of the values that define us as a school and as a community—kindness, compassion, resilience, and respect. Today, we gather to honor a young person who exemplified these values in the most remarkable way.
>
> Let me tell you a story that will inspire you, a story about one of our very own—a 10th grader whose actions remind us of the extraordinary difference one person can make in someone else's life.
>
> Picture a young boy walking home from school, his backpack slung over his shoulder, his thoughts likely on the homework he has to finish and the dinner waiting for him

at home. But as he rounds a corner, something catches his attention. He sees a woman and her young son standing by the side of the road. Their clothes, slightly tattered and unfamiliar, don't resemble what people in this country usually wear. They look worried, glancing at street signs and buildings as if trying to orient themselves. Their conversation is in a language he doesn't recognize.

The boy pauses. It doesn't take long for him to realize that the woman and her son are not only lost but also likely hungry, confused, and unsure of where to turn. This boy, a 10th grader, had a choice. He could keep walking because he was already late. He knew his mother would be worried, and it was already starting to get dark. But his heart, shaped by his upbringing and the lessons about community and empathy he had learned at home and in our school, wouldn't let him. He approached them with a smile, determined to help. They couldn't understand each other's words, but kindness needed no translation. Using gestures and the paper and pencil from his backpack, he began to draw a map to his house. He signaled that he would call for help and mimed eating to let them know they could get food at his home.

Without hesitation, he led them to his house. As they got closer to his house, a neighbor noticed him and came over to say hello. Recognizing the clothing the woman and boy were wearing, the neighbor spoke to them in their native language. Relief washed over their faces; they had finally found someone who understood them. The neighbor learned that the mother and son were trying to find a cousin's grocery store but had gotten turned around. With the neighbor interpreting, the 10th grader didn't stop there. Together, they escorted the family to their cousin's store, ensuring they were safe, fed, and reunited with their loved one.

This story doesn't end there. Since that day, they have stayed in touch, sharing stories of their homeland and their gratitude for the high schooler's kindness. All this was interpreted by the neighbor and cousin. Today, we are here to celebrate the young man who acted with such empathy, courage, and generosity. He put someone else's needs above his own and showed us all what it means to live out the values of kindness, compassion, resilience, and respect.

There is student in our school who exemplifies these same values of kindness, compassion, resilience, and respect. Please join me in honoring our compassionate hero. (Student's name), you have shown us all what it means to be not only a good student but a great human being. Your actions reflect the very best of humanity, and we are so proud to call you one of our own.

The grade-level teacher who knows the student well shares reflections on the school's role in fostering values of community and global citizenship. Quotes from influential figures on kindness are possibly mentioned, such as Aesop's quote, "No act of kindness, no matter how small, is ever wasted." The teacher briefly describes the student's act of kindness and then says, "(Student's name), please stand and come to the stage." The student is presented with a certificate possibly titled "Compassionate Leadership Award" or a small commemorative token, such as a medal engraved with their name and the phrase, "For Making a Difference." The student paints his hand and slaps the "Wall of Kindness" and writes his name over his handprint.

Invite the family and the helpful neighbor to join the stage. Share a moment of gratitude, thanking the neighbor for their role in bridging the language gap.

If the student is willing, they can share their thoughts about the experience, what motivated them to act, and how they feel about being recognized.

In honor of the family and their cultural heritage, include a short performance, such as a dance or song from their native culture (coordinated in advance if possible).

If the family consents, share a brief story about how they are settling into the community and how acts of kindness make a difference in the lives of newcomers.

Invite attendees to recite a community pledge of kindness:

> We pledge to act with empathy, courage, and compassion in all our interactions, creating a community where everyone feels valued and supported.

The principal concludes the ceremony by celebrating the ripple effect of kindness and encouraging everyone to seek opportunities to help others in their daily lives.

Let this story inspire each of us to look for ways we can make a difference, no matter how small the gesture might seem. As we honor (Student's name), we also recommit ourselves to the values that make our school and community strong. Thank you, (Student's name), for reminding us all of the power of compassion. You are a true leader, and we are so proud of the person you are. Let's give a final round of applause to this incredible young man and the values he so beautifully represents.

▶ 2. CEREMONY: WE CARE, WE SHARE, WE DARE

Creating a ceremony, ritual, and symbol to capture the essence of the phrase, "We Care, We Share, We Dare" requires reflecting the values of compassion, generosity, and courage. The purpose of this event is to unite participants in a shared commitment to *care* for others, *share* generously, and *dare* to act with courage in the face of challenges.

Prior to the ceremony, ritual, and symbol display, a teacher team assigned to schedule and facilitate the event selects three colors to represent the values of a) caring, empathy, and compassion; b) sharing, collaboration, and community; and c) daring, courage, and taking action. Write on each of the banners or posters either "We Care," "We Share," or "We Dare" and attach each to a pole. Select three students deserving of the honor to carry each banner or poster. In an open space, such as a school gym or courtyard, arrange seating or standing in a circle to symbolize unity and interconnectedness. The three selected students enter the space in a single line holding their colored banner or poster and stand behind the podium and microphone. A student host deserving of the honor begins by explaining the meaning behind each value and saying, "The phrase 'We Care, We Share, We Dare' is not just a motto but a powerful reminder of shared purpose and action that can create a lasting impact and inspiration within the community."

A student, teacher team, parent, or community member is then called to the podium by the principal, student, or a member of the teacher planning team and a pin, badge, or necklace is presented as a reminder of their contribution and commitment to caring, sharing, and daring. Together, with those gathered in the circle recite a pledge:

We have a commitment to people: We Care! (for each other and recognize needs and struggles).

We have a commitment to partnership: We Share! (our knowledge, skills, mindsets, and commitment to make the world a better place).

We have a commitment to excellence: We Dare! (to challenge injustice and innovate).

Appendix 5: An Example of End-of-Chapter Bulleted Preliminary Plans to Be Expanded Into an Innovation Plan (for Chapter Eight)

▶ PRELIMINARY PLAN FOR ESTABLISHING AND MAINTAINING RELATIONAL TRUST

- Ask questions and actively listen regarding the needs of teachers, families, and students and also determine the degree to which there is a vision that guides all decision-making and whether a culture of collaboration exists.
- Informally assess the alignment of curriculum, assessments, materials, support services and other safety nets, professional development, parent engagement efforts, and budget.
- Share your leadership platform (who you are and what you stand for).
- Create a sense of urgency regarding the need for improvement based on global changes.
- Invite participation.
- Create a sense of community in which students, teachers, and parents feel welcomed and appreciated and participate in the decision-making process.
- Form a guiding coalition consisting of teacher teams and parents (in addition to school council).

▶ PRELIMINARY PLAN FOR COLLABORATIVELY ASSESSING CONTEXTUAL FACTORS AND CONDITIONS

Form data-collection teacher team(s) to assess the following:

- Current school vision, mission, and values.
- School culture.
- A sense of community in classrooms and school-wide.
- Professional learning community (collaboration).
- Power content and performance standards (curriculum) addressed in each subject in each grade level/department.
- Differentiated teaching and learning.
- Coordination of general education and support services.
- Alignment of power standards, common assessments, instructional approaches, multi-leveled materials, support services, professional development, and parent engagement with power standards.
- Student achievement data.

▶ PRELIMINARY PLAN FOR COLLECTIVELY DETERMINING A FOCUS FOR IMPROVEMENT

- Based on the collaboratively assessed contextual factors and conditions (previously listed).
- Data-collection teacher team(s) analyze the data.
- Data-collection teacher team(s) present findings to faculty.
- Faculty lead by the data-collection teacher team(s), in concert with the principal, develop a list of priority factors or conditions for faculty to consider.
- Faculty lead by the data-collection teacher team(s), in concert with the principal, select and determine one or two areas for focus (and set aside the others not selected for future reference).
- Faculty lead by the data-collection teacher team(s), in concert with the principal, reach consensus and agree that every faculty member will commit to addressing the one or two areas for collective focus.

▶ PRELIMINARY PLAN FOR COLLABORATIVELY DEVELOPING AN ACTION PLAN

- An action-plan teacher team is selected to collaboratively develop an action plan with short-term and long-term SMART goals, indicators of success, assigned responsibilities, and timelines.
- Faculty lead by the action-plan teacher team, in concert with the principal, reach consensus and agree that every faculty member will commit to addressing the goals of the action plan.

▶ PRELIMINARY PLAN FOR COLLABORATIVELY ASSESSING PROGRESS

- The action-plan teacher team, in concert with the principal, present the plan to parents and other school community members for feedback.
- Achieving the indicators of success of the action plan is included in the goal setting, observation, and evaluation process of faculty.

▶ PRELIMINARY PLAN FOR COLLECTIVELY ASSESSING PROGRESS

- An assess-progress teacher team is formed to review and use the indicators of success stated in the plan to assess progress (or the assess-progress teacher team may be the original data-collection teacher team, the action-plan teacher team, or a combination consisting of members from the two teams).
- The assess-progress teacher team, in concert with the principal, present their assessment of the degree to which the indicators of success have been achieved.
- The principal or department head assesses the degree to which individual faculty members or grade-level teams/department members have contributed to achieving the indicators of success.
- The faculty, lead by the principal, develop new plans to readdress the focus not achieved to the degree necessary

or set new action-plan goals and indicators based on those that were further down on the priority list and set aside.
- The principal communicates the assess-progress results and next steps to parents and other school community members.
- The principal establishes new indicators of success as part of the goal setting, observation, and evaluation process of faculty.

▶ PRELIMINARY PLAN FOR CELEBRATING GAINS

- A celebrate-gains teacher team is formed to create ceremonies, rituals, or traditions that reinforce the goals and indicators of success of the action plan.
- Faculty are asked to identify students, faculty, colleagues, or parents that have contributed to achieving the goals and indicators of success of the action plan.
- The celebrate-gains teacher team, along with the principal, selects students, faculty, colleagues, or parents to be acknowledged for contributing to achieving the goals and indicators of success of the action plan.
- A school-wide assembly is scheduled, and parents and other school community members are invited to participate in the ceremonies, rituals, or traditions created to acknowledge those students, teachers, and/or parents that contributed to achieving the goals and indicators of success of the action plan.

Appendix 6: A Rubric for Developing and Self-Assessing a Context-Specific Innovation Plan

Instructions: The following is a comprehensive rubric for developing an innovation plan using the Six-Point Conceptual Framework. The document should address reflective practice, outline a structured approach to systems thinking and strategic planning, emphasize collaboration, address data-informed decision-making, detail a plan of action, assess progress, and celebrate gains.

Rating Scale: 1 = Vague | 2 = Imprecise | 3 = Accurate | 4 = Detailed

Introduction

Describe the school or district and its demographics.	1	2	3	4
Define leadership position.	1	2	3	4
Provide an overview of the Six-Point Conceptual Framework.	1	2	3	4
Outline the innovation plan's content and how it is organized.	1	2	3	4

Build Relational Trust and a Sense of Community

Share values, vision, and leadership identity.	1	2	3	4
Define the foundational nature and importance of trust and a feeling of belonging.	1	2	3	4

Outline steps to build trust (e.g., establishing norms, transparency, communication).	1	2	3	4
Explain how you will create urgency and invite participation.	1	2	3	4

Collaboratively Collect Contextual Data

Introduce the teacher team selected and provide a rationale for gathering formative data.	1	2	3	4
Describe persistent problems in increasing student learning and their root causes.	1	2	3	4
Collaboratively identify possible areas to assess (e.g., culture, innovative curriculum, parent involvement).	1	2	3	4
Describe processes for data collection and suggest some possible assessment instruments and how and to whom the findings of the analysis will be reported.	1	2	3	4

Collaboratively Determine a *Collective* Focus

Have the teacher team identify the factors and conditions and the manner in which they were assessed and analyzed.	1	2	3	4
Emphasize that the collective focus selected will be for a whole grade-level, department, school, or district and that everyone will be working together on the collaboratively determined collective focus.	1	2	3	4
Collaboratively rate and prioritize factors and conditions and determine a collective focus for a whole grade-level, department, school, or district.	1	2	3	4
Guide the process for reaching consensus.	1	2	3	4

Determine who on the teacher collection and analysis team will report the data.	1	2	3	4
Identify the audiences that the data will be reported to.	1	2	3	4

Collaboratively Develop an Action Plan

State the collective focus and determine the teacher team that will develop the goals, objectives, and outcomes to actualize the collective focus.	1	2	3	4
Mention that short-term wins and accountability measures should be included in the innovation plan. Specify audiences for feedback and communication.	1	2	3	4
Include steps that will be taken to align budget and job-embedded staff development necessary to build capacity in achieving the goals, objectives, and outcomes for the identified collective focus.	1	2	3	4

Revisit Building Relational Trust and a Sense of Community

Describe the process that will be used to communicate to members of the organization and the community at large regarding how the plan was developed and how consensus was achieved for adoption of the plan by the faculty who will be expected to implement the plan.	1	2	3	4
Describe efforts that will be taken to invite engagement from the community at large, parents, shareholders, other stakeholders and support the plan (e.g., request for feedback or input).	1	2	3	4

Collaboratively Assess Progress

Detail the processes for collecting and analyzing summative data, who will collect and analyze the data, and who will report the findings to the faculty.	1	2	3	4
State how the findings will be communicated to parents and members of the school community at large.	1	2	3	4
Describe accountability efforts and adjustments to goals.	1	2	3	4
Specify next steps.	1	2	3	4

Celebrate Gains

Identify goals to intentionally celebrate and describe the location of the celebration.	1	2	3	4
Collaboratively identify who will develop, organize, and schedule the celebrations.	1	2	3	4
Determine when the celebration will be developed and scheduled and how the honorees will be selected.	1	2	3	4
Brainstorm ideas for ceremonies, traditions, rituals, and stories that might be developed or selected to reinforce the collaboratively selected collective focus of the action plan.	1	2	3	4

THE 6-POINT CONCEPTUAL FRAMEWORK

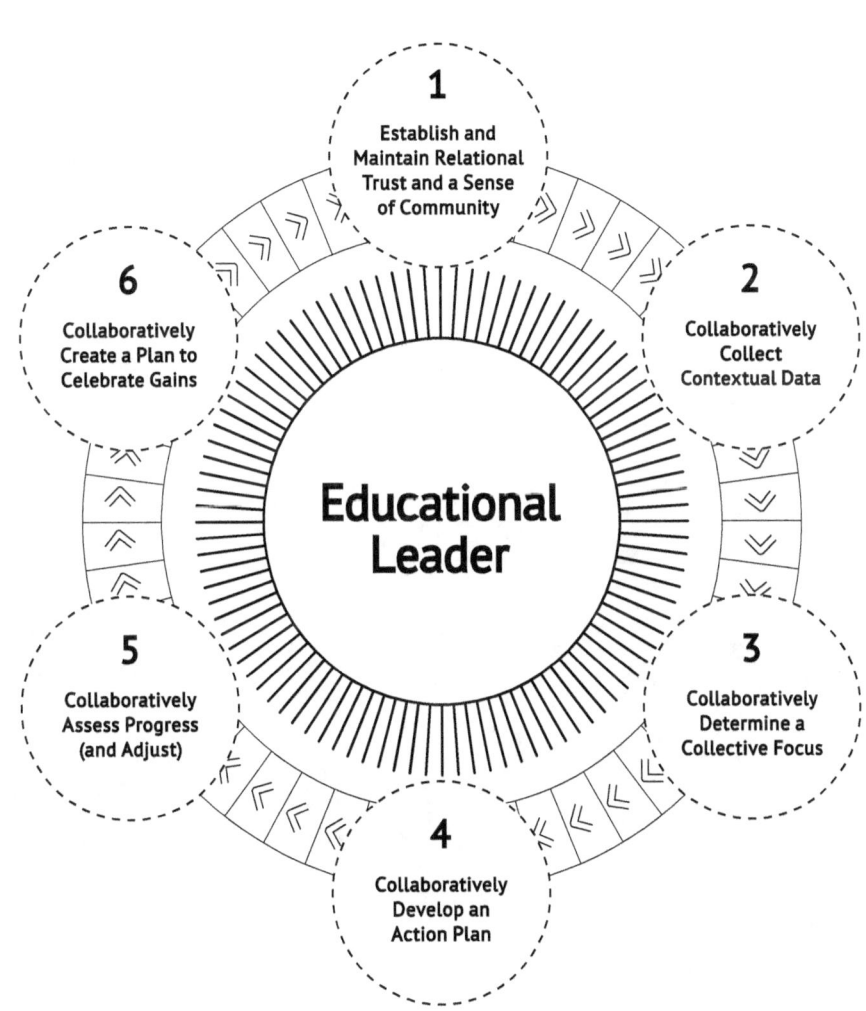

Conceptual Framework design and chapter openers designed by Christian Arichabala.

For Product Safety Concerns and Information please contact our EU
representative GPSR@taylorandfrancis.com
Taylor & Francis Verlag GmbH, Kaufingerstraße 24, 80331 München, Germany

www.ingramcontent.com/pod-product-compliance
Lightning Source LLC
Chambersburg PA
CBHW061438300426
44114CB00014B/1733